Phonetic Transcription for Lyric Diction

A graded method of phonetic transcription that employs frequently occurring words from Italian, German, French, Latin, and English lyrics

Expanded Version

Cheri Montgomery

S.T.M. Publishers
Nashville, TN

Copies of this book may be ordered by contacting:

S.T.M. Publishers
P.O. Box 111485
Nashville, TN 37222
Tel: (615) 831-9859
Fax: (615) 831-7148
Email: info@studenttextmfg.com
Website: www.stmpublishers.com
Facebook: *Lyric Diction Workbook Series*

Phonetic Transcription for Lyric Diction, Expanded Version, Student Manual: 978-0-9975578-5-5

Resources for voice and diction from S.T.M. Publishers:

ISBN 978-1-7338631-0-0 (spiral bound)	Singer's Diction
ISBN 978-1-7352114-0-4 (spiral bound)	The Singer's Daily Practice Journal, volume I
ISBN 978-0-9975578-7-9 (spiral bound)	The Singer's Daily Practice Journal, volume II
ISBN 978-1-7338631-6-2 (spiral bound)	The Singer's Daily Practice Journal, volume III
ISBN 978-1-7338631-2-4 (spiral bound)	IPA Handbook for Singers, 2nd edition
ISBN 978-0-9975578-3-1 (spiral bound)	Phonetic Readings for Lyric Diction, 3rd edition
ISBN 978-0-9975578-0-0 (spiral bound)	Phonetic Transcription for Lyric Diction
ISBN 978-0-9975578-5-5 (spiral bound)	Phonetic Transcription for Lyric Diction, expanded version
ISBN 978-1-7338631-5-5 (spiral bound)	English Lyric Diction Workbook, 4th edition
ISBN 978-0-9818829-8-7 (spiral bound)	Italian Lyric Diction Workbook, 3rd edition
ISBN 978-0-9916559-2-2 (spiral bound)	Latin Lyric Diction Workbook
ISBN 978-0-9818829-6-3 (spiral bound)	German Lyric Diction Workbook, 5th edition
ISBN 978-0-9916559-1-5 (spiral bound)	French Lyric Diction Workbook, 4th edition
ISBN 978-0-9916559-5-3 (spiral bound)	Advanced French Lyric Diction Workbook
ISBN 978-1-7352114-4-2 (spiral bound)	Russian Lyric Diction Workbook
ISBN 978-1-7352114-9-7 (spiral bound)	Spanish Lyric Diction Workbook

Cover image: Camille Pissarro, *The Artist's Garden at Eragny,* 1898. Courtesy of the National Gallery of Art

Technical Support: Verlan Kliewer

To my students at the Blair School of Music
at
Vanderbilt University

PREFACE

Phonetic Transcription for Lyric Diction offers an efficient approach to the study of Italian, German, French, and Latin transcription. It is second in a two-part series. *Phonetic Readings for Lyric Diction* is the introductory text. Together, these workbooks address enunciation and transcription respectively. Italian, German, French, and Latin enunciation rules with English rules for transcription are established in part one so that students are adequately prepared for the rigorous approach to transcription provided in part two.

This text is the expanded version of *Phonetic Transcription for Lyric Diction.* It contains an additional 10 units to cover English transcription.

The word lists in this text were generated from the lyrics of more than 6,000 art songs. Lyric words were organized in order of frequency of occurrence and categorized according to Italian, German, French, Latin, and English speech sounds as defined by the International Phonetic Alphabet. Worksheets were created from the word lists and arranged according to a strategic order of rules. This design streamlines the approach to teaching lyric diction and allows the instructor to cover transcription in an efficient manner.

Each unit highlights a specified set of symbols by providing rules for transcription, a group assignment, and 12 individually assigned word lists. Units progress in cumulative order culminating with exercises that allow students to transcribe and enunciate phrases from art song lyrics and Liturgical Latin texts. A study of articulatory phonetics is included with consonant and vowel charts for student application and definition of terms. Comprehensive exams and a review of rules are provided for each language.

I invite the reader to see the appendix of *Exploring Art Song Lyrics,* published by Oxford University Press, for a comparative analysis of my method of transcription.

This text would not be possible without generous help from many individuals. I wish to thank Dr. Corradina Caporello, Professor of Italian diction at the Juilliard School, for her excellent guidance. She finalized the rules for enunciation and transcription in the *Italian Lyric Diction Workbook* which were again applied in the Italian portions of this book. Dr. Daniel Solomon, professor of Classical Studies at Vanderbilt University, is the Latin and Italian language and translation editor. Sarah Köllner, editor of the *Athenäum - Jahrbuch der Friedrich Schlegel-Gesellschaft*, is the German text and translation editor. Cecile Moreau is the French language and translation editor. Their expertise is much appreciated.

The *Lyric Diction Workbook Series* was created to make the lyric languages accessible to singers. Familiarity is gained as numerous words are encountered. The series was designed to make grading easier for instructors. Accurate transcription and proficiency of memorized rules is assessed through in-class enunciation. Further discussion and sample syllabus schedules are available by clicking on the blue button titled "How the workbooks function in the classroom" on the home page at www.stmpublishers.com. *Phonetic Readings for Lyric Diction* and *Phonetic Transcription for Lyric Diction* accommodate various pedagogical approaches and course lengths. Together, they introduce students to the lyric languages through transcription and enunciation of a rich vocabulary.

Cheri Montgomery

TABLE OF CONTENTS

UNIT 1:

Italian classification of symbols

GENERAL TERMS

IPA. The *International Phonetic Alphabet* was established by the International Phonetic Association around 1888. Each symbol stands for one phonetic sound and is enclosed in brackets. Authentic pronunciation, accurate formation, and precise resonance must be defined for each symbol within the respective language.
Pronunciation: conversion of letters into the proper choice of speech sounds as represented by IPA
Enunciation and Articulation: the act of speaking or singing phonetic sounds
Expression: the act of conveying mood, color and sentiment of lyric texts
Monosyllable: a word with one syllable – polysyllabic words contain two or more syllables
Monophthong: a vowel sound that maintains one articulatory position throughout the course of the syllable
Rising Diphthong: two vowel sounds in the same syllable with a lengthening of the second vowel
Falling Diphthong: two vowel sounds in the same syllable with a lengthening of the first vowel
Triphthong: three vowel sounds within the same syllable
Hiatus: adjacent vowel sounds that occupy consecutive syllables
Prevocalic: a consonant preceding a vowel
Intervocalic: a consonant that stands between vowels
Postvocalic: a consonant following a vowel
Initial: the first letter or sound of a word
Medial: a letter or sound in the middle of a word
Final: the last letter or sound of a word
Apocopation or truncation: a vowel or group of letters omitted from the end of a word
Apostrophe: used to replace the vowel of an unstressed word in vowel groups within the phrase
Aspirate: a consonant that is sounded with an audible release of breath (English *p, t, k*)

SCHOLARLY AUTHORITY

Transcription rules in this text are based upon Evelina Colorni's *Singer's Italian.* Specified rules have been updated to accommodate current performance practice. Dr. Corradina Caporello, Professor of Italian Diction at the Juilliard School, edited and finalized the rules for enunciation and transcription. The dictionary source follows her recommendation: *Dizionario d'ortografia e di pronunzia* (http://www.dizionario.rai.it)

CHARACTERISTICS OF THE ITALIAN LANGUAGE

1) Italian uses several letters in addition to the English alphabet: grave *à, è, ì, ò, ù,* acute *é, ó,* circumflex *î*
2) Vowel sounds are deliberate, strong, precise and frontal in placement.
3) Stressed syllables are distinguished by a lengthened vowel sound, not a punched stress as in English
4) Monophthongs maintain their formation throughout vocalization - avoid on or off-glides of vowels. In spelling, each Italian vowel represents one sound (for English, one vowel often represents two sounds)
5) A single vowel is lengthened when followed by one consonant
6) There is no glottal stop or neutral vowel sound present in Italian (no schwa [ə])
7) Dental consonants: tongue tip contacts the back of the upper front teeth for consonants *d, n, t, l, r*
8) Plosive consonants: a nonaspirate quality is required for consonants [b], [d], [g], [p], [t], [k]
9) Double consonants require deliberate lengthening of the consonant sound with a short preceding vowel
10) Additional sounds not familiar to English include prepalatal consonants [ɲ] and [ʎ]

WARNINGS

1) Do not assign a medial placement to vowel sounds
2) Do not diphthongize monophthongs
3) Do not articulate a glottal stop before initial vowel words
4) Employ a fully vocalized tone for articulation of voiced consonants (avoid partial aspiration)
5) Do not substitute an English consonantal point of contact for the Italian dentals (*d, n, t, l, r*)
6) Do not aspirate plosive consonants ([b], [d], [g], [p], [t], [k])
7) Do not reduce the length of double consonants or long vowels

PRONUNCIATION GUIDE

FRONT VOWELS

IPA	ENGLISH (approximation)	ITALIAN
[i]	greet, evening	vita, ivi, sospiri [ˈvita][ˈivi][sosˈpiɾi]
[e]	chaos, décor	cheto, entra, mercé [ˈketo] [ˈentra] [merˈtʃe]
[ɛ]	heaven, friend	cielo, erba, ahimè [ˈtʃɛlo][ˈɛrba][aːiˈmɛ]

BACK VOWELS

IPA	ENGLISH (approximation)	ITALIAN
[u]	truth, moon	giusto, umile, virtù [ˈdʒusto][ˈumile][virˈtu]
[o]	obey, protect	dolce, ombra, solo [ˈdoltʃe][ˈombra][ˈsolo]
[ɔ]	dawn, autumn	core, occhi, però [ˈkɔɾe][ˈɔkki][peˈɾɔ]

CENTRAL VOWEL

IPA	ENGLISH (approximation)	ITALIAN
[a]		mare, alma, città [ˈmaɾe][ˈalma][tʃitˈta]

SEMICONSONANTS / SEMIVOWELS

IPA	ENGLISH (approximation)	ITALIAN
[j]	yield, view	fiore, chiara, insieme [ˈfjoɾe][ˈkjaɾa][inˈsjɛme]
[w]	willow, sweet	suono, guardia, quale [ˈswɔno][ˈgwardja][ˈkwale]

DIACRITICAL MARKS

IPA	ENGLISH (approximation)	ITALIAN
[ː] (long vowel)	day, shadow [dɛːɪ][ˈʃædoːʊ]	mio, bei, lauro [miːo][bɛːi][ˈlaːuɾo]
[ˈ] (stressed syllable)	believe, prevail [bɪˈliv] [pɹɪˈvɛːɪl]	semplice, libertà [ˈsemplitʃe][liberˈta]

HIATUS (adjacent vowel sounds that occupy consecutive syllables)

ENGLISH (approximation)	ITALIAN
noel, create, triumph	leone, fluire, paese, vialetto, realtà
[noˈɛl] [kɹiˈɛːɪt] [ˈtɹɑːɪ-əmf]	[leˈone] [fluˈiɾe] [paˈeze] [vi-aˈletto] [re-alˈta]

RISING DIPHTHONG (two vowel sounds in the same syllable with a longer duration of the second vowel - a glide rapidly introduces the following vowel)

music, view, dwell	lieta, piano, chiusa, quando, uomini
[ˈmjuzɪk] [vju] [dwɛl]	[ˈljɛta] [ˈpjano] [ˈkjuza] [ˈkwando] [ˈwɔmini]

FALLING DIPHTHONG (two vowel sounds in the same syllable with a longer duration of the first vowel - length is more deliberate in Italian)

eyes, ray, note	io, sei, coi, tuo, mai, aura, neutro
[ʔɑːɪz][ɹɛːɪ][noːʊt]	[iːo][sɛːi][koːi][tuːo][maːi][ˈaːuɾa][ˈnɛːutro]

When accented within the phrase, final stressed falling diphthongs of select words may be set in separate syllables: *io* [ˈi-o] *coi* [ˈko-i] *tuo* [ˈtu-o] *miei* [ˈmjɛ-i] *tuoi* [ˈtwɔ-i]

TRIPHTHONG (three vowel sounds within the same syllable)

fire, power, cure	miei, tuoi, quiete, guai, quei, aiuola
[fɑːɪə][pɑːʊə] [kjʊːə]	[mjɛːi][twɔːi][[ˈkwjɛte][gwaːi][kweːi][aˈjwɔla]

LONG MONOPHTHONG ("the tonic stress in Italian words is given by lengthening the stressed vowel. This helps the singers not to punch stressed syllables as one would do in English."[1])

IPA	ITALIAN
[iː]	dito, ira, primo, fine [ˈdiːto][ˈiːɾa][ˈpriːmo][ˈfiːne]
[eː] [ɛː]	vero, neve, tema, bene [ˈveːɾo][ˈneːve][ˈtɛːma][ˈbɛːne]
[uː]	lumi, oscuro, duca, muro [ˈluːmi][osˈkuːɾo][ˈduːka][ˈmuːɾo]
[oː] [ɔː]	dono, voto, sposa coro [ˈdoːno][ˈvoːto][ˈspɔːza][ˈkɔːɾo]
[aː]	mano, spada, prato, capo [ˈmaːno][ˈspaːda][ˈpraːto][ˈkaːpo]

Note: The following text provides phonetic indications for vowel length in falling diphthongs only

[1] Dr. Corradina Caporello, e-mail instructions to author, May 29, 2008

DENTAL CONSONANTS (the following are alveolar in English)

IPA	ENGLISH (approximation)	ITALIAN
[d]	dream, delight	dì, onde, addio [di][ˈonde][adˈdiːo]
[n]	noon, linen	nome, fontana, donna [ˈnome][fonˈtana][ˈdɔnna]
[t]	trust, teach	tanto, istante, detto [ˈtanto][isˈtante][ˈdetto]
[l]	life, blissful	luna, velo, stelle [ˈluna][ˈvelo][ˈstelle]
[ɾ]	thread, throne	amore, puro, sperare [aˈmoɾe][ˈpuɾo][speˈɾaɾe]
[r]		ardor, rose, terra [arˈdor][ˈrɔze][ˈtɛrra]

PLOSIVE CONSONANTS (Qualities that differ from English examples: articulation in Italian is unaspirated - examples of plosive *d* and *t* are listed above)

IPA	ENGLISH (approximation)	ITALIAN
[b]	bright, beauty	barca, nubi, labbra [ˈbarka][ˈnubi][ˈlabbra]
[g]	grace, garden	grave, vago, agguato [ˈgrave][ˈvago][agˈgwato]
[p]	peace, pleasant	pietà, aprile, coppa [pjeˈta][aˈprile][ˈkɔppa]
[k]	candle, quick	caldo, sacra, staccato [ˈkaldo][ˈsakra][stakˈkato]

PREPALATAL CONSONANTS (There are no English equivalents)

IPA	ENGLISH (approximation)	ITALIAN
[ɲ]		ognora, degno, sogni [oɲˈɲoɾa][ˈdeɲɲo][ˈsoɲɲi]
[ʎ]		voglia, gigli, figlio [ˈvɔʎʎa][ˈdʒiʎʎi][ˈfiʎʎo]

Other sounds familiar to English and Italian: [ʃ] *sheep*, [tʃ] *chair*, [dʒ] *judge*, [ŋ] *sing*

Classification of Symbols: Consonants

Voicing: A voiced consonant engages vocal cords. A voiceless consonant does not employ vocal cords.

Point of Articulation	Italian	English
Bilabial [bɑɪˈleɪbɪəl] Refers to the lips	[b] [p] [m] [w]	[b] [p] [m] [w] [ʍ]
Labiodental [leɪbɪoˈdɛntəl] Involves the lower lip and the upper front teeth	[v] [f]	[v] [f]
Dental [ˈdɛntəl] Involves the tip of the tongue and the back of the upper row of teeth	[d] [t] [z] [s] [l] [n] [ɾ] [r] [dz] [ts]	[ð] [θ]
Alveolar [ʔælˈviələ] Involves the tip of the tongue and the ridge behind the upper teeth	some sources classify Italian *r* as alveolar	[d] [t] [z] [s] [l] [n] [ɾ] [ɹ]
Prepalatal [pɹɪˈpælətəl] Involves the tongue and the area between the alveolar ridge and hard palate	[ʃ] [dʒ] [tʃ] [j] [ɲ] [ʎ]	[ʒ] [ʃ] [dʒ] [tʃ]
Palatal [ˈpælətəl] Involves a front arch of the tongue and the hard palate		[j]
Velar [ˈvilə] Involves the back of the tongue and the soft palate	[g] [k] [ŋ]	[g] [k] [ŋ]
Glottal [ˈglɑtəl] Involves the air flow and the opening between the vocal cords		[ʔ] [h]

Manner of Articulation	Italian	English
Plosive [ˈploʊsɪv] or **Stop** [stɑp] A momentary closure of the air flow passage	[b] [p] [d] [t] [g] [k]	[b] [p] [d] [t] [g] [k] [ʔ]
Fricative [ˈfɹɪkətɪv] Produced by directing the air flow past a set of articulators	[v] [f] [z] [s] [ʃ]	[v] [f] [z] [s] [ʍ] [ʒ] [ʃ] [h] [ð] [θ]
Affricate [ˈʔæfɹɪkət] A plosive or stop that is followed by a fricative	[dz] [ts] [dʒ] [tʃ]	[dʒ] [tʃ]
Nasal [ˈneɪzəl] Produced by directing vocalized tone through the nasal passages	[m] [n] [ŋ] [ɲ]	[m] [n] [ŋ]
Lateral [ˈlætərəl] Produced by directing vocalized tone over the sides of the tongue	[l] [ʎ]	[l]
Glide [glɑɪd] Produced by directing vocalized tone past a set of articulators without friction	[j] [w]	[j] [w]
Trill [tɹɪl] Formed by taps with the tip of the tongue against the ridge or teeth	[ɾ] [r]	[ɾ]
Retroflex [ˈɹɛtɹoʊflɛks] Produced with the tongue tip curled up		[ɹ]

WORKSHEET #1: Classification of Consonants

Provide IPA to complete the following chart for Italian consonants:

	Bilabial	Labiodental	Dental	Alveolar	Prepalatal	Palatal	Velar	Glottal
Plosive voiced voiceless								
Fricative voiced voiceless								
Affricate voiced voiceless								
Nasal voiced								
Lateral voiced								
*Trill voiced								
Glide voiced								

Provide IPA to complete the following chart for English consonants:

	Bilabial	Labiodental	Dental	Alveolar	Prepalatal	Palatal	Velar	Glottal
Stop voiced voiceless								
Fricative voiced voiceless								
Affricate voiced voiceless								
Nasal voiced								
Lateral voiced								
Trill voiced								
Glide voiced								
Retroflex voiced								

*Formation of Italian *r* is initiated with the tongue tip touching the alveolar ridge and trilling between the ridge and upper front teeth. For this reason, sources differ concerning the point of articulation for *r*.

Classification of Symbols: Vowels

Quality	**Italian**	**English**
Closed Requires a closer proximity between the tongue and roof of the mouth	[i] [e] [u] [o]	[i] [u] [o]
Open Requires more space between the tongue and roof of the mouth	[ɛ] [ɔ]	[ɪ] [ɛ] [ʊ] [ɔ]

Peak of tongue arch	**Italian**	**English**
Front (tongue vowel) The arch of the tongue is forward with tip down during enunciation	[i] [e] [ɛ]	[i] [ɪ] [ɛ]
Back (lip vowel) The arch of the tongue is back with tip down during enunciation	[u] [o] [ɔ]	[u] [ʊ] [o] [ɔ]
Central Tongue maintains a central position during enunciation	bright [a]	dark [ɑ] [ʌ] [æ] [ɜ]

See vowel chart on page 234

WORKSHEET #1: Classification of Vowels

Provide vowel descriptions for the following symbols:

Italian Vowels

IPA	Quality	Peak tongue arch
[i]		
[e]		
[ɛ]		
[u]		
[o]		
[ɔ]		
[a]		

English Vowels

	IPA	Quality	Peak tongue arch
greet	[i]		
bit	[ɪ]		
said	[ɛ]		
blue	[u]		
look	[ʊ]		
obey	[o]		
ought	[ɔ]		
sat	[æ]		
father	[ɑ]		
bird	[ɜ]		
up	[ʌ]		

UNIT 2:

Italian vowels and semivowels

RULES FOR TRANSCRIPTION

Italian vowels and semivowels

Spelling	IPA	Sample Words
Initial vowel words (there are no glottal stops in Italian)	[ʔ] Glottal Stop	amanti [a'manti]
Stressed syllable (the stress mark precedes the stressed syllable)	['] Stress Mark	lampada ['lampada]
a	[a] Bright [a]	farfalla [far'falla]
e in stressed syllable (*dictionary required)	[ɛ] Open Front	etɛrno [e'tɛrno]
e in stressed syllable (*dictionary required)	[e] Closed Front	fedele [fe'dele]
e in unstressed syllables	[e]	serenate [seɾe'nate]
h (*h* is silent in Italian)	[h] Glottal Fricative	hanno ['anno]
i (as the single vowel in the syllable)	[i] Closed Front	infinito [infi'nito]
i + vowel	[j] Prepalatal Glide	pensiɛro [pen'sjɛɾo]
o in stressed syllable (*dictionary required)	[ɔ] Open Back	confɔrto [kon'fɔrto]
o in stressed syllable (*dictionary required)	[o] Closed Back	profondo [pro'fondo]
o in unstressed syllables	[o]	giocondo [dʒo'kondo]
u (as the single vowel in the syllable)	[u] Closed Back	futura [fu'tuɾa]
u + vowel	[w] Bilabial Glide	nuɔvo ['nwɔvo]
Double consonant (all double consonants are doubled)	[ll]	brillare [bril'laɾe]

STRESS MARK

The stress mark is placed before a single consonant: *anɛllo* [a'nɛllo], between double consonant *cammino* [kam'mino], or after the first *r, m, n, s,* or *l* of a consonant cluster: *beltà* [bel't. (memory aid: *harmoniously*).

* A dictionary is required in order to determine the closed or open quality of *e* and *o* in a stress syllable. It is not possible to identify the stressed syllable without a dictionary. The followi worksheets provide pronunciation indications within the Italian text. The vowel of the stress syllable is underlined with transcription of *e* and *o* indicated within the underlined text. Wor with vowels in hiatus have one vowel underlined. Example: *affettuoso* [affettu'ozo]

:LASSWORK #2: Italian vowels and semivowels

rovide IPA:

1.	mattina	(morning)	5.	novɛlla	(short story)
2.	onde	(waves)	6.	liɛve	(light)
3.	lamenti	(complaints)	7.	buɔno	(good)
4.	veduto	(seen)	8.	dɔnne	(women)

'RANSCRIPTION WITHIN THE PHRASE #2: Vowel clusters

'owel clusters within the phrase occur before initial vowel words. Identical vowels that are djacent within the phrase are not rearticulated: *pɛrle elɛtte* [ˈpɛrleˈlɛtte]. An unstressed final *i* ɔllowed by an initial vowel word becomes a [j] glide: *dɔrmi amore* [ˈdɔrmjaˈmoɾe]. Provide IPA:

and from me she hopes only for bread and not for gold.
Classwork: e da me sola aspɛtta del pan e non dell'ɔr.

1. *Without hope of happiness,*
   Sɛnza spɛme di dilɛtto
   ts

2. *of your glimmering shoulders,*
   de le nitide spalle,

3. *Don't you hear in your soul?*
   Non sɛnti tu ne l'anima

4. *on the path of the stars*
   pel cammino delle stelle
   k

5. *Invitation to the dance*
   Invito alla danza
   ts

6. *Do not rise at the new sun.*
   non ti dɛsti al nɔvo sole.

7. *in the veil of the night.*
   de la nɔtte nel velo.

8. *Don't you smell in the air?*
   Non sɛnti tu ne l'aria
   ɾ

9. *you cast upon my heart:*
   nel pɛtto m'avvɛnti:

10. *full of passion*
    piɛna di passione

11. *you only, you only*
    tu soltanto, tu soltanto

12. *The ladies on the balcony*
    Le dɔnne sul balcone
    k

WORKSHEET #2: Italian vowels and semivowels

Provide IPA:

#1

aiuɔle	(flower boxes)
volto	(face)
nɔbile	(noble)
dilɛtto	(delight)
meno	(less)
fiume	(river)
potuto	(been able)

#2

inutile	(useless)
bionda	(blond)
muɔio	(I die)
venti	(twenty)
lɛtto	(read)
nome	(name)
pɔpoli	(peoples)

#3

vuɔto	(empty)
avete	(you have)
dopo	(after)
mɔlle	(soft)
punto	(point)
viɛni	(you come)
lɛnto	(slow)

#4

ove	(where)
muto	(mute)
piɛdi	(feet)
neve	(snow)
talvɔlta	(sometimes)
bɛllo	(attractive)
duɔle	(it hurts)

WORKSHEET #2: Italian vowels and semivowels

Provide IPA:

#5

volo	(flight)
umile	(humble)
momento	(moment)
fɔlle	(deranged)
vɛnto	(wind)
pietate	(pity)
duɔmo	(cathedral)

#6

nume	(heavens)
monti	(mountains)
vɔlle	(wanted)
pianto	(I plant)
ɛbbe	(he had)
buɔn	(good)
mente	(mind)

#7

affɛtto	(affection)
nɔve	(nine)
venuto	(come)
fonte	(source)
benedetto	(blessed)
tiɛni	(you hold)
muɔvo	(I move)

#8

udite	(you hear)
l'uɔmo	(the man)
dove	(where)
nebbia	(fog)
tɔlto	(removed)
vede	(sees)
poɛta	(poet)

WORKSHEET #2: Italian vowels and semivowels

Provide IPA:

#9

dolεnte	(hurting)
nɔdo	(knot)
appena	(hardly)
vuɔle	(wants)
mondo	(world)
niεnte	(nothing)
tutto	(all)

#10

l'ultimo	(the last)
volete	(you want)
pεtto	(chest)
empia	(wicked)
fondo	(deep)
nɔte	(notes)
tuɔno	(thunder)

#11

lume	(light)
anεllo	(ring)
nɔtte	(night)
uɔmini	(men)
piume	(feathers)
molto	(a lot)
vene	(veins)

#12

almeno	(at least)
pupille	(students)
tεmpo	(time)
dɔle	(hurts)
piεno	(full)
voti	(vows)
nuɔto	(swimming)

UNIT 3:

Italian *s*, *z*, and *r* spellings

RULES FOR TRANSCRIPTION

Italian *s*, *z*, and *r* spellings

Spelling	IPA	Sample Words
Intervocalic *r*	[ɾ] Flipped *r*	parole [pa'ɾɔle]
All other *r*	[r] Rolled *r*	ritorno [ri'torno] per [per]
rr	[rr] Rolled *r*	torre ['torre]
* Intervocalic *s*	[z] Dental Fricative	presente [pre'zɛnte]
s + voiced consonant	[z] Dental Fricative	fantasma [fan'tazma]
All other *s, ss*	[s]/[ss] Dental Fricative	sussurro [sus'surro]
z (dictionary required)	[ts] Dental Affricate	sɛnza ['sɛntsa]
zz (dictionary required)	[tts] Dental Affricate	carezze [ka'ɾettse]
z (dictionary required)	[dz] Dental Affricate	garzone [gar'dzone]
zz (dictionary required)	[ddz] Dental Affricate	mɛzzo ['mɛddzo]

* LYRIC DICTION RULES FOR INTERVOCALIC *S*

Specified words have two pronunciations for intervocalic *s*. Dictionary transcription indicates a voiceless [s] pronunciation for the words *casa* ['kasa], *così* [ko'si], and *cosa* ['kɔsa]. Dictionary IPA represents the spoken form of the language. The correct pronunciation of intervocalic *s* for lyric diction is [z]: ['kaza], [ko'zi], and ['kɔza].

Lyric diction rules for the proper pronunciation of intervocalic *s* were codified by Evelina Colorni, author of *Singer's Italian*. A voiced pronunciation of intervocalic *s* is an elegant manner of speech that is appropriate for poetry and singing.

Exceptions: compound words (*stasera*), words with prefixes (*risuonare*), and words containing the pronoun *si* (*dicesi*) retain a voiceless pronunciation of *s* for spoken and lyric pronunciation.

CLASSWORK #3: Italian *s*, *z*, and *r* spellings

Provide IPA:

1. istante (instant)
2. basso (low)
3. speranza (*z* [ts]) (hope)
4. rɛsta (it remains)
5. paradiso (paradise)
6. sleale (disloyal)
7. allora (then)
8. zɛffiri (*z* [dz]) (zephyrs)

TRANSCRIPTION WITHIN THE PHRASE #3: Intervocalic *r*

Intervocalic *r* within the phrase is flipped: *vaghi rai* [ˈvagi ɾaːi]. Provide IPA:

Classwork: *The beautiful crimson rose*
Bɛlla rɔsa porporina

1. *The fervent desire*
Il fɛrvido desidɛrio

2. *its fragrance troubled my thoughts!*
m'ha l'olezzo turbato 'l pensiɛr!
ddz

3. *a tempestuous sea;*
un tempestoso mare;

4. *do not learn misfortune.*
non impara la sventura.

5. *perfumed with roses,*
profumato di rɔsa

6. *Solitary little breeze,*
Solitario zeffiretto,
dz

7. *you announce her paradise,*
tu l'annunzi il paradiso,
ts

8. *An amorous flame*
Un amoroso fɔco

9. *but by past experience*
ma per usanza antica
ts

10. *the shady valleys, the deep forests,*
valli ombrose, ɛrme forɛste,

11. *the miserable delight*
il misero dilɛtto

12. *Return, charming Phyllis,*
Torna, vezzosa Fillide,
tˈts

WORKSHEET #3: Italian *s*, *z*, and *r* spellings

Provide IPA:

#1

spesso	(often)
[ˈspesso]	
bellezza (*zz* is [tts])	(beauty)
[belˈlettsa]	
ripɔso	(rest)
[riˈpɔzo]	
smetti	(you stop)
[ˈzmetti]	
pɛnso	(I think)
[ˈpɛnzo] ← s	
forse	(perhaps)
[ˈforse]	
sereno	(good weather)
[seˈreno]	

#2

mentre	(while)
[ˈmentre]	
snɔdo	(junction)
[ˈsnɔdo] z	
fɛsta	(party)
[ˈfɛsta]	
azzurro (*zz* is [ddz])	(blue)
[adˈdzurro]	
lassa	(relaxed)
[ˈlassa]	
pɔvero	(poor)
[ˈpɔvero]	
rɔse	(roses)
[ˈrɔze]	

#3

smania	(agitation)
[ˈzmania] zmanja	
dolor	(pain)
[doˈlor]	
silɛnzio (*z* is [ts])	(silence)
[siˈlɛntsjo]	
fossi	(I were)
[ˈfossi]	
viso	(face)
[ˈvizo]	
ora	(now)
[ˈora]	
splɛnde	(shines)
[ˈzplɛnde] s	

#4

stesso	(same)
[ˈztesso] s	
ɛra	(was)
[ˈɛra]	
zeffiretto (*z* is [dz])	(little zephyr)
[dzeffiˈretto]	
amorosa	(loving)
[amoˈroza]	
snɛllo	(slender)
[ˈznɛllo]	
tɛrra	(earth)
[ˈtɛrra]	
spine	(thorns)
[ˈzpine] s	

WORKSHEET #3: Italian *s*, *z*, and *r* spellings

Provide IPA:

#5

altro	(other)
smɔrte	(pale)
vero	(true)
innanzi (*z* is [ts])	(ahead)
riso	(laughter)
bellissima	(most attractive)
suɔno	(sound)

#6

sasso	(stone)
anzi (*z* is [ts])	(on the contrary)
tempɛsta	(storm)
smalto	(enamel)
morire	(to die)
spɔsa	(bride)
pensiɛr	(thought)

#7

spada	(sword)
pietoso	(compassionate)
smarrita	(lost)
amore	(love)
essa	(it)
sospir	(sigh)
fɔrza (*z* is [ts])	(force)

#8

serenata	(serenade)
pose	(poses)
stanza (*z* is [ts])	(room)
lasso	(lapse)
sventura	(misfortune)
ride	(laughs)
tɛsta	(head)

WORKSHEET #3: Italian *s*, *z*, and *r* spellings

Provide IPA:

#9

misero	(wretched)
vezzosa (*zz* is [tts])	(charming)
svanito	(vanished)
sera	(evening)
pɔsso	(I am able)
sɛmpre	(always)
destino	(destiny)

#10

sorriso	(smile)
riva	(shore)
insiɛme	(together)
adɛsso	(now)
smeraldi	(emeralds)
tɛnero	(tender)
lenzuɔla (*z* is [ts])	(sheets)

#11

sponda	(bank)
desidɛrio	(desire)
brezza (*zz* is [ddz])	(breeze)
spirito	(spirit)
mɔsse	(movements)
fior	(flower)
svɛntola	(slap)

#12

danza (*z* is [ts])	(dance)
sɔrte	(sort)
tesɔro	(treasure)
basta	(enough)
sbadato	(careless)
vivere	(to live)
passo	(step)

UNIT 4:

Italian *c*, *ch,* *sc*, and *nc* spellings

RULES FOR TRANSCRIPTION

Italian *c*, *ch, sc*, and *nc* spellings

Spelling	IPA	Sample Words
c + *a, o, u,* or consonant	[k] Velar Plosive (Stop)	cɔre [ˈkɔɾe] lacrime [ˈlakrime]
cc + *a, o, u,* or consonant	[kk]	accanto [akˈkanto] ɛccola [ˈɛkkola]
sc + *a, o, u,* or consonant	[sk]	scolpita [skolˈpita] fresca [ˈfreska]
ch (silent *h*)	[k]	chiama [ˈkjama] schermo [ˈskermo]
cch (silent *h*)	[kk]	ɔcchi [ˈɔkki] ricche [ˈrikke]
c + *e* or *i*	[tʃ] Prepalatal Affricate	vicino [viˈtʃino] dolce [ˈdoltʃe]
cc + *e* or *i*	[ttʃ]	uccɛlli [utˈtʃɛlli] lacci [ˈlattʃi]
c + *i* + vowel (silent *i*)	[tʃ]	ciɛlo [ˈtʃɛlo] guancia [ˈgwantʃa]
cc + *i* + vowel (silent *i*)	[ttʃ]	braccio [ˈbrattʃo] goccia [ˈgottʃa]
sc + *e* or *i*	[ʃʃ] Prepalatal Fricative	ruscɛllo [ruʃˈʃɛllo] pesci [ˈpeʃʃi]
sc + *i* + vowel (silent *i*)	[ʃʃ]	lascia [ˈlaʃʃa] conosciuta [konoʃˈʃuta]
nc + *a, o, u,* consonant	[ŋ] Velar Nasal	manca [ˈmaŋka] incontro [iŋˈkontro]

CLASSWORK #4: Italian *c*, *ch, sc*, and *nc* spellings

Provide IPA:

1. conosco (I know)
2. faccia (makes)
3. nasce (is born)
4. vecchio (old)
5. ancora (still)
6. ɛcco (here)
7. cime (tops)
8. gradisci (you appreciate)
9. pace (peace)
10. l'uscio (the door)

TRANSCRIPTION WITHIN THE PHRASE #4: Elision and phrasal doubling

Elision is formed when an apostrophe replaces the vowel of a monosyllabic word in order to connect it with a following initial vowel word: *d'ɛsser tu l'amor mio* [ˈdɛsser tu laˈmor miːo]. The spelling *c'* [tʃ] is an abbreviated form of the personal pronoun *ci.*

Phrasal doubling is the doubling of an initial consonant within the phrase. The decision to double is based upon the musical setting and text (see page 236 for additional information). Phrasal doubling suggestions are indicated with an asterisk.

Provide IPA:

Do you still remember the day that we met?
Classwork: Ricɔrdi ancora il dì *che c'incontrammo;

1. *Why are you sad when you live happily?*
di chi vi dolete se *viver felici

2. *And the little bird sings to the serene heaven:*
e l'uccellino canta al ciɛl sereno:

3. *Cut down are the flowers and the hopes,*
cadon recisi i fiori e le speranze

4. *the sweet old flame*
la dolce fiamma antica

5. *without refuge, love has constrained me . . .*
sɛnza ricɛtto amor m'ha *costretto . . .

6. *Nina, remember the kisses that I gave you!*
Nina, rammenta i baci che t'hɔ dato!

7. *Now that heaven gives you to me,*
or che il ciɛlo a *me ti rɛnde,

8. *I seek you, I call you, I hope and I sigh.*
cerco te, chiamo te, spɛro e *sospiro.

9. *Indeed you have spoken, O beautiful mouth,*
Pur dicesti, | o *bocca bɛlla,

10. *I feel in my heart a certain pain,*
Sɛnto nel cɔre cɛrto dolore,

11. *Stop, cruel one, all the torment!*
Cɛssa, crudɛl, tanto rigor!

12. *you were born with the roses;*
nasceste colle rɔse;

WORKSHEET #4: Italian *c*, *ch*, *sc*, and *nc* spellings

Provide IPA:

#1

usciva	(he exited)	[uʃ'ʃiva]
pɔco	(little)	['pɔko]
dolci	(sweets)	['doltʃi]
asciutto	(dry)	[aʃ'ʃutto]
spelonche	(caves)	[spe'lonke]
marciamo	(we march)	[mar'tʃamo]
rinasce	(it revives)	[ri'naʃʃe]
chiamo	(I call)	['kjamo]
face	(it does)	['fatʃe]
scritto	(written)	['skritto]

#2

conosciuto	(known)	[konoʃ'ʃuto]
barchetta	(small boat)	[bar'ketta]
felice	(happy)	[fe'litʃe]
anco	(still)	['aŋko]
scintilla	(spark)	[skin'tilla]
fisco	(revenue)	['fisko]
guancie	(cheeks)	['gwantʃe]
canto	(song)	['kanto]
scɛna	(stage)	['skɛna]
placido	(calm)	['platʃido]

#3

ufficio	(office)	[uf'fitʃo]
ascendere	(to rise)	[a'skendere]
spɛcchio	(mirror)	['spɛkkio]
fugaci	(fleeting)	[fu'gatʃi]
inchino	(bow)	[in'kino]
scivola	(it slides)	['ʃʃivola]
contɛnto	(content)	[kon'tɛnto]
accɛnti	(accents)	[ak'kɛnti]
cresciuta	(grown)	[kreʃʃuta]
scolpire	(to sculpt)	[skol'pire]

#4

scelta	(chosen)	['ʃʃelta]
dice	(says)	['ditʃe]
cheto	(quiet)	['keto]
ferisci	(you hurt)	[fe'riʃʃi]
bocca	(mouth)	['bokka]
vincitor	(winner)	[vintʃi'tor]
scampo	(escape)	[skampo]
anche	(also)	['anke]
pɔscia	(later)	['pɔʃʃa]
capriccio	(whim)	[ka'prittʃo]

WORKSHEET #4: Italian *c*, *ch, sc*, and *nc* spellings

Provide IPA:

#5

chi<u>ɔ</u>me	(foliage)	[ˈkjɔme]
bi<u>a</u>nca	(white)	[ˈbjaŋka]
usci<u>a</u>mo	(we go out)	[uʃˈʃamo]
felicit<u>à</u>	(happiness)	[felitʃiˈta]
c<u>o</u>me	(like)	[ˈkome]
osc<u>u</u>ra	(dark)	[oˈskura]
sc<u>i</u>sso	(split)	[ʃˈʃisso]
r<u>i</u>ccioli	(curls)	[ˈrittʃoli]
svan<u>i</u>sce	(it vanishes)	[zvaˈniʃʃe]
c<u>ɛ</u>nto	(hundred)	[ˈtʃɛnto]

#6

sc<u>ɛ</u>ttro	(scepter)	[ʃˈʃɛttro]
pescat<u>o</u>re	(fisherman)	[peskaˈtoɾe]
fi<u>a</u>nco	(flank)	[ˈfjaŋko]
sch<u>e</u>rza (*z* is [ts])	(jokes)	[ˈskertsa]
dolc<u>i</u>ssimo	(sweetest)	[doltˈʃissimo]
sciag<u>u</u>ra	(disaster)	[ʃʃaˈgura]
c<u>a</u>po	(head)	[ˈkapo]
br<u>a</u>ccia	(arms)	[ˈbrattʃa]
len<u>i</u>sci	(you soothe)	[leˈniʃʃi]
c<u>ɛ</u>rto	(certain)	[ˈkɛrto]

#7

scient<u>i</u>fico	(scientific)	[ʃʃenˈtifiko]
circond<u>a</u>re	(encircle)	[tʃirkonˈdaɾe]
f<u>ɔ</u>co	(fire)	[ˈfɔko]
v<u>o</u>ce	(voice)	[ˈvotʃe]
asc<u>o</u>lta	(listen to)	[aˈskolta]
scintill<u>a</u>nte	(sparkling)	[ʃʃintilˈlante]
c<u>o</u>nca	(basin)	[ˈkoŋka]
disc<u>e</u>nde	(comes down)	[diʃˈʃende]
ci<u>ɛ</u>co	(blind)	[ˈtʃɛko]
schi<u>ɛ</u>ra	(ranks)	[ˈskjɛra]

#8

f<u>a</u>scia	(band)	[ˈfaʃʃa]
tronc<u>a</u>to	(cropped)	[troŋˈkato]
sc<u>e</u>nde	(comes down)	[ʃˈʃende]
fanci<u>u</u>lla	(child)	[fanˈtʃulla]
p<u>a</u>sco	(I graze)	[ˈpasko]
ch<u>i</u>na	(slope)	[ˈkina]
recitat<u>i</u>vo	(recitative)	[retʃitaˈtivo]
crud<u>ɛ</u>le	(cruel)	[kruˈdɛle]
ard<u>i</u>sci	(you dare)	[arˈdiʃʃi]
c<u>e</u>rco	(I seek)	[ˈtʃerko]

WORKSHEET #4: Italian *c*, *ch, sc*, and *nc* spellings

Provide IPA:

#9

fascino	(glamor)	[ˈfaʃʃino]
chiɛde	(asks)	[ˈkjɛde]
arciɛro	(archer)	[arˈtʃɛro]
ɛsce	(exits)	[ˈɛʃʃe]
casa	(house)	[ˈkasa]
bɔsco	(forest)	[ˈbɔsko]
principe	(prince)	[ˈprintʃipe]
incanto	(spell)	[iŋkanto]
luce	(light)	[ˈlutʃe]
scialba	(colorless)	[ʃˈʃalba]

#10

scɔpo	(purpose)	[ˈskɔpo]
mesci	(pour)	[ˈmeʃʃi]
bacio	(kiss)	[ˈbatʃo]
finisce	(it ends)	[fiˈniʃʃe]
piccino	(tiny)	[pitˈtʃino]
lɔco	(place)	[ˈlɔko]
arranca	(it hobbles)	[arˈraŋka]
sciɔcco	(stupid)	[ʃˈʃɔkko]
celɛste	(celestial)	[tʃeˈlɛste]
chiaro	(clear)	[ˈkjaro]

#11

confɔrto	(comfort)	[konˈfɔrto]
piacere	(to please)	[pjatˈʃere]
lasci	(you leave)	[ˈlaʃʃi]
sciɔlto	(relaxed)	[ʃˈʃɔlto]
chiɛsa	(church)	[ˈkjɛza]
fosco	(dark)	[ˈfosko]
fiorisce	(it flowers)	[fjoˈriʃʃe]
baci	(kisses)	[ˈbatʃi]
stanco	(tired)	[ˈstaŋko]
caccia	(hunting)	[ˈkattʃa]

#12

tace	(it is silent)	[ˈtatʃe]
anca	(hip)	[ˈaŋka]
disciɔlto	(dissolved)	[diʃˈʃɔlto]
scaccia	(it dispels)	[ˈskattʃa]
caro	(beloved)	[ˈkaro]
intenerisci	(you move)	[inteneˈriʃʃi]
laccio	(lace)	[ˈlattʃo]
fatiche	(toils)	[faˈtike]
ciprɛsso	(cypress)	[tʃiˈprɛsso]
cresce	(it grows)	[ˈcreʃʃe]

UNIT 5:

Italian *g*, *gh, gli*, and *gn* spellings

RULES FOR TRANSCRIPTION

Italian *g*, *gh*, *gli*, and *gn* spellings

Spelling	IPA	Sample Words
g + *a, o, u,* or consonant	[g] Velar Plosive (Stop)	lagrima ['lagrima] godere [go'deɾe]
gg + *a, o, u,* or consonant	[gg]	fugga ['fugga] struggo ['struggo]
gh (silent *h*)	[g]	preghiera [pre'gjɛɾa] spieghi ['spjɛgi]
ggh (silent *h*)	[gg]	agghiaccia [ag'gjattʃa]
g + *e* or *i*	[dʒ] Prepalatal Affricate	gentile [dʒen'tile] regina [re'dʒina]
gg + *e* or *i*	[ddʒ]	oggetto [od'dʒɛtto] raggi ['raddʒi]
g + *i* + vowel (silent *i*)	[dʒ]	giorno ['dʒorno] rifugio [ri'fudʒo]
gg + *i* + vowel (silent *i*)	[ddʒ]	maggio ['maddʒo] ondeggia [on'deddʒa]
gli	[ʎʎi] Prepalatal Lateral	egli ['eʎʎi] begli ['bɛʎʎi]
gli + vowel (silent *i*)	[ʎʎ]	figlio ['fiʎʎo] meraviglia [meɾa'viʎʎa]
gn	[ɲɲ] Prepalatal Nasal	ogni ['oɲɲi] bagnare [baɲ'ɲaɾe]

CLASSWORK #5: Italian *g*, *gh*, *gli*, and *gn* spellings

Provide IPA:

1. immagine (image)
2. meglio (better)
3. cinge (encircles)
4. prego (I pray)
5. ghirlande (wreaths)
6. raggio (ray)
7. signore (mister)
8. gigli (lilies)

TRANSCRIPTION WITHIN THE PHRASE #5

The spelling *gl'* [ʎʎ] is the abbreviated form of the article *gli*: *gl'inganni* [ʎʎiŋˈganni]

Provide IPA:

and I cry night and day:

Classwork: e *grido nɔtte e *giorno:

1. *embrace with the angels*
   cogl'angeli s'abbracciano

2. *The trip in a gondola*
   La gita in gondola

3. *that they make you wander far from life?*
   che *vagare ti fan lungi da *la vita?

4. *The unknown inhabitants*
   Gl'ignɔti abitatori

5. *Only our heart gives him every vigor!*
   Il nɔstro cɔre ogni vigore solo gli da!

6. *I cry, weeping continually:*
   grido piangɛndo ognora:

7. *into the sound of the gentle gavotte?*
   in suɔn di gavɔtta gentile?

8. *turn your eyes, oh desolate,*
   vɔlgi gl'ɔcchi desolata

9. *today Silvia will choose,*
   ɔggi Silvia sceglierà,

10. *Lovely moon, you who turn silver*
    Vaga luna, che inargɛnti

11. *he took nothing from the angels.*
    nulla agli angeli levò.

12. *Leap, turn, every couple goes around,*
    Salta, gira, ogni cɔppia a *cɛrchio va,

WORKSHEET #5: Italian *g*, *gh*, *gli*, and *gn* spellings

Provide IPA:

#1

giɔco	(game)
dirgli	(say to them)
angelo	(angel)
piglia	(it takes)
segno	(sign)
grave	(serious)
vɔlgi	(you turn)
mugghiando	(roaring)

#2

piangi	(you cry)
vɔglio	(I want)
frange	(fringes)
ignɔto	(unknown)
bɛgli	(fine)
gorgheggia	(trills)
lago	(lake)
stagione	(season)

#3

gite	(trips)
montagna	(mountain)
vermigli	(vermilion)
allegro	(cheerful)
ciglia	(eyelashes)
gregge	(flocks)
spiɛghi	(you explain)
piɔggia	(rain)

#4

legge	(law)
voghi	(you row)
grazia	(grace)
sdegno	(scorn)
ɔggi	(today)
bisbigliare	(to whisper)
giardino	(garden)
quegli	(those)

VORKSHEET #5: Italian *g*, *gh*, *gli*, and *gn* spellings

rovide IPA:

#5

magico	(magical)
larghi	(wide)
giɔia	(joy)
sveglia	(awake)
punge	(it stings)
dagli	(from the)
grillo	(cricket)
compagna	(girlfriend)

#6

giro	(turn)
sugli	(on the)
rugiada	(dew)
cɔglie	(picks)
benigni	(favorable)
segreto	(secret)
leghi	(building blocks)
gelato	(frozen)

#7

grigi	(grey)
scɔglio	(obstacle)
neghi	(you deny)
argɛnto	(silver)
piaga	(plague)
giovane	(young)
legno	(wood)
degli	(of the)

#8

gradita	(appreciated)
bisogno	(need)
leggɛra	(light)
agli	(to the)
giova	(is useful)
spargi	(you scatter)
fɔglie	(leaves)
margherita	(daisy)

WORKSHEET #5: Italian *g*, *gh*, *gli*, and *gn* spellings

Provide IPA:

#9

ragione	(reason)
laguna	(lagoon)
pɔrgi	(you offer)
consiglio	(council)
sfoghi	(outlets)
gɛme	(groans)
gli	(the)
vergogna	(disgrace)

#10

fuggi	(you flee)
grande	(great)
sogni	(dreams)
periglio	(peril)
vaghi	(vague)
oggɛtto	(object)
scɔgli	(obstacles)
giusto	(just)

#11

stringi	(you tighten)
ciglio	(edge)
piɛghe	(folds)
refrigɛrio	(refreshment)
negli	(in the)
voga	(to be fashionable)
ognuno	(everyone)
giunge	(arrives)

#12

cordɔglio	(grief)
maggiore	(greater)
regno	(reign)
saggi	(tests)
grɛmbo	(lap)
tɔgli	(you remove)
ghiaccio	(ice)
sorge	(rises)

UNIT 6:

Accent marks, vowel length, *gu, qu*, and *ng* spellings

RULES FOR TRANSCRIPTION

Accent marks, vowel length, *gu, qu,* and *ng* spellings

Spelling	IPA	Sample Words
à	[a] Bright [a]	pietà [pje'ta] già [dʒa]
é (dictionary required)	[e] [ɛ] Front Vowels	finché [fiŋ'ke] ohimé [o:i'mɛ]
è (dictionary required)	[e] [ɛ] Front Vowels	è [ɛ] mercè [mer'tʃe] piè [pjɛ]
ì	[i] Closed Front	desìo [de'zi:o] ferì [fe'ɾi]
Final ò	[ɔ] Open Back	vedrò [ve'drɔ] ciò [tʃɔ]
ù	[u] Closed Back	servitù [servi'tu] giù [dʒu]
gu + vowel	[gw] Stop + Glide	guardo ['gwardo] seguire [se'gwiɾe]
ng + *a, o, u,* or consonant	[ŋ] Velar Nasal	lungo ['luŋgo] solingo [so'liŋgo]
n + *qu*	[ŋ]	dunque ['duŋkwe] tranquillo [traŋ'kwillo]
qu	[kw]	quando ['kwando] qua [kwa]
* Final stressed vowel groups The first *a, e, o* of a diphthong	[:] Long Vowel	mio [mi:o] Lucia [lu'tʃi:a] causa ['ka:uza]

ACCENT MARKS

Acute and grave marks do not indicate an open or closed pronunciation of *e* and *o* in Italia Consult a dictionary. Exceptions: final ò verb ending is always open [ɔ] and final *ché/chè* a always closed: *perché/perchè* [per'ke]. The purpose of an accent mark is to:

1. Indicate the stressed syllable: *divinità* [divini'ta]
2. Distinguish between words of like spelling: *sì* (yes) / *si* (himself)
3. Indicate the syllabic vowel in words with final vowel groups: *può* [pwɔ] and *più* [pju]

* FINAL STRESSED VOWEL GROUPS

Two, three, and four letter words with final vowel groups (*io, mio, tuo, sia, miei, tuoi* and other are transcribed as polysyllables in the dictionary: ['i-o], ['mi-o], ['tu-o], ['si-a], ['mjɛ-i], ['twɔ-i These words are often set on one note by the composer. Since stress is characterized by vow length in Italian, these polysyllables are appropriately transcribed as monosyllables for lyr diction: [i:o], [mi:o], [tu:o], [si:a], [mjɛ:i], [twɔ:i].

The penultimate vowel is long (or syllabic) in a polysyllable with a vowel cluster at the end the word and stress on the final syllable: *melodia* [melo'di:a]

LASSWORK #6: Accent marks, vowel length, *gu, qu,* and *ng* spellings

rovide IPA:

1. questo	(this)	5. più	(more)
2. conviɛne	(agrees)	6. montagne	(mountains)
3. vuɔi	(you want)	7. tuo	(yours)
4. rimango	(I remain)	8. sangue	(blood)

RANSCRIPTION WITHIN THE PHRASE #6: Syllabic Vowels

ne vowel in a vowel cluster within the phrase must be selected as long. The syllabic vowel is chosen ased upon its emphasis within the phrase. Emphasized vowels include the vowel of a stressed syllable: *eltà infinita* [belˈtaːinfiˈnita], the long vowel of a diphthong: *miti augɛi* [ˈmitjaːuˈdʒɛːi], or a strong onosyllabic monophthong: *la vita è *brɛve* [la ˈvitaɛːˈbrɛve] (strong words are listed on page 236). The rst *a, e, o,* or *u* is syllabic in vowel clusters of unstressed syllables: *trɔppo ardore* [ˈtrɔppoːarˈdoɾe]. ook for initial vowel words to find vowel clusters and place a long mark after the syllabic vowel.

When will that day come when to my heart I will hold you,
Classwork: Quando verrà quel dì *che in sen t'accoglierò, (*che* is a strong word)

1. *why do you burn with love?*
perché ardete d'amore?

2. *What is this thing, alas?*
che cɔsa è *questo ahimè? (*è* [ɛ] is strong)
ε

3. *this beautiful infinity*
quella beltà infinita

4. *temper my love*
temprate i miɛi ardori

5. *in such a bitter moment*
in così amaro istante

6. *this desire that worries my heart;*
quel desìo, che il cɔr m'affanna; (*che* is strong)

7. *I will kiss you again*
ti bacerò ancora

8. *I feel the breathlessness, alas!*
sɛnto gli affanni, ohimè
ε

9. *he will give his heart*
donerà il cɔre

10. *love wants this*
vuɔl così amore

11. *every word is mute*
è muta ɔgni parɔla
ε

12. *what will be praiseworthy?*
qual havrà i lɔdi?

WORKSHEET #6: Accent marks, vowel length, *gu, qu,* and *ng* spellings

Provide IPA:

#1

benigna	(favorable)
qui	(here)
vittɔria	(victory)
luɔgo	(place)
fango	(mud)
può	(can)
chiunque	(whoever)
sɛi	(you are)

#2

stuɔlo	(crowd)
lunghe	(long)
guɛrra	(war)
nɔi	(we)
diɛtro	(behind)
estingue	(it extinguishes)
così	(therefore)
sognare	(to dream)

#3

fuɔra	(outside)
spɛgne	(extinguishes)
piɛtra	(stone)
vɔi	(you)
inquiɛta	(restless)
guise	(manners)
lusinghiɛro	(gratifying)
sarà	(will be)

#4

sia	(is)
luɔghi	(places)
inganno	(deceit)
tregua	(truce)
fiorito	(bloomed)
ovunque	(wherever)
piè (*è* is [ɛ])	(foot)
segni	(signs)

WORKSHEET #6: Accent marks, vowel length, *gu, qu,* and *ng* spellings

Provide IPA:

#5

degna	(worthy)
miεi	(mine)
segue	(follows)
languido	(languid)
suɔna	(sounds)
perché	(because)
io	(I)
vεnga	(comes)

#6

magna	(main)
sguardo	(look)
cinque	(five)
sentiεro	(path)
ohimè (*è* is [ε])	(oh dear)
Dio	(God)
scuɔla	(school)
piango	(I cry)

#7

tranquilla	(calm)
lεi	(she)
compagno	(companion)
piεna	(full)
fuɔco	(fire)
verrà	(will come)
quiεte	(quiet)
giunga	(reaches)

#8

pɔi	(then)
dilegua	(it vanishes)
langue	(languishes)
fiato	(breath)
ingrata	(ungrateful)
suɔlo	(ground)
regna	(reigns)
ciò	(that)

WORKSHEET #6: Accent marks, vowel length, *gu, qu,* and *ng* spellings

Provide IPA:

#9

lingua	(language)
cui	(which)
tuɔi	(yours)
beltà	(will beautify)
pegno	(pledge)
guida	(guide)
stringo	(I tighten)
memɔria	(memory)

#10

lenzuɔla	(sheets)
soffio	(breath)
mai	(never)
ignɔte	(unknown)
qua	(here)
ramingo	(wandering)
già	(already)
pingui	(fat)

#11

prɛmio	(prize)
suɔi	(its)
languire	(to languish)
signori	(sirs)
cinga	(it surrounds)
vivrò	(I will live)
quella	(that one)
dei	(of the)

#12

pugna	(fight)
quale	(what)
solitaria	(lonely)
buɔno	(good)
libertà	(freedom)
dovunque	(wherever)
suo	(its)
tɛnga	(holds)

Provide IPA:

1. smeraldo (emerald)
   [zme'raldo]
2. gioventù (youth)
   [dʒoven'tu]
3. albɛrgo (hotel)
   [al'bɛrgo]
4. miɛi (mine)
   [mjɛ:i]
5. tranquillo (calm)
   [traŋ'kwillo]
6. felicità (happiness)
   [felitʃi'ta]
7. insiɛme (together)
   [in'sjɛme]
8. seguirò (I will follow)
   [segwi'rɔ]
9. qui (here)
   [kwi]
10. angosciare (to upset)
    [aŋgoʃ'ʃare]
11. snɛlla (slender)
    [znɛlla]
12. più (more)
    [pju]
13. fanciullo (child)
    [fan'tʃullo]
14. piaghe (plagues)
    ['pjage]
15. riposar (to rest)
    [ripo'zar]
16. tuɔi (yours)
    [twɔ:i]
17. fiorisce (it flowers)
    [fjo'riʃʃe]
18. consigli (councils)
    [kon'siʎʎi]
19. passeggɛro (fleeting)
    [passed'dʒɛro]
20. fierezza (*zz* is [tts]) (pride)
    [fie'rettsa]
21. hai (have)
    [ha'i]
22. grato (grateful)
    ['grato]
23. compagna (girlfriend)
    [kom'paɲɲa]
24. azzurre (*zz* is [ddz]) (blue)
    [ad'dzurre]
25. fuggitivo (fugitive)
    [fuddʒi'tivo]
26. sbocciare (to bloom)
    [sbot'tʃare]
27. può (ò is [ɔ]) (can)
    [pwɔ]
28. lucɛnte (shining)
    [lu'tʃɛnte]
29. figliuɔlo (son)
    [fi'ʎʎwɔlo]
30. uccɛlli (birds)
    [ut'tʃɛlli]
31. l'ɔcchio (the eye)
    ['lɔkkjo]
32. pietosa (compassionate)
    [pje'toza]
33. zɛffiro (*z* is [dz]) (zephyr)
    ['dzɛffiro]
34. vigile (watchful)
    ['vidʒile]
35. sembianza (*z* is [ts]) (appearance)
    [sem'bjantsa]
36. poiché (since)
    [poi'ke]

37. piè (è is [ɛ]) (foot)
[pi'ɛ]
38. sguardi (looks)
[sgwardi]
39. desìo (desire)
[de'zi:o]
40. schiɛra (rank)
[ˈskjɛra]
41. gelsomino (jasmine)
[dʒelso'mino]
42. piɔggia (rain)
[ˈpjɔddʒa]
43. ghiaccio (ice)
[ˈgjattʃo]
44. pescatore (fisherman)
[peska'toce]
45. gaudio (joy)
[ˈgaudjo]
46. sia (is)
[si:a]

Provide IPA for the following phrases (phrasal doubling is suggested with an asterisk):

1. la voce del ciɛlo è amor (the voice of the sky is love)
[la'votʃe del'tʃɛlo ɛ a'mor]
2. il sogno ɛra bɛllo (the dream was beautiful)
[il ˈsoɲɲo ˈɛra ˈbɛllo]
3. ridɛndo va incontro all'ignɔto (laughing he goes toward the unknown)
[ri'dɛndo va iŋ'kontro alliɲ'ɲɔto]
4. le luci hɔ *lagrimose (I have weeping eyes)
[le'lutʃi hɔ laggri'moze]
5. che *sì affranto mi tiɛne (yes, distress holds me)
[ke ssi af'franto mi tjɛne]
6. l'ultima aurɔra splɛnde (the last dawn shines)
['lultima aurɔra splɛnde]
7. o *luci amate (oh dear eyes)
[o lut'tʃi a'mate]
8. amor mi tiɛne in pugno (love holds me in its grasp)
[a'mor mi 'tjɛne in ˈpuɲɲo]
9. il mondo esulta (the world rejoices)
[il ˈmondo e'sulta]
10. in una nɔtte estiva (in a summery night)
[in ˈuna ˈnɔtte es'tiva]

UNIT 7:

German classification of symbols

INTRODUCTORY NOTES

GENERAL TERMS

IPA. The *International Phonetic Alphabet* was established by the International Phonetic Association around 1888. Each symbol stands for one phonetic sound and is enclosed in brackets. Authentic pronunciation, accurate formation, and precise resonance must be defined for each symbol within the respective language.
Pronunciation: conversion of letters into the proper choice of speech sounds as represented by IPA
Enunciation and Articulation: the act of speaking or singing phonetic sounds
Expression: the act of conveying mood, color and sentiment of lyric texts
Monophthong: a vowel sound that maintains one articulatory position throughout the course of a syllable – a diphthong contains two vowel sounds per syllable; a triphthong contains three vowel sounds per syllable
Aspirate: a consonant that is sounded with an audible release of breath (English *p, t, k*)
Prevocalic: refers to a consonant that precedes a vowel sound
Intervocalic: refers to a consonant that stands between vowel sounds
Postvocalic: refers to a consonant that follows a vowel sound
Initial: the first letter or sound of a word
Medial: a letter or sound in the middle of a word
Final: the last letter or sound of a word

INTRODUCTION

This text highlights a lyric vocabulary of the classical period. Archaic words and spellings are represented. Some spellings reflect a former usage of the Eszett. Words that are commonly truncated within lyrics are included. Recommendations for pronunciation are based upon Siebs' *Deutsche Aussprache* with adjustments made for lyric diction. The 1969 edition provides a clear distinction for the pronunciation of *r. Die Laute im einzelnen* offers transcription rules with an exhaustive list of exception words. The recommended online multilingual dictionary and app is http://pons.eu. Pons provides sound examples with IPA for each language.

CHARACTERISTICS OF THE GERMAN LANGUAGE AND IPA

1) All nouns are capitalized
2) German uses several letters in addition to the English alphabet: Umlaut *ä, ö, ü* and Eszett *ß*
3) Additional IPA symbols include the ich-Laut [ç], ach-Laut [x], long vowel [:], and mixed [y:], [ʏ], [ø:], and [œ] vowels
4) Vowels are precisely formed, pure, and frontal in resonance
5) Monophthongs are predominant (words with one vowel sound per syllable)
6) Consonants clusters are prevalent (articulate in a quick, crisp and energetic manner)
7) An aspirate quality is required for the voiceless stops *p, t* and *k*
8) An alveolar point of contact is required for voiced *d* and voiceless *t*
9) Dental articulation is required for voiced lateral *l*
10) Long vowels and double consonants require a deliberate lengthening of the sound

WARNINGS

1) Do not diphthongize monophthongs
2) Do not assign a medial placement to vowels
3) Do not omit consonants from consonant clusters
4) Do not allow an intervening pause or schwa to divide consonant clusters
5) Do not substitute an English point of contact for the German dental *l*

PRONUNCIATION GUIDE

FRONT VOWELS

IPA	ENGLISH (approximation)	GERMAN
[iː]	eat, greet	ihm, Liebe, dir [ʔiːm] [ˈliːbə] [diːʁ]
[ɪ]	bit, quick	Kind, Himmel [kɪnt] [ˈhɪmməl]
[eː]	chaos, décor	mehr, Leben, Seele [meːɾ] [ˈleːbən] [ˈzeːlə]
[ɛ] / [ɛː]	met, friend	Herz, Mädchen [hɛɾts] [ˈmɛːtçən]

BACK VOWELS

IPA	ENGLISH (approximation)	GERMAN
[uː]	food, blue	Uhr, Blume [ʔuːɾ] [ˈbluːmə]
[ʊ]	look, put	Duft, Stunde [dʊft] [ˈʃtʊndə]
[oː]	obey, protect	Sohn, Vogel, Boot [zoːn] [ˈfoːgəl] [boːt]
[ɔ]	talk, ought	Wonne, Morgen [ˈvɔnnə] [ˈmɔɾgən]

CENTRAL VOWELS

IPA	ENGLISH (approximation)	GERMAN
[ɑː] dark *a*	father, honor	Jahr, Abend, Saal [jɑːɾ] [ˈʔɑːbənt] [zɑːl]
[a] bright *a*		Wald, Schatten [valt] [ˈʃattən]
[ʁ] vowel *r*		für, wandern [fyːʁ] [ˈvandəʁn]

MIXED VOWELS

IPA	ENGLISH	GERMAN
[yː]		früh, Hügel [frʏː] ['hyːgəl]
[ʏ]		Glück, Lüfte [glʏkk] ['lʏftə]
[øː]		schön, fröhlich [ʃøːn] ['frøːlɪç]
[œ]		öffnen, Töchter ['ʔœffnən] ['tœçtəʁ]

SCHWA

(The schwa is an undefined vowel sound in an unstressed syllable. In German, the schwa is pronounced as [ʊ] when followed by a vowel *r* or when final in the word or element, and [ɛ] for all other spellings. The English schwa has many pronunciations.)

[ə]	sofa, angel	meine, gegeben ['maenə] [gə'geːbən]

DENTAL CONSONANTS

(The following consonants are classified as dental in German but alveolar in English)

[z]	zoo, wise	Sonne, Weise ['zɔnnə] ['vaezə]
[s]	festive, house	Fest, Haus, müssen [fɛst] [hɑos] ['mʏssən]
[l]	loyal, little	Lied, als, Stille [liːt] [ʔals] ['ʃtɪllə]

ALVEOLAR CONSONANT

[ɾ]	thread, throne	Recht, Frieden, Herr [ɾɛçt] ['friːdən] [hɛɾɾ]

PREPALATAL CONSONANTS

IPA	ENGLISH	GERMAN
[ʃ]	short, passion	Stein, spricht, rasch [ʃtaen] [ʃpɾɪçt] [ɾaʃ]
[tʃ]	chair, latch	Deutsch, plätschert [dɔøtʃ] [ˈplɛtʃəʁt]

PALATAL CONSONANTS

IPA	ENGLISH	GERMAN
[ç]	huge, humor	gleich, nicht ewig [glaeç] [nɪçt] [ˈʔeːvɪç]
[j]	yet, year	jung, Jäger [jʊŋ] [ˈjɛːgəʁ]

VELAR CONSONANTS

IPA	ENGLISH	GERMAN
[x]		Buch, machen [buːx] [ˈmaxən]
[ŋ]	finger, link	Engel, danke [ˈʔɛŋəl] [ˈdaŋkə]

GLOTTAL STOP

IPA	ENGLISH	GERMAN
[ʔ]	age, ever	Auge, uralt [ˈʔɑogə][ˈʔuːɾʔalt]

DIACRITICAL MARKS

IPA	ENGLISH	GERMAN
[ː] long vowel		Meer, Wogen [meːɾ] [ˈvoːgən]
[ˈ] stress mark	ret<u>u</u>rn, ag<u>ai</u>n [ɹɪˈtɜn] [ʔʌˈgɛn]	Gesicht, zurück [gəˈzɪçt] [tsuˈɾʏkk]

INDICATIONS WITHIN THE TEXT

Primary stress typically falls on the first syllable in German. Stress on a consecutive syllable is indicated within the word by an underlined vowel.

Note: This text highlights a lyric vocabulary of the classical period. Archaic words and spellings are represented. Some spellings reflect a former usage of the Eszett. Words that are commonly truncated within lyrics are also included.

Classification of Symbols: Consonants

Voicing: A voiced consonant engages vocal cords. A voiceless consonant does not employ vocal cords.

Points of Articulation	**German**	**English**
Bilabial [bɑɪˈlɛɪbɪəl] Refers to the lips	[b] [p] [m]	[b] [p] [m] [w] [ʍ]
Labiodental [lɛɪbɪoˈdɛntəl] Involves the lower lip and the upper front teeth	[v] [f] [pf]	[v] [f]
Dental [ˈdɛntəl] Involves the tip of the tongue and the back of the upper row of teeth	[z] [s] [l]	[ð] [θ]
Alveolar [ʔælˈviələ] Involves the tip of the tongue and the ridge behind the upper teeth	[d] [t] [n] [ɾ] [ts]	[d] [t] [z] [s] [l] [n] [ɾ] [ɹ]
Prepalatal [pɹɪˈpælətəl] Involves the tip of tongue and the area between the alveolar ridge and hard palate	[ʃ] [tʃ]	[ʒ] [ʃ] [dʒ] [tʃ]
Palatal [ˈpælətəl] Involves a front arch of the tongue and the hard palate	[j] [ç]	[j]
Velar [ˈvilə] Involves the back of the tongue and the soft palate	[g] [k] [ŋ] [x]	[g] [k] [ŋ]
Glottal [ˈglɑtəl] Involves the air flow and the opening between the vocal cords	[ʔ] [h]	[ʔ] [h]

Manner of Articulation	**German**	**English**
Stop [stɑp] A momentary closure of the air flow passage	[b] [p] [d] [t] [g] [k] [ʔ]	[b] [p] [d] [t] [g] [k] [ʔ]
Fricative [ˈfɹɪkətɪv] Produced by directing the air flow past a set of articulators	[v] [f] [z] [s] [ʃ] [h] [ç] [x]	[v] [f] [z] [s] [ʍ] [ʒ] [ʃ] [h] [ð] [θ]
Affricate [ˈʔæfɹɪkət] A stop that is followed by a fricative	[tʃ] [pf] [ts]	[dʒ] [tʃ]
Nasal [ˈnɛɪzəl] Produced by directing vocalized tone through the nasal passages	[m] [n] [ŋ]	[m] [n] [ŋ]
Lateral [ˈlætərəl] Produced by directing vocalized tone over the sides of the tongue	[l]	[l]
Glide [glɑɪd] Produced by directing vocalized tone past a set of articulators without friction	[j]	[j] [w]
Trill [tɹɪl] Formed by taps with the tip of the tongue against the alveolar ridge	[ɾ]	[ɾ]
Retroflex [ˈɹɛtɹoʊflɛks] Produced with tongue tip curled up		[ɹ]

Worksheet #7: Classification of Consonants

Provide IPA to complete the following chart for German consonants:

	Bilabial	Labiodental	Dental	Alveolar	Prepalatal	Palatal	Velar	Glottal
Stop voiced voiceless								
Fricative voiced voiceless								
Affricate voiced voiceless								
Nasal voiced								
Lateral voiced								
Trill voiced								
Glide voiced								

Provide IPA to complete the following chart for English consonants:

	Bilabial	Labiodental	Dental	Alveolar	Prepalatal	Palatal	Velar	Glottal
Stop voiced voiceless								
Fricative voiced voiceless								
Affricate voiced voiceless								
Nasal voiced								
Lateral voiced								
Trill voiced								
Glide voiced								
Retroflex voiced								

Classification of Symbols: Vowels

Length: Closed vowels in stressed syllables are long [:]. Open vowels are short. (*ä* can be short or long [ɛ:])

Quality	German	English
Closed Requires a closer proximity between the tongue and roof of the mouth	[i:] [e:] [u:] [o:] [y:] [ø:]	[i] [u] [o]
Open Requires more space between the tongue and roof of the mouth	[ɪ] [ɛ] [ʊ] [ɔ] [ʏ] [œ]	[ɪ] [ɛ] [ʊ] [ɔ]

Peak of tongue arch	German	English
Front (tongue vowel) The arch of the tongue is forward with tip down during enunciation	[i:] [ɪ] [e:] [ɛ]	[i] [ɪ] [ɛ]
Back (lip vowel) The arch of the tongue is back with tip down during enunciation	[u:] [ʊ] [o:] [ɔ]	[u] [ʊ] [o] [ɔ]
Mixed (rounded front vowel) The arch of the tongue is forward with lips rounded during enunciation	[y:] [ʏ] [ø:] [œ]	
Central The tongue maintains a low position during enunciation	dark [ɑ:] bright [a] vowel *r*: [ʁ]	dark [ɑ] [æ] [ʌ] retroflex [ɜ]

The schwa represents an undefined vowel sound in an unstressed syllable. In German, the assigned pronunciation is [ʊ] or [ɛ]. The schwa symbol cannot be categorized by length, quality, or tongue arch.

Worksheet #7: Classification of Vowels

Provide vowel descriptions for the following symbols:

German Vowels

IPA	Length of vowel	Quality	Peak of tongue arch
[i:]			
[ɪ]			
[e:]			
[ɛ]			
[u:]			
[ʊ]			
[o:]			
[ɔ]			
[y:]			
[ʏ]			
[ø:]			
[œ]			
[ɑ:]			
[a]			
[ʁ]			

English Vowels

	IPA	Quality	Peak tongue arch
greet	[i]		
bit	[ɪ]		
said	[ɛ]		
blue	[u]		
look	[ʊ]		
obey	[o]		
ought	[ɔ]		
sat	[æ]		
father	[ɑ]		
bird	[ɜ]		
up	[ʌ]		

See vowel chart on page 234

UNIT 8:

German front vowels, double consonants, *r, h, w*

RULES FOR TRANSCRIPTION

German front vowels, double consonants, *r, h,* and *w*

Spelling	IPA	Sample Words
Initial vowel words and elements	[ʔ] Glottal Stop	umarmen [ʔʊmˈʔaɾmən]
e + one consonant, *eh, ee*	[eː] Long Closed Front	Regen [ˈɾeːgən] geht [geːt] leer [leːɾ]
e or *ä* + two or more consonants	[ɛ] Short Open Front	Stern [ʃtɛɾn] Gäste [ˈgɛstə]
ä + one consonant, *äh*	[ɛː] Long Open Front	Fäden [ˈfɛːdən] Nähe [ˈnɛːə]
Initial *h* of word or element	[h] Glottal Fricative	Händen [ˈhɛndən] (*h* in consonant clusters is silent: *ph* is [f] *th* is [t])
i + one consonant, *ih, ie*	[iː] Long Closed Front	Stil [ʃtiːl] ihn [ʔiːn] Miene [ˈmiːnə]
i + two or more consonants	[ɪ] Short Open Front	Bild [bɪlt]
* *e* in unstressed syllables	[ə] Schwa	Liebende [ˈliːbəndə]
** Schwa + *r* (except intervocalic *r*)	[əʁ] Schwa + Vowel *r*	Silber [ˈzɪlbəʁ] Wanderer [ˈvandəɾəʁ]
All other *r*	[ɾ] Flipped *r*	Ring [ɾɪŋ] empor [ʔɛmˈpoːɾ]
w	[v] Labiodental Fricative	Wimpern [ˈvɪmpəʁn]
Double consonants (all double consonants are doubled)	[mm]	Zimmer [ˈtsɪmməʁ] irre [ˈʔɪɾɾə]

STRESSED SYLLABLE

Primary stress often falls on the first syllable. Stress on a consecutive syllable is indicated by an underlinec vowel: *Geheimnis* [gəˈhaemnɪs]. Stress affects pronunciation of *ik* and *ie.* Stressed *ik* and *ie* are closed [iː] *Musik* [muˈziːk] *Melodie* [meloˈdiː]. Unstressed *ik* / *ie* are [ɪk] / [jə]: *Chronik* [ˈkɾoːnɪk] *Familie* [faˈmiːljə].

* SCHWA

Unstressed *e* within an element is transcribed with a schwa. Exceptions apply. A knowledge of the multiple elements of the German language is needed in order to identify schwa (see page 80).

** VOWEL [ʁ]

Vowel *r* possesses less carrying power than flipped *r* and should be reserved for words and syllables that are unstressed within the phrase. The [ʁ] symbol originated with Siebs' German pronunciation dictionary 1969 edition. It was applied to lyric diction by Dr. William Odom, author of *German for Singers.* The [ɐ symbol is found in dictionary transcriptions. This symbol is ideal for spoken practice but is not suitable fo lyric diction. The [ɐ] symbol merges a schwa with an *r*-colored vowel. For singing, the schwa must be separated from the *r*-colored vowel. Note both transcriptions of *Lieder*: [ˈliːdəʁ] (lyric diction), [ˈliːdɐ (spoken practice).

CLASSWORK #8: German front vowels, double consonants, *r, h,* and *w*

Provide IPA:

1.	wider	(against)	5.	Felder	(fields)
2.	dämmert	(dawns)	6.	gehen	(to go)
3.	Klee	(clover)	7.	Linde	(linden tree)
4.	hier	(here)	8.	edel	(noble)

TRANSCRIPTION WITHIN THE PHRASE #8: Exception Words

German exception words are listed on page 88. The closed vowel exception words follow patterns in spelling. The open vowel exception words are few in number but frequently occurring. It is necessary to memorize the open vowel exception words and vowel *r* words before completing the following phrases. Provide IPA:

Classwork: *in my heart is peace, in my heart is rest,*
Im Herzen ist Friede, im Herzen ist Ruh,
ts ts uː

1. *love's gentle fragrance.*
Der Liebe linden Duft.
ʊ

2. *poisoned me with her tears.*
Vergiftet mit ihren Tränen.
fɛʁ

3. *the love ever again!*
Die Liebe immer wieder!

4. *nearness of the beloved*
Nähe des Geliebten
p

5. *the world is empty.*
Die Welt ist leer.

6. *and brings hers back to her.*
Und nimmt die ihren mit.
ʔʊnt

7. *against the wind's opposition,*
Dem Wind entgegen,
t

8. *Love awakens the songs!*
Die Liebe weckt die Lieder!

9. *in my heart is peace,*
Im Herzen ist Friede,
ts

10. *You worlds, you thunder,*
Ihr Welten, ihr donnert,
ɔ

11. *many tears fell down.*
Fielen die Tränen nieder.

12. *in the empty window arches.*
In den leeren Fensterbogen.
oː

WORKSHEET #8: German front vowels, double consonants, *r, h,* and *w*

Provide IPA:

#1

Glieder	(limbs)
Kehle	(throat)
Tränen	(tears)
dem	(the)
ihren	(their)
Wilder	(savage)
Herr	(gentleman)
Beeren	(berries)

#2

Kälte	(cold)
tief	(deep)
immer	(always)
Lehre	(apprenticeship)
Fibel	(introduction)
weben	(to weave)
Berge	(mountains)
Heer	(army)

#3

wäre	(would be)
Feen	(fairies)
Ritter	(knights)
Liebe	(love)
geben	(to give)
ihn	(him)
mehr	(more)
Helden	(heros)

#4

Räder	(wheels)
eben	(even)
helle	(brightness)
Frieden	(peace)
Meer	(sea)
will	(wants)
wehen	(to blow)
Bibel	(Bible)

WORKSHEET #8: German front vowels, double consonants, *r, h,* and *w*

Provide IPA:

#5

Beet	(patch)
Lippen	(lips)
wieder	(again)
den	(the)
ihre	(their)
Hähne	(roosters)
nehmen	(to take)
ferne	(distance)

#6

midi	(length)
leer	(empty)
ende	(end)
flehen	(to beg)
nieder	(down)
Wipfel	(treetop)
heben	(to lift)
Blätter	(sheets)

#7

finden	(to find)
hehrer	(noble)
Mädel	(girl)
Klee	(clover)
ihrem	(their)
legen	(to put)
wie	(like)
Bett	(bed)

#8

liegen	(to lie)
Winde	(winds)
Feen	(fairies)
hätte	(have)
Tiger	(tiger)
kehrt	(turns)
gern	(gladly)
Feder	(feather)

WORKSHEET #8: German front vowels, double consonants, *r, h,* and *w*

Provide IPA:

#9

ihnen [Inən]	(them)
Täler [Telər]	(valleys)
Leben [Lebə]	(life)
Himmel [hIməl]	(sky)
Beet [bet]	(patch)
Perlen [perlən]	(beads)
fehlt [fɛlt]	(it is missing)
wiegen [vegə]	(to weigh)

#10

hinter [hIntəʁ]	(behind)
Knie (*kn* is [kn]) [kne]	(knee)
Beeren [berən]	(berries)
Lämmer [lɛmər]	(lambs)
wem [vem]	(whom)
rig<u>i</u>de [rIgidə]	(rigid)
drehen [drehə]	(to turn)
Fremde [frɛmdə]	(stranger)

#11

hegen [hegən]	(to cherish)
Titel [titəl]	(title)
leeren [lerən]	(to empty sth.)
Welt [vɛlt]	(world)
Ehre [ɛhrə]	(honor)
die [de]	(the)
Männer [mɛnəʁ]	(men)
Blick [blIc]	(gaze)

#12

Kinder [kIndəʁ]	(children)
Reh [re]	(deer)
fliegen [flegən]	(to fly)
Hände [hɛndə]	(hands)
Meer [mer]	(sea)
Wellen [vɛllən]	(waves)
ihm [Im]	(him)
Nebel [nebəl]	(mist)

UNIT 9:

German back vowels and *v*

RULES FOR TRANSCRIPTION

German back vowels and *v*

Spelling	IPA	Sample Words
o + one consonant	[oː] Long Closed Back	Loben [ˈloːbən]
oh	[oː]	Wohnung [ˈvoːnʊŋ]
oo	[oː]	Boot [boːt]
Final *o*	[oː]	so [zoː]
o + two or more consonants	[ɔ] Short Open Back	Pforte [ˈpfɔɾtə]
u + one consonant	[uː] Long Closed Back	Tugend [ˈtuːgənt]
uh	[uː]	Ruhe [ˈɾuːə]
Final *u*	[uː]	tu [tuː]
u + two or more consonants	[ʊ] Short Open Back	Wunder [ˈvʊndəʁ]
Initial and final *v*	[f] Labiodental Fricative	Vater [ˈfɑːtəʁ] brav [bɾɑːf] (intervocalic *v* [v]: Klav<u>ie</u>r [klɑˈviːɾ])
v in words of foreign origin	[v] Labiodental Fricative	Violine [vioˈliːnə]

CLASSWORK #9: German back vowels and *v*

Provide IPA:

1. Vogel (bird)
2. Munde (mouth)
3. Boot (boat)
4. holder (gentle)
5. Wehmut (melancholy)
6. Ohr (ear)
7. du (you)
8. Ton (tone)

TRANSCRIPTION WITHIN THE PHRASE #9: Exception Words

German exception words are listed on page 88. The closed vowel exception words follow patterns in spelling. The open vowel exception words are few in number but frequently occurring. It is necessary to memorize the open vowel exception words and vowel *r* words before completing the following phrases. Provide IPA:

Classwork: *the hat flew off my head,*
Der Hut flog mir vom Kopfe,
k

1. *he comes to you nevermore.*
Er kommt dir nimmermehr.

2. *in God's clear morning!*
In Gottes hellen Morgen!

3. *O death, how bitter are you*
O Tod, wie bitter bist du,
t

4. *you find rest there!*
Du fändest Ruhe dort!

5. *and the breath of the beasts*
und der Odem des Viehes
t

6. *the sky until morning*
Der Himmel bis zum Morgen
ts

7. *for love and love's pain.*
Vor Liebe und Liebesweh.
t

8. *then you would go in a golden cloud,*
Gehst du in gold'ner Wolke,

9. *the morning will come*
Kommen wird der Morgen,
t

10. *mother advised me wisely,*
Mutter, die rät' mir klug,
k

11. *like the kiss from her mouth*
Wie der Kuss von ihrem Mund,
t

12. *You are the rest, you are the peace,*
Du bist die Ruh, du bist der Frieden,

WORKSHEET #9: German back vowels and *v*

Provide IPA:

#1

goldenen	(golden)
drohen	(to threaten)
Flur	(hall)
oder	(or)
<u>v</u>er<u>g</u>essen (*r* is [ʁ])	(to forget)
Runde	(round)
wo	(where)

#2

Wolken	(clouds)
viel	(much)
Bruder	(brother)
Moor	(moor)
Ruhm	(fame)
oben	(above)
Luft	(air)

#3

wogen	(to surge)
kommen	(to come)
Blut	(blood)
Rohr	(pipe)
Mutter	(mother)
also (s is [z])	(thus)
vorn	(in front of)

#4

Väter	(fathers)
tut	(do)
bunten	(multicolored)
Ruhe	(rest)
wollen	(to want)
du	(you)
Chor	(choir)

WORKSHEET #9: German back vowels and *v*

Provide IPA:

#5

Lohn [lon]	(wage)
munter [mʊntəʁ]	(lively)
vier [fer]	(four)
Echo (*ch* is [ç]) [ɛço]	(echo)
fort [fɔrt]	(away)
Mut [mut]	(courage)
Bogen [bogən]	(bow)

#6

Wunden [vʊndən]	(wounds)
Dom [dom]	(cathedral)
hoffen [ˈhɔfən]	(to hope)
Vieh [fe]	(cattle)
Boot [bot]	(boat)
Ufer [ufəʁ]	(bank)
frohe [froə]	(merry)

#7

Krone [crɔnə]	(crown)
fuhren [forə]	(drove)
o [o]	(oh)
verg<u>e</u>hen (*r* is [ʁ]) [fəʁgeən]	(to go by)
Grunde [grʊndə]	(reason)
Blumen [blumə]	(flowers)
Wonne [vɔnə]	(delight)

#8

zu (*z* is [ts]) [tsu]	(to)
wohnen [vonən]	(to live)
Glut [glut]	(glow)
Volk [fɔlk]	(people)
Not [not]	(need)
Kummer [kʊməʁ]	(grief)
Ort [ɔrt]	(place)

WORKSHEET #9: German back vowels and *v*

Provide IPA:

#9

Rot (red)
[rot]

nun (now)
[nun]

Vesper (vespers)
[fɛspəʁ]

Wort (word)
[vɔrt]

ohne (without)
[onə]

Turm (tower)
[tʊrm]

desto (the more)
[dɛsto]

#10

Duft (scent)
[dʊft]

oft (often)
[ɔft]

Flut (flood)
[flut]

Moos (moss)
[mos]

buhlen (to court)
[bulən]

Brot (bread)
[brot]

Vetter (cousin)
[fɛtəʁ]

#11

tu (do)
[tu]

Tor (gate)
[tor]

Brunnen (well)
[brʊnən]

vern<u>o</u>mmen (*r* [ʁ]) (heard)
[fəʁn ɔmən]

gut (good)
[gut]

Morgen (tomorrow)
[mɔrgən]

wohl (probably)
[vol]

#12

Boden (soil)
[bodə]

voll (fully)
[fɔll]

hohen (high)
[hoən]

nur (only)
[nur]

dort (there)
[dɔrt]

so (*s* is [z]) (so)
[zo]

unter (under)
[ʊntəʁ]

UNIT 10:

German mixed vowels, central *a,* and final *b, d, g*

RULES FOR TRANSCRIPTION

German mixed vowels, central *a,* and final *b, d, g*

Spelling	IPA	Sample Words
a + one consonant or final	[ɑ:] Long Dark [ɑ:]	Atem [ˈʔɑ:təm] da [dɑ:]
ah	[ɑ:]	Zahl [tsɑ:l]
aa	[ɑ:]	Saaten [ˈzɑ:tən]
a + two or more consonants	[a] Short Bright [a]	Kraft [kɾaft]
ö + one consonant	[ø:] Long Closed Mixed	Öden [ˈʔø:dən]
öh	[ø:]	Söhne [ˈzø:nə]
ö + two or more consonants	[œ] Short Open Mixed	Schöpfer [ˈʃœpfəʁ]
ü or *y* + one consonant	[y:] Long Closed Mixed	Trüben [ˈtɾy:bən] Lyrik [ˈly:ɾɪk]
üh	[y:]	Frühling [ˈfɾy:lɪŋ]
ü or *y* + two or more consonants	[ʏ] Short Open Mixed	Wünsche [ˈvʏnʃə] Myrte [ˈmʏɾtə]
* *b* + consonant or final	[p] Bilabial Stop	Herbst [hɛɾpst] Laub [lɑop]
* *d* + consonant or final	[t] Alveolar Stop	Stadt [ʃtatt] Wind [vɪnt]
* *g* + consonant or final	[k] Velar Stop	Magd [mɑ:kt] Berg [bɛɾk]

TRUNCATED WORDS

An apostrophe at the end of a word indicates a clipped schwa. The final *b, d*, or *g* of a truncated word becomes voiceless: *sag'* [zɑ:k]. Retain some voicing when this sequence is followed by a word that begins with a vowel: *ein' Lind' in jenem Tal* [ʔaen lɪnt(d) ʔɪn ˈje:nəm tɑ:l]

* EXCEPTION SPELLINGS

When *b, d,* or *g* is followed by *l, r,* or *n* within the same element, it indicates a clipped *e* or *i* (memory aid: learn). Voicing and vowel length are retained:

Ebne (*Ebene*) [ˈʔe:bnə]
Adliger (*Adeliger*) [ˈʔɑ:dlɪgəʁ]
Vöglein (*Vögelein*) [ˈfø:glaen]

Voicing of *b, d* and *g* is retained for initial consonant blends with *l, r, n*: *bleiben*, *drei*, *Gnom*

CLASSWORK #10: German mixed vowels, central *a,* and final *b, d, g*

Provide IPA:

1.	flüsternd	(whispering)	6.	gönnen	(to grant)
2.	dröhnt	(roars)	7.	mag	(likes)
3.	Haar	(hair)	8.	kühlen	(to cool)
4.	andern	(others)	9.	Flöte	(flute)
5.	trüb	(cloudy)	10.	nahen	(to approach)

TRANSCRIPTION WITHIN THE PHRASE #10: Intervocalic *r*

Intervocalic *r* within the phrase may be flipped when a following initial vowel word or element is unstressed within the phrase: *Der Winter ist aus* [deːʁ ˈwɪntəʁ(ɾ) ʔɪst ʔɑos]. Provide IPA:

There familiar birds greet him over the sea,
Classwork: Da grüßen ihn Vögel bekannt überm Meer,
yːss

1. *Now the days drag over the world,*
Nun ziehen Tage über die Welt,
ts

2. *lamenting and whispering,*
Und es klaget und es flüstert,

3. *it blooms forth so that one can pluck,*
Da blüht es hervor, da pflückt man es ab,

4. *and could fly over the sea,*
Und zöge über das Meer,
ts

5. *above the wander- and wonderland.*
Über Wander - und Wunderland.

6. *As if in a garden*
Als müßte in dem Garten,
ss

7. *Green-adorned are woods and heights.*
Grünend umkränzet Wälder und Höh.
ts

8. *the day lost its glow,*
Der Tag verglühte all,

9. *the blossoms faded, life old,*
Die Blüte welk, das Leben alt,

10. *for soon her beloved returns.*
Denn der Geliebte kehrt bald zurück.
ts

11. *To wander is the miller's joy,*
Das Wandern ist des Müllers Lust,

12. *now you are fond of green!*
Nun hab' das Grüne gern!

WORKSHEET #10: German mixed vowels, central *a,* and final *b, d, g*

Provide IPA:

#1

Glück	(luck)
fühlend	(feeling)
barg	(saved)
ahnen	(to suspect)
Möwe	(sea gull)
Trab	(trot)
Hügel	(hill)
Völker	(peoples)
Paar	(pair)

#2

füllen	(to fill)
trüg	(deceive)
Grab	(grave)
Vögel	(birds)
Wahl	(choice)
niemand	(nobody)
Höhle	(cave)
wühlen	(to rake)
öffne	(open)

#3

trag	(carry)
Mühle	(mill)
wahr	(true)
Körper	(body)
brüllend	(roaring)
Abgrund	(abyss)
Übel	(evil)
ha	(ha)
Nöten	(difficulties)

#4

rühme	(praise)
blöde	(silly)
Lüfte	(winds)
nahm	(took)
wütend	(furiously)
Höhe	(height)
abwärts	(downward)
fördern	(to promote)
trug	(carried)

WORKSHEET #10: German mixed vowels, central *a,* and final *b, d, g*

Provide IPA:

#5

Müller	(miller)
Tür	(door)
Bahn	(path)
können	(can)
Abbild	(image)
frag	(ask)
Röte	(blush)
Haaren	(hair)
glühend	(glowing)

#6

Güte	(kindness)
da	(there)
halb	(half)
Höcker	(bumps)
Trümmer	(rubble)
Bahre	(stretcher)
Frühlingstag (*ng* [ŋ])	(spring day)
Löwe	(lion)
Abend	(evening)

#7

dröhnt	(roars)
Hölle	(hell)
Mahl	(meal)
arg	(bad)
Töne	(tones)
blühend	(flowering)
Knab	(boy)
Hütte	(hut)
über	(over)

#8

tönen	(to sound)
Hand	(hand)
wölbt	(curves)
klag	(complain)
Blüten	(blossoms)
la	(la)
Gründe	(reasons)
fahren	(to drive)
Mühe	(trouble)

WORKSHEET #10: German mixed vowels, central *a,* and final *b, d, g*

Provide IPA:

#9

mahnt	(reminds)
hören	(to hear)
rührend	(agitating)
Hülle	(cover)
Allerliebste	(all-dearest)
wölben	(to bend)
Brüder	(brothers)
Tag	(day)
dröhnen	(to roar)

#10

Land	(country)
hab'	(have)
müden	(tired)
Kahn	(boat)
Löwenburg	(lion castle)
öffnen	(to open)
früh	(early)
Brücke	(bridge)
höhnen	(to scoff)

#11

mög	(like)
Hahnen	(rooster)
Düfte	(scents)
Wald	(forest)
Haare	(hair)
öfter	(more often)
kühn	(bold)
gab	(gave)
Flügel	(wing)

#12

Wahn	(delusion)
Höhen	(heights)
hübsch (*sch* is [ʃ])	(pretty)
Öde	(desert)
lag	(lay)
grünen	(green)
bald	(soon)
Götter	(Gods)
führe	(carry)

UNIT 11:

German diphthongs, *ich* Laut and *ach* Laut

RULES FOR TRANSCRIPTION

German diphthongs, *ich* Laut and *ach* Laut

Spelling	IPA	Sample Words
ei and *ai*	[ae]	Freiheit [ˈfraehaet] Hain [haen]
au	[ɑo]	Raum [ɾɑom]
eu and *äu*	[ɔø]	Freude [ˈfɾɔødə] säuseln [ˈzɔøzəln]
Front vowel, mixed vowel, consonant + *ch*	[ç] Palatal Fricative	lächeln [ˈlɛçəln] möchte [ˈmœçtə]
Back vowel or *a* + *ch*	[x] Velar Fricative	Tochter [ˈtɔxtəʁ] Pracht [pɾaxt]
Final *ig*	[ɪç]	König [ˈkøːnɪç]
ig + consonant	[ɪç]	Königs [ˈkøːnɪçs]
Intervocalic *ig*	[ɪg]	Königin [ˈkøːnɪgɪn]
ig + *lich* or *reich*	[ɪk]	königlich [ˈkøːnɪklɪç] Königreich

EXCEPTION WORDS

Spelling *chs* is [ks] in specified words: *Achse, Achsel, Büchse*, *Dachs, Flachs, Fuchs, Füchsin, Luchs, Ochs, sechs,* all forms of *wachsen* (to grow) and *Wechsel*

CLASSWORK #11: German diphthongs, *ich* Laut and *ach* Laut

Provide IPA:

1. Licht (light)
2. Bläue (blueness)
3. flüchtigen (volatile)
4. Haupt (head)
5. all<u>ei</u>n (alone)
6. kräftig (strong)
7. teuer (expensive)
8. Dach (roof)

TRANSCRIPTION WITHIN THE PHRASE #11

Provide IPA:

Classwork: *Ah! just a little while,*
Ach! nur ein kleines Weilchen,

1. *O were I but a little bird*
O wär ich doch ein Vögelein nur

2. *and teach me Your holy law*
Und lehre mich dein heilig Recht,

3. *I alone, I poor tormented,*
Ich allein, ich armer Trauriger,

4. *"I am forever yours,"*
»Ich bin auf ewig Dein,«

5. *one stays yet gladly awake by the fire,*
Bleibt man noch gern am Feuer wach,

6. *yet my limbs rest not:*
Doch meine Glieder ruh'n nicht aus:

7. *that I will weep upon you.*
Die will ich auf euch weinen.

8. *I must also mourn the loss of the pearl*
Muß auch ich die Perle weinend
ss

9. *What I suffer, I know not,*
Was ich traure, weiß ich nicht,
ss

10. *Should I wake him up now? Ah no!*
Weck ich ihn nun auf? – Ach nein!

11. *however veiled my sorrows,*
Wie mich Leiden auch umfloren,

12. *there I'll peer perhaps a little inside!*
Da guck' ich wohl ein wenig 'nein!

WORKSHEET #11: German diphthongs, *ich* Laut and *ach* Laut

Provide IPA:

#1

lacht	(laughs)
heftiger	(more violent)
weit	(far)
Traum	(dream)
Fräulein	(young lady)
innig	(dearly)
deute	(interpret)
recht	(right)

#2

Honig	(honey)
Träume	(dreams)
Frau	(woman)
Pein	(torment)
durch	(through)
beugen	(to bend)
auch	(also)
wonnigen	(lovely)

#3

heulen	(to howl)
wenige	(few)
bei	(with)
euch	(you)
doch	(however)
freudig	(joyful)
Augen	(eyes)
träumen	(to dream)

#4

Leiden	(suffering)
räumen	(to vacate)
ewigen	(eternal)
gleich	(same)
Nacht	(night)
Baum	(tree)
teuren	(dearly)
heilig	(holy)

WORKSHEET #11: German diphthongs, *ich* Laut and *ach* Laut

Provide IPA:

#5

träuft	(drip)
willig	(willing)
noch	(still)
Gläubige	(believer)
blauen	(blue)
ein	(a)
möcht	(would like to)
Leute	(people)

#6

ich	(I)
Glaube	(faith)
Frucht	(fruit)
heilige	(holy)
läuten	(to ring)
weinen	(to weep)
mächtig	(powerful)
Beute	(prize)

#7

Äuglein	(little eyes)
laut	(loud)
gnädig	(gracious)
Heute	(today)
Bächlein	(little brook)
mutiger	(more courageous)
dennoch	(nevertheless)
keine	(none)

#8

eure	(your)
kaum	(hardly)
macht	(makes)
ruhigen	(calm)
Liebchen	(sweetheart)
traurig	(sad)
Bräute	(brides)
nein	(no)

WORKSHEET #11: German diphthongs, *ich* Laut and *ach* Laut

Provide IPA:

#9

Räuber	(robbers)
dein	(your)
Braut	(bride)
ewig	(eternal)
freundlich	(friendly)
Nachtigall	(nightingale)
Woche	(week)
treu	(loyal)

#10

Hauch	(breath)
nicht	(not)
läute	(ring)
einmal	(once)
Tau	(dew)
Bräutigam	(groom)
wenig	(little)
Reue	(regret)

#11

feurig	(fiery)
auf	(on)
wacht	(wakes)
bäumen	(to rise)
mein	(mine)
lächelt	(smiles)
neu	(new)
trauriger	(sadder)

#12

Bäume	(trees)
Mädchen (*ä* is [ɛ:])	(girl)
weil	(because)
Lauf	(run)
grimmige	(grim)
fleugt	(flies)
ruhig	(calm)
Knochen	(bones)

UNIT 12:

German consonants
[j], [ŋ], [ʃ], *qu, s, x, z*

RULES FOR TRANSCRIPTION

German consonants [j], [ŋ], [ʃ], *qu, s, x, z*

Spelling	IPA	Sample Words
j	[j] Palatal Glide	Jugend [ˈju:gənt]
ng	[ŋ] Velar Nasal	Finger [ˈfɪŋəʁ]
n + [k]	[ŋ]	dunkel [ˈdʊŋkəl]
qu	[kv]	Quelle [ˈkvɛllə]
sch	[ʃ] Prepalatal Fricative	Schimmer [ˈʃɪmməʁ]
Initial *sp* of word or element	[ʃp]	Spiel [ʃpi:l]
Medial and final *sp*	[sp]	Knospen [ˈknɔspən]
Initial *st* of word or element	[ʃt]	Stimme [ˈʃtɪmmə]
Medial and final *st*	[st]	Angst [ʔaŋst]
Prevocalic *s*	[z] Dental Fricative	See [ze:] Felsen [ˈfɛlzən] (except: Rätsel [ˈɾɛ:tsəl] unsre [ˈʔʊnzɾə])
ss and the Eszett *ß*	[ss]	besser [ˈbɛssəʁ] Roß [ɾɔss]
All other *s*	[s] Dental Fricative	Winters [ˈvɪntəʁs]
x	[ks]	Exempel [ɛksˈɛmpəl] (affects preceding vowel as two consonants)
z	[ts]	Tanz [tants]

INFLECTIONAL ENDINGS

Certain spellings indicate the presence of an ending. The spellings to be alerted to are *s, t,* and *st* at the end of a word. The root of a word must be identified in order to accurately transcribe nouns and adjectives with endings. The most common endings involve conjugated verbs. It is necessary to retain the vowel quality of the infinitive. Example: *gibst* [gi:pst] is closed since its infinitive, *geben* [ˈge:ben], is closed. Frequently occurring words with inflectional endings are:

bebt	[be:pt]	(trembles)	hebt	[he:pt]	(lifts)	regt	[ɾe:kt]	(moves)
betrübt	[bəˈtɾy:bt]	(sad)	hörst	[hø:ɾst]	(hear)	schönste	[ʃø:nstə]	(prettiest)
bewegt	[bəˈve:kt]	(moved)	hört	[hø:ɾt]	(hears)	schönsten	[ʃø:nstən]	(prettiest)
erhebt	[ʔɛʁˈhe:pt]	(raises)	lebt	[le:pt]	(lives)	schwebt	[ʃve:pt]	(floats)
gebt	[ge:pt]	(give)	legt	[le:kt]	(puts)	strebt	[ʃtɾe:pt]	(strives)
gibst	[gi:pst]	(give)	löst	[lø:st]	(solves)	strömt	[ʃtɾø:mt]	(flows)
gibt	[gi:pt]	(gives)	mögt	[mø:kt]	(like)	tönt	[tø:nt]	(it sounds)

CLASSWORK #12: German consonants [j], [ŋ], [ʃ], *qu, s, x, z*

Provide IPA:

1.	Schatz	(treasure)	5.	schnell	(fast)
2.	Fenster	(window)	6.	Morgens	(in the morning)
3.	Rosen	(roses)	7.	Sturm	(storm)
4.	Wangen	(cheeks)	8.	Jäger	(hunter)

TRANSCRIPTION WITHIN THE PHRASE #12

Provide IPA:

The stones themselves are so heavy,
Classwork: Die Steine selbst so schwer sie sind,

1. *sinks in my quiet window!*
In mein stilles Fenster sinkt!

2. *I'd like to train a young starling*
Ich möcht mir ziehen einen jungen Star,

3. *then she starts to sing!*
Dann fängt sie an zu schlagen!

4. *The day is beautiful! O be not anxious!*
Der Tag ist schön! O sei nicht bang!

5. *More gently sway the branches,*
Leiser schwanken die Äste,

6. *I went to the rosebush at night,*
Ging zum Rosenbusch zur Nacht,

7. *Quietly I sit on the hill's slope,*
Still sitz ich an des Hügels Hang,

8. *The farther my voice reaches,*
Je weiter meine Stimme dringt,

9. *My heart within itself quietly sings*
Mein Herz still in sich singet

10. *The sun has risen! Wake up!*
Die Sonn' ist aufgegangen! Steh' auf!

11. *Is she lovely and good as well?*
Ist sie schön und gut dazu?

12. *so proud, so bold, so spiteful,*
So stolz, so keck, so schadenfroh,

WORKSHEET #12: German consonants [j], [ŋ], [ʃ], *qu, s, x, z*

Provide IPA:

#1

Dank	(thank)
Spur	(trail)
lustig	(merry)
Schein	(light)
übers	(over)
jener	(that, those)
zwei	(two)
selbst	(even)

#2

wirst	(will)
Schnee	(snow)
Ding	(thing)
Spiegel	(mirror)
Lebens	(life's)
Stolz	(pride)
Jasmin	(jasmine)
sie	(she)

#3

ganz	(whole)
Strom	(river)
Hügels	(hill's)
rauschen	(to murmur)
Jahr	(year)
Sinn	(mind)
Liebsten	(most loved)
singt	(sings)

#4

Vaters	(father's)
Junge	(the young)
schon	(already)
Antlitz	(face)
so	(so)
Hoffnung	(hope)
finster	(dark)
spät	(late)

WORKSHEET #12: German consonants [j], [ŋ], [ʃ], *qu, s, x, z*

Provide IPA:

#5

Meister	(master)
Seele	(soul)
Klang	(tone)
Zeit	(time)
Himmels	(heaven's)
Stunde	(hour)
Jammer	(misery)
scheiden	(to separate)

#6

ja	(yes)
singen	(to sing)
jetzt	(now)
Liebste	(dearest)
spricht	(speaks)
Abends	(in the evening)
sind	(are)
frisch	(fresh)

#7

Strahl	(ray)
zurück	(back)
Schatten	(shadow)
Fels	(rock)
bringt	(brings)
sei	(is)
lispelt	(whisper)
jedem	(every)

#8

schön	(beautiful)
Gestern	(yesterday)
lange	(long)
zog	(pulled)
jemand	(anyone)
Spiel	(game)
Hals	(neck)
sah	(saw)

WORKSHEET #12: German consonants [j], [ŋ], [ʃ], *qu, s, x, z*

Provide IPA:

#9

Bergs	(mountain's)
ging	(went)
Schmerz	(pain)
soll	(shall)
jeder	(all)
Stand	(rank)
Flüstern	(whisper)
Menschen	(humans)

#10

sein	(his)
Schlaf	(sleep)
Knospe	(bud)
Tags	(day's)
zieht	(pulls)
Sterne	(stars)
Frühling	(spring)
je	(each)

#11

jagen	(to hunt)
steht	(stands)
Weins	(wine's)
Sonne	(sun)
Glanz	(gleam)
Engel	(angel)
schaut	(looks)
Osten	(the east)

#12

Herz	(heart)
Geister	(spirits)
Eins	(one)
still	(calm)
sich	(itself)
Jüngling	(youth)
schwer	(heavy)
rings	(around)

UNIT 13:

German prefixes and suffixes

RULES FOR TRANSCRIPTION

German prefixes and suffixes

Each element of a word is transcribed independently:

WORD	PREFIX	ROOT	ENDING	SUFFIX	TRANSCRIPTION	DEFINITION
Blümchen		Blüm		chen	[ˈbly:m-çən]	(little flower)
weggebracht	weg - ge	brach	t		[ˈvɛk-gə-bɾaxt]	(carried away)
unendlich	un	end		lich	[ʔʊn-ˈʔɛnt-lɪç]	(infinite)

Become familiar with common elements of the German language:

OPEN VOWEL & DIPHTHONG PREFIXES		MEANING	CLOSED VOWEL PREFIXES		MEANING
ab-	[ʔap]	off, down, away	da-	[dɑ:]	there, here
an-	[ʔan]	at, to, on	dar-	[dɑ:ɾ]	to present
auf-	[ʔɑof]	on, upon	* ˈher-	[he:ʁ]	hither, here
aus-	[ʔɑos]	from, out, of	über-	[ˈʔy:bəʁ]	motion to, past, over
be-	[bə]	verb prefix	ur-	[ʔu:ɾ]	denotes origin
bei-	[bae]	by, near, with	vor-	[fo:ʁ]	before, previous
durch-	[dʊɾç]	through, across	zu-	[tsu:]	to, towards, up to
ein-	[ʔaen]	a, one	nach-	[nɑ:x]	after, behind
emp-	[ʔɛmp]	x	SUFFIXES		
ent-	[ʔɛnt]	denotes separation	-bar	[bɑ:ɾ]	able, *-able*
er-	[ʔɛʁ]	denotes start	-chen	[çən]	diminutive
fort-	[fɔɾt]	away, off, forth	-haft	[haft]	denotes manner, *-ish*
ge-	[gə]	denotes collectivity	-heit	[haet]	designates condition
* herˈ-	[hɛʁ]	hither, here	-keit	[kaet]	denotes character trait
hin-	[hɪn]	away from, undone	-lein	[laen]	has a diminutive effect
miß-	[mɪss]	indicates opposite	-lich	[lɪç]	denotes quality, *-ly*
mit-	[mɪt]	with, along with	-los	[lo:s]	free of, *-less*
um-	[ʔʊm]	round about, again	-nis	[nɪs]	denotes result
un-	[ʔʊn]	indicates negation	-sal	[zɑ:l]	condition
unter-	[ˈʔʊntəʁ]	beneath, among	-sam	[zɑ:m]	denotes attributes
ver-	[fɛʁ]	indicates change	-schaft	[ʃaft]	indicates condition, group
weg-	[vɛk]	away, gone, lost	-tum	[tu:m]	denotes entities or ideas
zer-	[tsɛʁ]	indicates breaking	** -ung	[ʊŋ]	consequence of an action
		apart of something	-voll	[fɔll]	full of something

There is no glottal stop before an initial vowel *prefix* that is preceded by *her-, hin-, dar-, vor-*: *herab* [hɛˈɾap] (intervocalic *r* is flipped), *hinein* [hɪˈnaen], *daraus* [dɑˈɾɑos], *voran* [foˈɾan]

* *her-* is closed when stressed and open when unstressed: *herkommen*: [ˈhe:ʁ] *hernieder*: [hɛʁˈ]

** There is no glottal stop before *-ung* (*b, d* and *g* retain voicing): *Brandung* [ˈbɾandʊŋ]

CLASSWORK #13: German prefixes and suffixes

Underline the prefixes and suffixes:

1. verschwunden (disappeared)
   [fɛʁ'ʃvʊndən]
2. umarmte (embraced)
   [ʔʊm'ʔaɾmtə]
3. schicksalhaft (fateful)
   ['ʃɪkkzɑ:lhaft]
4. Gedanken (thoughts)
   [gə'daŋkən]
5. danieder (down below)
   [dɑ:'ni:dəʁ]
6. Vorbild (example)
   ['fo:ʁbɪlt]
7. Heiligtum (sanctuary)
   ['haelɪçtu:m]
8. zuwider (adverse)
   [tsu:'vi:dəʁ]
9. Nachsicht (indulgence)
   ['nɑ:xzɪçt]
10. Botschaft (message)
    ['bo:tʃaft]
11. Untergang (downfall)
    ['ʔʊntəʁgaŋ]
12. Entzücken (delight)
    [ʔɛnt'tsʏkkən]
13. übermannt (overpowers)
    [ʔy:bəʁ'mannt]
14. abflauen (to abate)
    ['ʔapflɑoən]
15. hinlaufen (to run there)
    ['hɪnlɑofən]
16. Mitherrscher (co-regent)
    ['mɪthɛɾɾʃəʁ]
17. Röslein (little rose)
    ['ɾø:slaen]
18. fortbleiben (to stay away)
    ['fɔɾtblaebən]
19. herstellen (to make sth.)
    ['he:ʁʃtɛllən]
20. wegbegeben (to negotiate)
    ['vɛkbəge:bən]
21. lenksam (manageable)
    ['lɛŋkzɑ:m]
22. Andacht (devotion)
    ['ʔandaxt]
23. heimlich (secretly)
    ['haemlɪç]
24. Traurigkeit (sadness)
    ['tɾɑoɾɪçkaet]
25. dartun (to display)
    ['dɑ:ɾtu:n]
26. erbaut (built)
    [ʔɛʁ'bɑot]
27. Gottheit (diety)
    ['gɔtthaet]
28. Blümchen (little flower)
    ['bly:mçən]
29. Urfehde (oath of truce)
    ['ʔu:ɾfe:də]
30. abgefallen (fallen off)
    ['ʔapgəfallən]
31. schalkhaft (waggish)
    ['ʃalkhaft]
32. zerreißt (tears up)
    [tsɛʁ'ɾaesst]
33. beginnt (begins)
    [bə'gɪnnt]
34. unendlich (infinitely)
    [ʔʊn'ʔɛntlɪç]
35. Einhundert (one hundred)
    ['ʔaenhʊndəʁt]
36. wonnevoll (wonderful)
    ['vɔnnəfɔll]
37. Aufenthalt (abode)
    ['ʔɑofʔɛnthalt]
38. wunderbar (marvelous)
    ['vʊndəʁbɑ:ɾ]
39. empfangen (to receive)
    [ʔɛmp'faŋən]
40. Trennung (separation)
    ['tɾɛnnʊŋ]
41. hoffnungslos (hopeless)
    ['hɔffnʊŋslo:s]
42. Mißbehagen (displeasure)
    ['mɪssbəhɑ:gən]
43. durchdringen (to permeate)
    ['dʊɾçdɾɪŋən]
44. Finsternis (darkness)
    ['fɪnstəʁnɪs]

WORKSHEET #13: German prefixes and suffixes

Underline the prefixes and suffixes:

#1

missgönnte	(begrudged)
[mɪss'gœnntə]	
Weilchen	(a little while)
['vaelçən]	
Freundschaft	(friendship)
['frɔøntʃaft]	
überdies	(besides)
[ʔy:bəʁ'di:s]	
Dankbarkeit	(gratitude)
['daŋkbɑ:ɾkaet]	
fortschleicht	(crept away)
['fɔɾtʃlaeçt]	
darüberlegen	(to superimpose)
[dɑ:'ɾy:bəʁle:gen]	
erscheinen	(appear)
[ʔɛʁ'ʃaenən]	
Rößlein	(pony)
['ɾœsslaen]	
Trunkenheit	(drunkenness)
['tɾʊŋkənhaet]	
zerfällt	(disintegrates)
[tsɛʁ'fɛllt]	
Andenken	(keepsake)
['ʔandɛŋkən]	
tränenvoll	(tearful)
['tɾɛ:nənfɔll]	
geschieden	(divorced)
[gə'ʃi:dən]	
dabeistehen	(to stand by)
[dɑ:'baeʃte:ən]	
weggeworfen	(thrown away)
['vɛkgəvɔɾfən]	
friedlich	(peacefully)
['fɾi:tlɪç]	
beklommen	(uneasy)
[bə'klɔmmən]	

#2

seltsam	(strange)
['zɛltzɑ:m]	
namenlos	(nameless)
['nɑ:mənlo:s]	
umhüllt	(coated)
['ʔʊmhʏllt]	
mitgekommen	(to accompany)
['mɪtgəkɔmmən]	
vorüberwallt	(boiled over)
[fo:'ɾy:bəʁvallt]	
durchbricht	(breaks through)
['dʊɾçbɾɪçt]	
nachsingen	(to imitate singing)
['nɑ:xzɪŋən]	
Urteil	(judgement)
['ʔʊɾtael]	
entbehren	(to miss)
[ʔɛnt'be:ɾən]	
Auftrag	(order)
['ʔaoftɾɑ:k]	
einkehren	(to stop by)
['ʔaenke:ɾən]	
Finsternis	(darkness)
['fɪnstəʁnɪs]	
unterscheidet	(differentiates)
[ʔʊntəʁ'ʃaedət]	
Zuversicht	(assurance)
['tsu:fɛʁzɪçt]	
untreu	(unfaithful)
['ʔʊntɾɔø]	
verlor	(lost)
[fɛʁ'lo:ɾ]	
empfindsam	(sentimental)
[ʔɛmp'fɪntzɑ:m]	
hernieder	(down)
[hɛʁ'ni:dəʁ]	

WORKSHEET #13: German prefixes and suffixes

Underline the prefixes and suffixes:

#3

weggeschwemmt	(washed away)
[ˈvɛkgəʃvɛmmt]	
mißgönnen	(to grudge)
[mɪssˈgœnnən]	
empfinden	(to feel)
[ʔɛmpˈfɪndən]	
Engelbildnis	(angel portrait)
[ˈʔɛŋəlbɪltnɪs]	
Schätzchen	(dearie)
[ˈʃɛttsçən]	
grausam	(cruel)
[ˈgɾɑozɑ:m]	
Gestalt	(shape)
[gəˈʃtalt]	
fieberhaft	(feverish)
[ˈfi:bəʁhaft]	
nachgesandt	(forwarded)
[ˈnɑ:xgəzantt]	
verlassen	(left)
[fɛʁˈlassən]	
durchwaten	(to wade through)
[ˈdʊɾçvɑ:tən]	
erschallt	(resounds)
[ʔɛʁˈʃallt]	
dahinwelken	(to pine away)
[dɑ:ˈhɪnvɛlkən]	
Ungeduld	(impatience)
[ˈʔʊngədʊlt]	
fortgeschritten	(sophisticated)
[ˈfɔrtgəʃɾɪttən]	
dargestellt	(depicted)
[ˈdɑ:ɾgəʃtɛllt]	
hersehen	(to look here)
[ˈhe:ʁze:ən]	
zerfallen	(to decay)
[tsɛʁˈfallən]	

#4

angefacht	(fanned)
[ˈʔangəfaxt]	
schwermutsvollen	(melancholic)
[ˈʃve:ɾmu:tsfɔllən]	
Freiheit	(liberty)
[ˈfraehaet]	
Abschiedsgruß	(parting greeting)
[ˈʔapʃi:tsgɾu:ss]	
Wohnung	(dwelling)
[ˈvo:nʊŋ]	
zuleid	(hurt)
[tsu:ˈlaet]	
betrübt	(sad)
[bəˈtɾy:pt]	
Klugheit	(cleverness)
[ˈklu:khaet]	
unzerreißbar	(untearable)
[ʔʊntsɛʁˈɾaessbɑ:ɾ]	
Wissenschaft	(science)
[ˈvɪssənʃaft]	
übernachten	(to stay overnight)
[ʔy:bəʁˈnaxtən]	
grausenhaft	(horrible)
[ˈgɾɑozənhaft]	
vorbeigehst	(pass)
[fo:ʁˈbaege:st]	
auserlesen	(choice)
[ˈʔɑosʔɛʁle:zən]	
umflossen	(flowed around)
[ʔʊmˈflɔssən]	
Hinsicht	(regard)
[ˈhɪnzɪçt]	
herrlich	(wonderful)
[ˈhɛɾɾlɪç]	
ausgegossen	(poured out)
[ˈʔɑosgəgɔssən]	

WORKSHEET #13: German prefixes and suffixes

Underline the prefixes and suffixes:

#5

umfassen	(to cover)
[ʔʊm'fassən]	
anschauen	(to behold)
['ʔanʃɑoən]	
unendlichen	(infinite)
[ʔʊn'ʔɛntlıçən]	
geboren	(born)
[gə'bo:ɾən]	
Bündnis	(alliance)
['bʏntnıs]	
hergeben	(to give away)
['he:ʁge:bən]	
Urlaub	(vacation)
['u:ɾlɑop]	
Fröhlichkeit	(gladness)
['frø:lıçkaet]	
Zufall	(coincidence)
['tsu:fall]	
abgetrennt	(separated)
['ʔapgətrɛnnt]	
Weggenosse	(companion)
['vɛkgənɔssə]	
Gebiet	(area)
[gə'bi:t]	
eingeschlafen	(fallen asleep)
['ʔaengəʃlɑ:fən]	
Wanderschaft	(journey)
['vandəʁʃaft]	
Hinweis	(hint)
['hınvaes]	
aufgeführt	(presented)
['ʔɑofgəfy:ɾt]	
dagegen	(however)
[dɑ:'ge:gən]	
empfange	(receive)
[ʔɛmp'faŋə]	

#6

überbreitet	(spread over)
['ʔy:bəʁbraetət]	
Unterricht	(instruction)
['ʔʊntəʁrıçt]	
Mitgefühl	(sympathy)
['mıtgəfy:l]	
Geselligkeit	(sociability)
[gə'zɛllıçkaet]	
Kindlein	(little child)
['kıntlaen]	
Schöpfung	(creation)
['ʃœpfʊŋ]	
fortgeschlichen	(crept away)
['fɔɾtgəʃlıçən]	
Dunkelheit	(darkness)
['dʊŋkəlhaet]	
begehrt	(desired)
[bə'ge:ɾt]	
aufspringt	(jumps up)
['ʔɑofʃprıŋt]	
vereint	(united)
[fɛʁ'ʔaent]	
uraltes	(ancient)
['ʔu:ɾʔaltəs]	
Einfalt	(simplemindedness)
['ʔaenfalt]	
entfernt	(removed)
[ʔɛnt'fɛɾnt]	
hoffnungslosen	(hopeless)
['hɔffnʊŋslo:zən]	
Mißgeschick	(mishap)
['mıssgəʃıkk]	
Abglanz	(reflection)
['ʔapglants]	
Reichtum	(wealth)
['ɾaeçtu:m]	

WORKSHEET #13: German prefixes and suffixes

Underline the prefixes and suffixes:

#7

Unsterblichkeit	(immortality)
[ˈʔʊnʃtɛɾplɪçkaet]	
sichtbarlich	(visibly)
[ˈzɪçtbɑːɾlɪç]	
unbekanntes	(unknown)
[ˈʔʊnbəkanntəs]	
kummervoll	(sorrowful)
[ˈkʊmməʁfɔll]	
Vorsitz	(chairmanship)
[ˈfoːʁzɪtts]	
hinwollen	(to aim at)
[ˈhɪnvɔllən]	
eingezogen	(drawn in)
[ˈʔaengətsoːgən]	
dargereicht	(handed)
[ˈdɑːɾgəɾaeçt]	
Unterströmung	(undercurrent)
[ˈʔʊntəʁʃtɾøːmʊŋ]	
Liebesbotschaft	(love's message)
[ˈliːbəsboːtʃaft]	
Köpfchen	(brains)
[ˈkœpfçən]	
ernsthaft	(earnest)
[ˈʔɛɾnsthaft]	
erfüllt	(fulfilled)
[ʔɛʁˈfʏllt]	
empfand	(felt)
[ʔɛmpˈfant]	
Schicksal	(fate)
[ˈʃɪkkzɑːl]	
auferstehen	(to arise)
[ˈʔɑofʔɛʁʃteːən]	
weggekehret	(turned away)
[ˈvɛkgəkeːɾət]	
durchschossen	(shot through)
[ˈdʊɾçʃɔssən]	

#8

Lüftchen	(breeze)
[ˈlʏftçən]	
Ahnung	(notion)
[ˈʔɑːnʊŋ]	
mithin	(consequently)
[ˈmɪthɪn]	
überschaute	(overlooked)
[ʔyːbəʁˈʃɑotə]	
durchschritt	(paced)
[ˈdʊɾçʃɾɪtt]	
wonnesam	(joyful)
[ˈvɔnnəzɑːm]	
entzwei	(divide)
[ʔɛntˈtsvae]	
Mägdelein	(little servant girl)
[ˈmɛːkdəlaen]	
vorübergehen	(to pass)
[foːˈɾyːbəʁgeːən]	
darbieten	(to present)
[ˈdɑːɾbiːtən]	
umzäunen	(to enclose)
[ʔʊmˈtsɔønən]	
gottlosigen	(godless)
[ˈgɔttloːzɪgən]	
nachgegangen	(to go after)
[ˈnɑːxgəgaŋən]	
ausruhen	(to rest)
[ˈʔɑosɾuːən]	
Unterzeichnung	(signature)
[ʔʊntəʁˈtsaeçnʊŋ]	
ergreift	(seizes)
[ʔɛʁˈgɾaeft]	
zerbrochen	(broken)
[tsɛʁˈbɾɔxən]	
traulich	(truly)
[ˈtɾɑolɪç]	

WORKSHEET #13: German prefixes and suffixes

Underline the prefixes and suffixes:

#9

Vögelein	(small bird)
[ˈfø:gəlaen]	
gottlos	(godless)
[ˈgɔttlo:s]	
Anfang	(beginning)
[ˈʔanfaŋ]	
zerbrechen	(to break)
[tsɛʁˈbɾɛçən]	
glücklich	(lucky)
[ˈglʏkklɪç]	
leidvoll	(sorrowfully)
[ˈlaetfɔll]	
Mißgeschicke	(misfortunes)
[ˈmɪssgəʃɪkkə]	
hergebracht	(traditional)
[ˈhe:ʁgəbɾaxt]	
nachgeflogen	(after-flown)
[ˈnɑ:xgəflo:gən]	
Verzweiflung	(despair)
[fɛʁˈtsvaeflʊŋ]	
umarmen	(to embrace)
[ʔʊmˈʔaɾmən]	
Dämmerung	(dawn)
[ˈdɛmməɾʊŋ]	
Einklang	(harmony)
[ˈʔaenklaŋ]	
boshaft	(maliciously)
[ˈbo:shaft]	
Täubchen	(little dove)
[ˈtɔøpçən]	
dargeboten	(presented)
[ˈdɑ:ɾgəbo:tən]	
entzückt	(overjoyed)
[ʔɛntˈtsʏkkt]	
dagegen	(however)
[dɑ:ˈge:gən]	

#10

Urkunde	(document)
[ˈʔu:ɾkʊndə]	
ausgespannt	(stretched)
[ˈʔɑosgəʃpannt]	
Mitläufer	(fellow traveler)
[ˈmɪtlɔøfəʁ]	
zufriedenen	(content)
[ˈtsu:fɾi:dənən]	
Gesang	(song)
[gəˈzaŋ]	
fortgerissen	(washed away)
[ˈfɔɾtgəɾɪssən]	
Altertum	(antiquity)
[ˈʔaltəʁtu:m]	
verderben	(to ruin)
[fɛʁˈdɛɾbən]	
umgeben	(surrounded)
[ʔʊmˈge:bən]	
bedeuten	(to mean)
[bəˈdɔøtən]	
überschneiden	(to intersect)
[ʔy:bəʁˈʃnaedən]	
entflohen	(escaped)
[ʔɛntˈflo:ən]	
gedankenvoll	(thoughtful)
[gəˈdaŋkənfɔll]	
wundersam	(wondrous)
[ˈvʊndəʁzɑ:m]	
Kindheit	(childhood)
[ˈkɪnthaet]	
herkömmlich	(conventional)
[ˈhe:ʁkœmmlɪç]	
abgetan	(dismissed)
[ˈʔapgətɑ:n]	
freudenlos	(joyless)
[ˈfɾɔødənlo:s]	

WORKSHEET #13: German prefixes and suffixes

Underline the prefixes and suffixes:

#11

hinreißen [ˈhɪnɾaessən]	(to carry along)
Ausgang [ˈʔaosgaŋ]	(exit)
täglich [ˈtɛːklɪç]	(daily)
Wahrheit [ˈvɑːɾhaet]	(truth)
Unrecht [ˈʔʊnɾɛçt]	(injustice)
Mißgeschick [ˈmɪssgəʃɪkk]	(misfortune)
Zickleine [ˈtsɪkklaenə]	(goatling)
Übermut [ˈʔyːbəʁmuːt]	(high spirits)
empfunden [ʔɛmpˈfʊndən]	(felt)
ratsam [ˈɾɑːtzɑːm]	(advisable)
schauderhaft [ˈʃaodəʁhaft]	(dreadful)
Geliebter [gəˈliːptəʁ]	(beloved)
Schicksal [ˈʃɪkkzɑːl]	(fate)
uralten [ˈʔuːɾʔaltən]	(ancient)
geheimnisvoll [gəˈhaemnɪsfɔll]	(mysterious)
abgeschieden [ˈʔapgəʃiːdən]	(remote)
aufgetan [ˈʔaofgətɑːn]	(opened)
Vorkämpfer [ˈfoːɾkɛmpfəʁ]	(pioneer)

#12

duftumrauscht [ˈdʊftʔʊmɾaoʃt]	(fragrance rustled around)
nachdenklich [ˈnɑːxdɛŋklɪç]	(reflective)
zufrieden [tsuːˈfɾiːdən]	(contently)
bewegt [bəˈveːkt]	(moved)
Herrlichkeit [ˈhɛɾɾlɪçkaet]	(glory)
furchtbar [ˈfʊɾçtbɑːɾ]	(terrible)
Dasein [ˈdɑːzaen]	(existence)
durchdrungen [ˈdʊɾçdɾʊŋən]	(permeated)
Teilbarkeit [ˈtaelbɑːɾkaet]	(divisibility)
zerstreut [tsɛʁˈʃtɾɔøt]	(scatters)
fortgemacht [ˈfɔɾtgəmaxt]	(made away)
mitleidsvoll [ˈmɪtlaetsfɔll]	(compassionate)
versunken [fɛʁˈzʊŋkən]	(sunk)
Leidenschaft [ˈlaedənʃaft]	(passion)
unterschätzen [ʔʊntəʁˈʃɛttsən]	(to underestimate)
sehnsuchtsvoll [ˈzeːnzʊxtsfɔll]	(full of longing)
Anblick [ˈʔanblɪkk]	(sight)
wegnehmen [ˈvɛkneːmən]	(to take away)

CLOSED VOWEL EXCEPTIONS

[e:rd]	
Beschwerde	(complaint)
Erde	(earth)
werden	(to become)

[e:rt]	
Erz (except as prefix)	(metal)
Herd	(hearth)
Pferd	(horse)
Schwert	(sword)
Wert	(worth)

[u:x]	[y:ç]	
Buch/Buche	Bücher	(book/beech/books)
Tuch	Tücher	(cloth/clothes)
Fluch	Psyche	(curse/psyche)
Kuchen		(cake)
ruchlos		(profane)
suchen		(seek)

[u:ss]	[y:ss]	
Buße	büßen	(repentance/to atone)
Fuß	Füße	(foot/feet)
Gruß	grüßen	(greet/greeting)
Muße	müßig	(leisure/leisurely)
	süß	(sweet)

[u:st]		
husten	düster	(cough/somber)
pusten	Rüster	(to puff/elm)
Schuster	Wüste	(shoemaker/desert)

[o:x]	[ø:çt]	
hoch Except: *Hochzeit*	höchst	(high/highest)

[o:nt]	
Mond	(moon)
Montag	(Monday)

[o:ss]	[ø:ss]	
bloß	Blöße	(bare/bareness)
groß	Größe	(large/greatness)
stoßen	stößt	(push/pushes)
Schoß floß	flöße	(lap/flowed/float)

[o:st]	[ø:st]	
Kloster		(cloister)
Ostern		(Easter)
Prost	rösten	(toast/roast)
Trost	trösten	(comfort/console)
getrost		(confident)

[ɑ:x]	
brach	(broke)
Schmach	(disgrace)
Sprache	(language)
stach	(pricked)

[ɑ:r]	
Art	(sort)
Arzt	(doctor)
Bart	(beard)
zart	(gentle)

[ɑ:ss]	
saß	(sat)
Spaß	(fun)
Straße	(street)

Other closed words:	
erst	(first)
stets	(always)
Geburt	(birth)
Wuchs	(growth)
Lotse	(pilot)
Obst	(fruit)
Vogt	(warden)
Psyche	(psyche)
Zypresse	(cypress)
atmen	(breathe)
Bratsche	(viola)
Jagd	(hunt)
Magd	(maid)

Closed vowel prefixes:

da-
dar-
'her-
über-
ur-
vor-
zu-
nach- [nɑ:x]
Except: *Nachbar*

Closed vowel suffixes:

-bar	-sam
-los	-tum
-sal	

OPEN VOWEL EXCEPTIONS: MEMORIZE

[ɪ]		
bin	(am)	viertel
in	(in)	vierzehn
bis	(until)	vierzig
hin	(there)	
im	(in the)	
mit	(with)	

[ɪ] prefixes and suffixes		
hin-	-ig	-nis
miß-	-in	
mit-	-lich	

[ɛ]		
es	(it)	
des	(of the)	
weg	(away)	Except: Weg [ve:k] (path)
gen	(towards)	

[ɛ] prefixes		
emp-	her'-	zer-
ent-	ver-	
er-	weg-	

[ʊ]		prefixes
um	(around)	durch-
zum	(to the)	um-, un-
drum	(around)	unter-
		suffix
		-ung

[ɔ]		prefix
ob	(whether)	fort-
von	(of)	**suffix**
vom	(of the)	-voll

[a]		prefixes
das	(that)	ab-
hat	(has)	an-
was	(what)	**suffixes**
an	(to, at)	-haft
man	(one)	-schaft
am	(to the)	
ab	(away)	

Schwa [ə]	prefixes	suffix
	be-	-chen
	ge-	

Penultimate letter is: [ʊ] [ɔ] [a]		
Jesus	Lotos	Bräutigam
ringsum	Marmor	Heimat
warum	Pathos	Monat

Vowel [ʁ] words		[ʁ] prefixes
der	(the)	er-
dir	(you)	her-
er	(he)	über-
für	(for)	unter-
ihr	(her, you)	ver-
mir	(me)	vor-
vor	(before)	zer-
wer	(who)	
wir	(we)	

[ə] + *r* (except when prevocalic)

Provide IPA:

1. vom (from)
2. Küsse (kisses)
3. Jahren (years)
4. wer (who)
5. Strauß (bunch)
6. räuchern (to smoke)
7. Brücke (bridge)
8. in (in)
9. Chronik (chronicle)
10. lag (lay)
11. schwache (weak)
12. wir (we)
13. lispeln (to whisper)
14. im (in the)
15. wandte (turned)
16. hat (has)
17. Paar (pair, couple)
18. moosigen (mossy)
19. zum (to the)
20. säuselt (murmurs)
21. heilige (holy)
22. Sphinx (sphinx)
23. gütigster (kindest)
24. blieb (remained)
25. der (the)
26. Pyramide (pyramid)
27. schüchtern (shy)
28. des (the)
29. jauchzend (cheering)
30. hier (here)
31. ob (whether)
32. stöhnen (groan)
33. ihr (her)
34. mächtig (powerful)
35. liegt (lies)
36. am (at, on)
37. Speer (spear)
38. er (he)
39. Frucht (fruit)
40. drum (around)
41. pochet (pound)
42. bis (until)
43. selbst (even)
44. nur (only)
45. Vögel (birds)
46. als (as)
47. weg (away)
48. Sympathie (*th* [t]) (sympathy)
49. bin (am)
50. Ochse (ox)
51. von (of)
52. war (was)
53. leuchtender (brighter)
54. dir (you)
55. Qualen (agonies)
56. Herrscher (ruler)
57. um (to)
58. Waffen (weapons)
59. mit (with)
60. vor (before)
61. gar (even)
62. Stuhl (chair)
63. Frühling (spring)

64. röchelte (groaned)
65. Musik (music)
66. schmeichelnd (flattering)
67. was (what)
68. Becher (mug)
69. Sehnen (longing)
70. ab (away)
71. Pflicht (duty)
72. Schäferin (shepherdess)
73. es (it)
74. für (for)
75. Kirche (church)
76. zur (to the)
77. das (the)
78. inniglich (dearly)
79. hin (there)
80. kränken (insult)
81. Maien (Mays)
82. man (one)
83. Weg (path)
84. unsere (ours)
85. an (to, at)
86. Phantasie (fantasy)
87. mir (to me)

Words with multiple elements: Circle the prefixes and suffixes in the following words

88. Ausgang ['ʔɑosgaŋ]
89. Bündnis ['bʏntnɪs]
90. dahinwelken [dɑ:'hɪnvɛlkən]
91. dargeboten ['dɑ:ɾgəbo:tən]
92. schicksalhaft ['ʃɪkkzɑ:lhaft]
93. herkömmlich ['he:ʁkœmmlɪç]
94. Klugheit ['klu:khaet]
95. Köpfchen ['kœpfçən]
96. missgönnte [mɪss'gœnntə]
97. Kindlein ['kɪntlaen]
98. abgetan ['ʔapgətɑ:n]
99. zuwider [tsu:'vi:dəʁ]
100. empfindsam [ʔɛmp'fɪntzɑ:m]
101. Fortbleiben ['fɔɾtblaebən]
102. umfassen [ʔʊm'fassən]
103. wegbegeben ['vɛkbəge:bən]
104. nachsingen ['nɑ:xzɪŋən]
105. namenlos ['nɑ:mənlo:s]
106. Reichtum ['ɾaeçtu:m]
107. Teilbarkeit ['taelbɑ:ɾkaet]
108. Unterströmung ['ʔʊntəʁʃtrø:mʊŋ]
109. versunken [fɛʁ'zʊŋkən]
110. Wissenschaft ['vɪssənʃaft]
111. erbaut [ʔɛʁ'baot]
112. Aufenthalt ['ʔaofʔɛnthalt]
113. eingeschlafen ['ʔaengəʃlɑ:fən]
114. zerfallen [tsɛʁ'fallən]
115. uraltes ['ʔu:ɾʔaltəs]
116. durchdringen ['dʊɾçdrɪŋən]
117. unendlich [ʔʊn'ʔɛntlɪç]
118. Andenken ['ʔandɛŋkən]
119. vorübergehen [fo:'ɾy:bəʁge:ən]
120. mitleidsvoll ['mɪtlaetsfɔll]

Provide IPA for conjugated verbs, nouns and adjectives with endings, and truncated words:

121. bebt (beben) (trembles)
122. Tags (day's)
123. schönste (most beautiful)
124. edlen (noble)
125. gibt (geben) (give)
126. regnen (to rain)

UNIT 14:

French classification of symbols

GENERAL TERMS

IPA. The *International Phonetic Alphabet* was established by the International Phonetic Association around 1888. Each symbol stands for one phonetic sound and is enclosed in brackets. Authentic pronunciation, accurate formation, and precise resonance must be defined for each symbol within the respective language.
Dialect: a form of pronunciation belonging to a specific geographic location. The appropriate pronunciation for French lyric diction is dialect free. It is the formal speech of the 19th to early 20th centuries (*style soutenu*). Recordings by Pierre Bernac with Poulenc and Ravel provide the authoritative source for authentic pronunciation of French art song literature.
Style soutenu [stil sutəny]: French term for the formal style. *Style soutenu* is an elite form of the language that represents traditional or noble speech. It is appropriate for the theatre, formal discourse, and French art song repertoire.
Langue courant [lɑ̃g kuɾɑ̃]: French term for the vernacular. It is also defined as colloquial or everyday speech.
Vocalic harmonization: a vowel sound that is altered to blend with the vowel sound of a consecutive syllable or word

PHONETIC TERMS (additional terms on pages 96 and 98)

Articulation and enunciation: the act of speaking or singing phonetic sounds.
Aspirate: a consonant that is articulated with an audible release of breath (English and German *p, t, k*)
Continuant: a consonant that maintains a continuous and even flow of sound (*l, n, m, r, s, z*)
Dental: a consonant that is articulated with the tongue tip touching the upper row of teeth (Italian and French *d, n, t, l*)

WORD STRUCTURE

Monosyllable: a word that contains one syllable. A polysyllabic word contains two or more syllables.
Monophthong: a word with one vowel sound per syllable. A diphthong contains two vowel sounds per syllable and a triphthong contains three vowel sounds per syllable. French words are strictly monophthongal in quality.
Hiatus: adjacent vowel sounds that occupy consecutive syllables
Prevocalic: a consonant that precedes a vowel sound
Intervocalic: a consonant that stands between vowel sounds
Postvocalic: a consonant that follows a vowel sound
Initial: the first letter or sound of a word
Medial: a letter or sound in the middle of a word
Final: the last letter or sound of a word

INTRODUCTION

The rules outlined in this text are based upon transcriptions in *Le Petit Robert* and upon recommendations given in *Singing in French* by Thomas Grubb. Symbol replacements are required for lyric diction. Open nasal [ɔ̃] is replaced with closed nasal [õ] as recommended by Thomas Grubb. The uvular [ʀ] of spoken French is replaced with a flipped [ɾ] as required for lyric diction. All schwas are indicated since they are typically syllabified in the musical setting. Variations of two standard IPA symbols are utilized to indicate a more accurate pronunciation of words with vocalic harmonization: the [(e)] symbol indicates the transformed vowel (as recommended by Grubb) and the [ɛ] symbol was created to define an additional sound not represented by the standard IPA.

CHARACTERISTICS OF THE FRENCH LANGUAGE AND IPA

1) Legato is the defining characteristic of the French language. Legato is movement from consonant to vowel and from pitch to pitch in a smooth and connected flow of sound. There are no glottal stops in French.
2) The French language is without strong cadences or resolutions. Syllabic stress is formed by an elongation of the vowel sound. Avoid a heavy or weighted accentuation of the stressed syllable as heard in English and German.
3) Primary stress is on the last syllable of a word, unless the word contains a final schwa. The primary stress of a word with a final schwa is placed on the penultimate syllable.
4) Vowels are precise, neat, pure, and frontal in placement. They maintain their formation throughout vocalization.
5) Consonants are quick, crisp, clean, and alternate with vowels in a regular consonant/vowel flow.
6) Dental consonants: the tongue tip contacts the back of the upper front teeth for consonants *d, n, t,* and *l.*
7) Plosive consonants: a non-aspirate quality is required for consonants *b, d, g, p, t,* and *k.*
8) Sounds not familiar to English include: closed [e], semi-closed [(e)], mixed [y], [ø], [œ], nasal [ɑ̃], [ɛ̃], [õ], [œ̃], semivowel [ɥ], and nasal [ɲ].
9) French uses many letters in addition to the English alphabet: grave *à, è, ù,* acute *é,* circumflex *â, ê, î, ô, û,* diæresis *ï* and *ë*, and the cedilla *ç*.
10) The French schwa must have an [œ] pronunciation for lyric diction (Bernac and Grubb). The legato line is dependent upon the accurate enunciation of a schwa that is neither weak nor varied within the vocalic flow.

PRONUNCIATION GUIDE

FRONT VOWELS

IPA	ENGLISH (approximation)	FRENCH
[i]	eat, greet	vie, ici [vi] [isi]
[e]		chez, été [ʃe] [ete]
[(e)]		laisser, plaisir [l(e)se] [pl(e)ziɾ]
[є]	chaos, bouquet	mais, palais [mє] [palє]
[ɛ]	met, friend	belle, chère [bɛlə] [ʃɛɾə]

BACK VOWELS

IPA	ENGLISH (approximation)	FRENCH
[u]	food, blue	douce, toujour [dusə] [tuʒuɾ]
[o]	obey, protect	rose, beau [ɾozə] [bo]
[ɔ]	talk, ought	poète, aurore [pɔɛtə] [ɔɾɔɾə]

CENTRAL VOWELS

IPA	ENGLISH (approximation)	FRENCH
[ɑ]	father, robin	lilas, âge [lilɑ] [ɑʒə]
[a]		moi, charme [mwa] [ʃaɾmə]

SCHWA (the schwa indicates the vowel of an unstressed syllable)

IPA	ENGLISH (approximation)	FRENCH
[ə]	sofa, angel	petite, chevelure [pətitə] [ʃəvəlyɾə]

SHADOW VOWEL (as set by composer)

IPA	ENGLISH (approximation)	FRENCH
[ᵊ]		destinée, pensée [dɛstineᵊ][pɑ̃seᵊ]

MIXED VOWELS

IPA	ENGLISH (approximation)	FRENCH
[y]		une, salut [ynə] [saly]
[ø]		feu, adieu [fø] [adjø]
[œ]		seule, bonheur [sœlə] [bɔnœɾ]

NASAL VOWELS

IPA	ENGLISH (approximation)	FRENCH
[ɑ̃]		dans, enfant [dɑ̃] [ɑ̃fɑ̃]
[õ]		mon, l'ombre [mõ] [lõbɾə]
[ɛ̃]		point, jardin [pwɛ̃] [ʒaɾdɛ̃]
[œ̃]		un, parfum [œ̃] [paɾfœ̃]

SEMICONSONANTS / SEMIVOWELS

IPA	ENGLISH (approximation)	FRENCH
[j]	yet, year	yeux, bien [jø] [bjɛ̃]
[ɥ]		nuit, suis [nɥi] [sɥi]
[w]	winter, web	oui, soir [wi] [swaɾ]

HIATUS (adjacent vowel sounds that occupy consecutive syllables)

ENGLISH: noel, create, naive
[no-ˈɛl] [kɹi-ˈɛɪt] [nɑ-ˈiv]

FRENCH: noël, poëte, aïeux, naïf
[nɔ-ɛl] [pɔ-ɛtə] [a-jø] [na-if]

DENTAL CONSONANTS The following consonants are classified as dental in French but alveolar in English (French *d* and *t* are dental plosives)

IPA	ENGLISH (approximation)	FRENCH
[d]	dance, decide	danse, monde [dɑ̃sə] [mɔ̃də]
[n]	noon, linen	nature, jeune [natyɾə] [ʒœnə]
[t]	trust, teach	toujour, cette [tuʒuɾ] [sɛtə]
[l]	loyal, blissful	larme, elle [laɾmə] [ɛlə]
[ɾ]	thread, throne	rire, sur [ɾiɾə] [syɾ]

PLOSIVE CONSONANTS (articulation in French is non-aspirate)

IPA	ENGLISH (approximation)	FRENCH
[b]	beauty, abide	beauté, sombre [bote] [sɔ̃bɾə]
[g]	give, agree	grâce, vague [gɾɑsə] [vagə]
[p]	pity, approve	pour, depuis [puɾ] [dəpɥi]
[k]	candle, back	cœur, encore [kœɾ] [ɑ̃kɔɾə]

NASAL CONSONANT

IPA	ENGLISH (approximation)	FRENCH
[ɲ]		vigne, seigneur [viɲə] [sɛɲœɾ]

INDICATIONS WITHIN THIS TEXT

Stress marks are not included in French transcription. The last syllable of a word is always stressed unless it contains a final schwa. The stress of a final schwa word is on the penultimate syllable. Stress is formed by lengthening the vowel, not by a weighted accentuation as in English or German.

This text highlights a lyric vocabulary of the 18th to early 20th centuries. Archaic words and spellings are represented.

Classification of Symbols: Consonants

Voicing: A voiced consonant engages vocal cords. A voiceless consonant does not employ the vocal cords.

Points of Articulation	French	English
Bilabial [baɪˈlɛɪbɪəl] Refers to the lips	[b] [p] [m] [w]	[b] [p] [m] [w] [ʍ]
Labiodental [lɛɪbɪoˈdɛntəl] Involves the lower lip and the upper row of teeth	[v] [f]	[v] [f]
Dental [ˈdɛntəl] Involves the tip of the tongue and the back of the upper row of teeth	[d] [t] [z] [s] [l] [n] [ɾ]	[ð] [θ]
Alveolar [ʔælˈviələ] Involves the tip of the tongue and the ridge behind the upper teeth		[d] [t] [z] [s] [l] [n] [ɾ] [ɹ]
Prepalatal [pɹɪˈpælətəl] Involves the tip of tongue and the area between the alveolar ridge and hard palate	[ʒ] [ʃ] [j] [ɲ] [ɥ]	[ʒ] [ʃ] [dʒ] [tʃ]
Palatal [ˈpælətəl] Involves a front arch of the tongue and the hard palate		[j]
Velar [ˈvilə] Involves the back of the tongue and the soft palate	[g] [k]	[g] [k] [ŋ]
Glottal [ˈglɑtəl] Involves the air flow and the opening between the vocal cords		[ʔ] [h]

Manner of Articulation	French	English
Stop [stɑp] or **Plosive** [ˈploʊsɪv] A momentary closure of the air flow passage	[b] [p] [d] [t] [g] [k]	[b] [p] [d] [t] [g] [k] [ʔ]
Fricative [ˈfɹɪkətɪv] Produced by directing the air flow past a set of articulators	[v] [f] [z] [s] [ʒ] [ʃ]	[v] [f] [z] [s] [ʍ] [ʒ] [ʃ] [h] [ð] [θ]
Affricate [ˈʔæfɹɪkət] A stop that is followed by a fricative		[dʒ] [tʃ]
Nasal [ˈnɛɪzəl] Produced by directing vocalized tone through the nasal passages	[m] [n] [ɲ]	[m] [n] [ŋ]
Lateral [ˈlætərəl] Produced by directing vocalized tone over the sides of the tongue	[l]	[l]
Glide [glɑɪd] Produced by directing vocalized tone past a set of articulators without friction	[j] [w] [ɥ]	[j] [w]
Trill [tɹɪl] Formed by taps with the tip of the tongue against the alveolar ridge	[ɾ]	[ɾ]
Retroflex [ˈɹɛtɹoʊflɛks] Produced with tongue tip curled up		[ɹ]

Worksheet #14: Classification of Consonants

Provide IPA to complete the following chart for French consonants:

	Bilabial	Labiodental	Dental	Alveolar	Prepalatal	Palatal	Velar	Glottal
Stop voiced voiceless								
Fricative voiced voiceless								
Affricate voiced voiceless								
Nasal voiced								
Lateral voiced								
Trill voiced								
Glide voiced								

Provide IPA to complete the following chart for English consonants:

	Bilabial	Labiodental	Dental	Alveolar	Prepalatal	Palatal	Velar	Glottal
Stop voiced voiceless								
Fricative voiced voiceless								
Affricate voiced voiceless								
Nasal voiced								
Lateral voiced								
Trill voiced								
Glide voiced								
Retroflex voiced								

Classification of Symbols: Vowels

Length: Syllabic stress within a word or phrase is formed by a lengthening of the vowel sound.

Quality	**French**	**English**
Closed Requires a closer proximity between the tongue and roof of the mouth	[i] [e] [o] [u] mixed [y] [ø] nasal [õ]	[i] [u] [o]
Open Requires more space between the tongue and roof of the mouth	[ɛ] [ɔ] mixed [œ] nasal [ɛ̃] [œ̃]	[ɪ] [ɛ] [ʊ] [ɔ]

Peak of tongue arch	**French**	**English**
Front (tongue vowel) The arch of the tongue is forward with tip down during enunciation	[i] [e] [ɛ] nasal [ɛ̃]	[i] [ɪ] [ɛ]
Back (lip vowel) The arch of the tongue is back with tip down during enunciation	[u] [o] [ɔ] nasal [õ]	[u] [ʊ] [o] [ɔ]
Mixed (rounded front vowel) The arch of the tongue is forward with lips rounded during enunciation	[y] [ø] [œ] nasal [œ̃]	
Central The tongue maintains a low position during enunciation	dark [ɑ] nasal [ɑ̃] bright [a]	dark [ɑ] [æ] [ʌ] retroflex [ɜ]

The schwa indicates a vowel in an unstressed syllable. It is not categorized by length, quality, or tongue arch.

Classification of Vowels Chart

Provide vowel descriptions for the following symbols:

French Vowels

IPA	Quality	Peak tongue arch
[i]		
[e]		
[ɛ]		
[u]		
[o]		
[ɔ]		
[a]		
[ɑ]		
[y]		
[ø]		
[œ]		
[ɑ̃]		
[õ]		
[ɛ̃]		
[œ̃]		

English Vowels

	IPA	Quality	Peak tongue arch
greet	[i]		
bit	[ɪ]		
said	[ɛ]		
blue	[u]		
look	[ʊ]		
obey	[o]		
ought	[ɔ]		
sat	[æ]		
father	[ɑ]		
bird	[ɜ]		
up	[ʌ]		

See vowel chart on page 234

UNIT 15:

French consonants

RULES FOR TRANSCRIPTION

French Consonants

Spelling	IPA	Sample Words
Initial vowel words	[ʔ] Glottal Stop	There are no glottal stops in French: été [ete]
Stress is not indicated in French transcription	[ˈ] Stress Mark	The penultimate syllable is stressed in final schwa words. The final syllable is stressed for other words: amie [ami]
c + a, â, o, ô, or consonant	[k] Velar Plosive (Stop)	calme [kalmə] éclate [eklatə]
c + i, y, e, é, è, ê	[s] Dental Fricative	docile [dɔsilə] céleste [selɛstə] descends [d(e)sɑ̃]
ç	[s]	garçon [garsõ]
ch	[ʃ] Prepalatal Fricative	chevalier [ʃəvalje] (except: écho [eko] and chœur [kœr])
g + a, â, o, ô, or consonant	[g] Velar Plosive (Stop)	goutte [gutə] glacé [glase]
g + i, y, e, é, è, ê	[ʒ] Prepalatal Fricative	givre [ʒivrə] songe [sõʒə]
gn	[ɲ] Prepalatal Nasal	montagne [mõtaɲə]
gu (silent *u*)	[g]	guérir [gerir]
h	[h] Glottal Fricative	*h* is silent in all positions: hélas [elɑs]
j	[ʒ] Prepalatal Fricative	jour [ʒur]
qu (silent *u*)	[k] Velar Stop	quelque [kɛlkə] qui [ki]
r	[r] Flipped *r*	regard [rəgar]
Spelling *z* and intervocalic *s*	[z] Dental Fricative	horizon [ɔrizõ] présence [prezɑ̃sə]
All other *s, ss*	[s] Dental Fricative	soupirs [supir] (final *s* is silent) aussi [osi]
Final *-tion, -tiel,* and *-tieux*	[s]	affection [afɛksjõ] essentiel [(e)sɑ̃sjɛl]
x + consonant	[ks]	extase [ɛkstɑzə] (except: fixe [fiksə] luxe [lyksə])
x + vowel or *h*	[gz]	exacte [ɛgzaktə] exhaler [ɛgzale]

Final consonants are silent except final *c, r, f, l* (memory aid: *careful*). See page 240 for exception Consonants that are doubled in spelling are not doubled in transcription except for initial *ill, irr, in,* and *imm*. The consonant *n* is silent when preceded by a nasal vowel. The spelling *b* becomes voiceless *p* when followed by an *s* or *t*: *obscur* [ɔpskyr]. Spellings *ph* is [f] and *th* is [t].

CLASSWORK #15: French consonants

1. délicate (delicate) [deli_atə]
2. chevaux (horses) [_əvo_]
3. visage (face) [vi_a_ə]
4. leçon (lesson) [lə_õ_]
5. unique (unique) [yni_ə]
6. toujours (always) [tu_u__]
7. fatigue (fatigue) [fati_ə]
8. signal (signal) [_i_a_]
9. beige (beige) [bɛ_ə]
10. grâces (thanksgiving) [_ɑ_ə_]

TRANSCRIPTION WITHIN THE PHRASE #15: Liaison

A final consonant is enunciated when followed by an initial vowel word. Exceptions apply. Forbidden liaison is indicated with a " | " mark. Phonetic changes occur. Final *d, f, g, s, and x* become [t], [v], [k], [z]: *Les oiseaux* | *avec leurs ailes* [lɛz wazo avɛk lœɾz ɛlə]. A summary of rules is given on page 240. Refer to *The Interpretation of French Song* by Pierre Bernac, *Singing in French* by Thomas Grubb, and *Sing French* by Eileen Davis for all rules governing liaison.

Classwork: *we will exchange one sole spark,*
Nous échangerons un éclair unique,
[nu_ e_ɑ̃_əɾõ_ œ̃_ e_lɛ_ yni_ə]

1. *searching for you on some roads unknown,*
cherchant jusqu'à toi des routes inconnues,
[_ɛɾ_ɑ̃ _ys_a twa dɛ ɾutə_ ɛ̃_ɔnyə_]

2. *I love your eyes, I love your mouth*
J'aime tes yeux, j'aime ta bouche
[_ɛmə tɛ_ jø _ɛmə ta bu_ə]

3. *the countryside, the woods, the charming shadows,*
La campagne, les bois, les ombrages charmants,
[la _ɑ̃pa_ə lɛ bwɑ lɛ_ õbɾa_ə _aɾmɑ̃_]

4. *the clouds, startled, have disappeared*
les nuages effarouchés | ont disparu.
[lɛ nɥa_ə_ (e)faɾu_e õ dispaɾy]

5. *a sweet, noble agreement:*
Un doux accord patricien:
[œ̃ du_ a_ɔ_ patɾi_jɛ̃_]

6. *Our love is a light thing*
Notre amour est chose légère
[nɔtɾ amu_ ɛ _o_ə le_ɛɾə]

7. *I will speak of your glory, O charm of the eyes,*
Je dirai ta gloire, ô charme des yeux,
[_ə diɾe ta _lwaɾ o _aɾmə dɛ_ jø_]

8. *to the hair with which I am enthralled.*
Des cheveux dont je suis épris.
[dɛ _əvø dõ _ə sɥi_ epɾi_]

9. *I am going to the setting sun,*
Je m'en vais au soleil couchant,
[_ə mɑ̃ vɛ_ o _ɔlɛj ku_ɑ̃_]

10. *the flying bees sing;*
Chantent les abeilles volages;
[_ɑ̃tə lɛ_ abɛjə vɔla_ə_]

11. *we may exchange our souls,*
Nous pouvons échanger nos âmes,
[nu puvõ_ e_ɑ̃_e no_ ɑmə_]

12. *In a dream which was charmed by your image*
Dans un sommeil que charmait ton image
[dɑ̃_ œ̃ sɔmɛj _ə _aɾmɛ tõ_ ima_ə]

WORKSHEET #15: French consonants

#1

guêpe	(wasp)
[_ɛpə]	
adoucir	(soften)
[adu_i_]	
épouse	(wife)
[epu_ə]	
ça	(it)
[_a]	
magique	(magic)
[ma_i_ə]	
cailloux	(pebbles)
[_aju_]	
signe	(sign)
[_i_ə]	
jamais	(never)
[_amɛ_]	
bouche	(mouth)
[bu_ə]	
lequel	(which)
[lə_ɛ_]	

#2

vague	(wave)
[va_ə]	
chair	(flesh)
[_ɛ_]	
atteigne	(reaches)
[atɛ_ə]	
sujet	(about)
[_y_ɛ_]	
câline	(cuddly)
[_ɑlinə]	
glaçon	(ice)
[_la_õ_]	
l'église	(the church)
[le_li_ə]	
berceau	(cradle)
[bɛ__o]	
rivages	(shores)
[_iva_ə_]	
musique	(music)
[my_i_ə]	

#3

gage	(token)
[_a_ə]	
prodigue	(prodigal)
[p_ɔdi_ə]	
désir	(desire)
[de_i_]	
baigne	(bathe)
[bɛ_ə]	
l'objet	(the object)
[lɔb_ɛ_]	
accolade	(embrace)
[a_ɔladə]	
soupçon	(suspicion)
[_up_õ_]	
racines	(roots)
[_a_inə_]	
chaste	(pure, innocent)
[_a_tə]	
tunique	(tunic)
[tyni_ə]	

#4

presque	(almost)
[p_ɛ__ə]	
majesté	(majesty)
[ma_ɛ_te]	
règne	(reigns)
[_ɛ_ə]	
cristal	(crystal)
[__i_ta_]	
écloses	(hatched)
[e_lo_ə_]	
guide	(guide)
[_idə]	
berçait	(rocked)
[bɛ__ɛ_]	
agile	(agile)
[a_ilə]	
chassez	(hunt)
[_a_e_]	
cilice	(sackcloth)
[_ili_ə]	

WORKSHEET #15: French consonants

#5

légère [le_ɛ_ə]	(light)
provençal [p_ɔvɑ̃_a_]	(Provencal)
vogue [vɔ_ə]	(vogue)
trésor [t_e_ɔ_]	(treasure)
célèbre [_elɛb_ə]	(famous)
charmes [_a_mə_]	(charms)
magnifique [ma_ifi_ə]	(magnificent)
beaucoup [bo_u_]	(a lot)
rustique [_y_ti_ə]	(rustic)
jettent [_ɛtə_]	(throw)

#6

image [ima_ə]	(image)
sourcil (*l* is silent) [_u___i]	(eyebrow)
digne [di_ə]	(worthy)
canards [_ana____]	(ducks)
guitare [_ita_ə]	(guitar)
jaunes [_onə_]	(yellow)
poésie [pɔe_i]	(poetry)
chaque [_a_ə]	(each)
balançant [balɑ̃_ɑ̃___]	(balancing)
lorsque [lɔ____ə]	(when)

#7

agite [a_itə]	(agitates)
reçois [_ə_wa_]	(receive)
l'école [le_ɔlə]	(the school)
bijoux [bi_u_]	(jewelry)
gagne [_a_ə]	(gain, win)
désert [de_ɛ___]	(desert)
cède [_ɛdə]	(yield)
quel [_ɛ_]	(what, which)
naguère [na_ɛ_ə]	(formerly)
péché [pe_e]	(sin)

#8

repose [_əpo_ə]	(rests)
bonjour [bɔ̃__u_]	(hello)
liquide [li_idə]	(liquid)
élégie [ele_i]	(elegy)
spectre [_pɛ_t_ə]	(ghost)
castagnettes [_a_ta_ɛtə_]	(castanets)
berçant [bɛ__ɑ̃___]	(rocking)
richesse [_i_ɛ_ə]	(wealth)
ciseaux [_i_o_]	(scissors)
guerre [_ɛ_ə]	(war)

WORKSHEET #15: French consonants

#9

bague [ba_ə]	(ring)
gênait [_ɛnɛ_]	(bother)
cercle [_ɛ__lə]	(circle)
fraîcheur [f_ɛ_œ_]	(freshness)
cascade [_a__adə]	(cascade)
reçu [_ə_y]	(received)
grise [__i_ə]	(gray)
quitter (*r* silent) [_ite]	(leave)
vignes [vi_ə_]	(vines)
joug [_u_]	(yoke)

#10

cierges [_jɛ__ə_]	(church candles)
écrit [e__i_]	(written)
dague [da_ə]	(dagger)
façons [fa_õ__]	(ways)
juste [_y_tə]	(just)
résonne [_e_ɔnə]	(resonates)
spécial [_pe_ja_]	(special)
quelle [_ɛlə]	(what, which)
lignage [li_a_ə]	(lineage)
couche [_u_ə]	(layer)

#11

l'orgue [lɔ__ə]	(organ)
génie [_eni]	(genius)
cygne [_i_ə]	(swan)
roseaux [_o_o_]	(reeds)
jade [_adə]	(jade)
français [f_ã_ɛ_]	(French)
calice [_ali_ə]	(chalice)
chez [_e_]	(at)
barque [ba__ə]	(boat)
accourt [a_u__]	(hurry up)

#12

l'éclat [le_la_]	(the glare)
chéris [_e_i_]	(cherished)
fragile [f_a_ilə]	(fragile)
guérir [_e_i_]	(heal)
résigne [_e_i_ə]	(resigns)
jaloux [_alu_]	(jealous)
cause [_o_ə]	(cause)
société [_ɔ_jete]	(society)
pâquerette [pa_ə_ɛtə]	(daisy)
conçu [_õ_y]	(designed)

UNIT 16:

French single vowel spellings

(A single vowel is a vowel that is in hiatus or not a part of a vowel cluster)

RULES FOR TRANSCRIPTION

French single vowel spellings

Spelling	IPA	Sample Words
Single *a*	[a] Bright [a]	ballade [baladə]
e + two or more consonants	[ɛ] Open Front	geste [ʒɛstə]
* *e* + double consonant + [ə]	[ɛ] Open Front	elle [ɛlə] clochette [klɔʃɛtə]
Single *i, y*	[i] Closed Front	triste [tɾistə] lys [lis]
o + pronounced consonant	[ɔ] Open Back	colore [kɔlɔɾə]
o + [z]	[o] Closed Back	osier [ozje]
o + *-tion*	[o] Closed Back	dévotion [devosjõ]
Single *u*	[y] Closed Mixed	crépuscule [kɾepyskylə]
** Final *-e* and *-es*	[ə] Schwa	le [lə] sourire [suɾiɾə] anges [ɑ̃ʒə]

EXCEPTION WORDS

The words *femme* [famə] and *solennelle* [sɔlanɛlə] are transcribed with a bright [a]. Words with *a* + [z] and medial *a* + *ss* spellings are transcribed with a dark [ɑ] but there are numerous exceptions. The word *ah* [ɑ] is dark (additional dark [ɑ] exception words are listed on page 240). The words *o* [o], *oh* [o], *fosse* [ˈfosə], and *grosse* [ˈgɾosə] are closed.

The pronunciation of *et* is [e]. A distinction must be made between *et* [e] (and) and the separate words *es/est* [ɇ] (is). Example: Voyant la rosée <u>et</u> le soleil clair [vwajɑ̃ la ɾoze <u>e</u> lə sɔlɛj klɛɾ] (*seeing the dew <u>and</u>* [e] *the clear sun*) not (*seeing the dew <u>is</u>* [ɇ] *the clear sun*)

MER/VER WORDS

Mer/ver words are transcribed with an open [ɛ]: *mer(s)* [mɛɾ] *vers* [vɛɾ] *amer(s)* [amɛɾ] *divers* [divɛɾ] *envers* [ɑ̃vɛɾ] *hiver(s)* [ivɛɾ] *travers* [tɾavɛɾ] *univers* [ynivɛɾ]. Other [ɛɾ] words: *cher(s)* [ʃɛɾ] *enfer* [ɑ̃fɛɾ] *éther* [etɛɾ] *fer(s)* [fɛɾ] *fier* [fjɛɾ] *hier* [jɛɾ] *sers* [sɛɾ]

* Additional rules apply for the *e* + double consonant spelling. See page 52 of the *Advanced French Lyric Diction Workbook* for more information.

** Final *-es* of articles have two pronunciations: *ces* [sɇ]/[s(e)], *des* [dɇ]/[d(e)], *les* [lɇ]/[l(e)], *mes* [mɇ]/[m(e)], *ses* [sɇ]/[s(e)], *tes* [tɇ]/[t(e)]. See transcription rules on page 119.

CLASSWORK #16: French single vowel spellings

Provide IPA:

1.	hymne	(hymn)	5.	rossignol	(nightingale)
2.	mer	(sea)	6.	jusque	(until)
3.	esprit	(spirit)	7.	l'hiver	(winter)
4.	choses	(things)	8.	tristesse	(sadness)

TRANSCRIPTION WITHIN THE PHRASE #16: Elision

A final schwa is dropped when followed by an initial vowel word: *un faible espoir* [œ̃ fɛbl ɛspwaɾ].

Provide IPA:

Classwork: *of a moon pink and gray,*
D'une lune rose et grise,

1. *Dear country, speak no more of her;*
   Cher pays, ne parle plus d'elle;
   pei

2. *He said to me: "What do you seek?"*
   Il me dit: "Que cherches-tu?"

3. *given by a rapid walk;*
   que donne une marche rapide;

4. *Neither man, nor woman,*
   Ni l'homme ni la femme,

5. *The little bells of digitalis*
   Les clochettes de digitales
   ɛ

6. *life bites death there*
   La vie y mord la mort
   vi

7. *The ghost of the rose*
   Le spectre de la rose

8. *like a false music.*
   Comme une musique fausse.
   o

9. *On the wings of music*
   Sur les ailes de la musique
   ɛ ɛ

10. *O divine nature,*
    Oh divine nature,

11. *and I come from paradise.*
    Et j'arrive du paradis.

12. *the swan paddles and approaches.*
    le cygne rame et s'approche.

WORKSHEET #16: French single vowel spellings

Provide IPA:

#1

issue (outcome)
[isyə]

lettres (letters)
[lɛtrə]

perdu (lost)
[pɛrdu]

mystique (mystic)
[mistikə]

l'orage (the storm)
[loraʒə]

ver (worm)
[vɛr]

rosine (rosin)
[rɔzinə]

#2

l'espace (the space)
[lɛspasə]

joli (nice, pretty)
[ʒoli]

presse (press)
[prɛssə]

solitude (solitude)
[solitydə]

travers (through)
[travɛr]

martyre (martyrdom)
[mɑrtirə]

closes (closed)
[klɔzə]

#3

cherche (looking for)
[ʃɛrʃə]

sonore (sound)
[sɔnɔrə]

appelle (calls)
[apɛllə]

zéphyre (zephyr)
[zefirə]

mer (sea)
[mɛr]

nocturne (nocturnal)
[nɔctyrnə]

rose (pink)
[rozə]

#4

satyre (satyr)
[satirə]

pudique (modest)
[pydikə]

terre (earth)
[tɛrə]

merci (thank you)
[mɛrsi]

adore (love)
[adorə]

univers (universe)
[ynivɛr]

philosophes (philosophers)
[filɔzofə]

WORKSHEET #16: French single vowel spellings

Provide IPA:

#5

humide	(damp)
paroles	(lyrics)
reste	(rest)
tyrannique	(tyrannical)
amer	(bitter)
morose	(inactive)
cesse	(stops)

#6

syllabe	(syllable)
cher	(dear)
homme	(man)
arrose	(sprinkles)
perdre	(lose)
elles	(they)
muse	(muse)

#7

perles	(pearls)
glose	(gloss)
l'unique	(unique)
mers	(seas)
collines	(hills)
rythmique	(rhythmic)
verre	(glass)

#8

chose	(thing)
vers	(towards, verse)
lyre	(lyre)
personne	(person)
force	(force)
coquette	(flirt)
brusque	(sudden)

WORKSHEET #16: French single vowel spellings

Provide IPA:

#9

l'univers	(the universe)
[lynivɛr]	
pose	(pose)
[pɔzə]	
fortune	(fortune)
[fɔrtynə]	
verte	(green)
[vɛrtə]	
monotone	(monotone)
[mɔnotɔnə]	
rythme	(rhythm)
[rithmə]	
caresses	(caresses)
[karɛsə]	

#10

proposes	(proposes)
[pɾopozə]	
chers	(dear)
[ʃɛr]	
myrte	(myrtle)
[mirtə]	
forme	(shape)
[fɔrmə]	
nectarine	(nectarine)
[nɛctarinə]	
azur	(azure)
[azyr]	
belles	(beautiful)
[bɛllə]	

#11

mettre	(put)
[mɛtrə]	
accords	(agreements)
[akɔr]	
fer	(iron)
[fɛr]	
prose	(prose)
[prozə]	
Sylvie	(Sylvie)
[silvi]	
l'herbe	(grass)
[lɛrbə]	
communique	(communicate)

#12

tonnerre	(thunder)
[tõ·nɛrə]	
charrue	(plow)
[ʃarуə]	
verse	(pour, shed tears)
[vɛrsə]	
mignonne	(cute)
[miɲɔnə]	
hiver	(winter)
[ivɛr]	
physique	(physical)
[fizikə]	
dispose	(incline)
[dispozə]	

UNIT 17:

French vowels with accent marks

RULES FOR TRANSCRIPTION

French vowels with accent marks

Spelling	IPA	Sample Words
à (grave)	[a] Bright [a]	voilà [vwala]
â (circumflex)	[ɑ] Dark [ɑ]	folâtre [fɔlɑtɾə]
é (acute)	[e] Closed Front	étoile [etwalə]
è (grave)	[ɛ] Open Front	lèvres [lɛvɾə]
ê (circumflex)	[ɛ] Open Front	fenêtre [fənɛtɾə]
ë (diaeresis indicates hiatus)	[ɛ] Open Front	poëte [pɔɛtə]
î (circumflex)	[i] Closed Front	abîme [abimə]
ï (diaeresis indicates hiatus)	[i] Closed Front	archaïque [aɾkaikə]
ô (circumflex)	[o] Closed Back	bientôt [bjɛ̃to]
û (circumflex)	[y] Closed Mixed	flûte [flytə]

CLASSWORK #17: French vowels with accent marks

Provide IPA:

1. noël (Christmas)
2. l'île (the island)
3. extrême (extreme)
4. déjà (already)
5. hôtesse (hostess)
6. apparût (appeared)
7. théâtre (theater)
8. naïf (naive)
9. charité (charity)
10. sévère (severe)

TRANSCRIPTION WITHIN THE PHRASE #17

Provide IPA:

luxury, calm and pleasure.
Classwork: Luxe, calme et volupté.

1. *to the shore of fidelity*
   À la rive fidèle

2. *that the waving grass breathes out . . .*
   Que l'herbe agitée expire. . .

3. *Ah! Faithful laughter*
   Ah! le rire fidèle

4. *from the church to the citadel,*
   De l'église à la citadelle,

5. *wrote: "Here lies a rose"*
   Écrivit: "Ci-gît | une rose"

6. *like a tear it may evaporate.*
   Comme une larme il s'évapore.

7. *sheds a tear unnoticed*
   Verse une larme méconnue

8. *Poem of April*
   Poème d'avril

9. *proclaims the distress at the top of its voice.*
   Clame la détresse à tue-tête.
   ɑ

10. *Diane, Selene, moon of beautiful metal,*
    Diane, Séléné, lune de beau métal,
    o

11. *That shore, my dear,*
    Cette rive, ma chère,

12. *vibrate the echo so pure;*
    Vibre l'écho si pur;
    o

WORKSHEET #17: French vowels with accent marks

Provide IPA:

#1

misérable	(miserable)
flèches	(arrows)
à	(at, to, in)
disgrâce	(disgrace)
éclôre	(hatch)
plût	(pleased)
cîme	(peak)
laïque	(layman)
suprême	(supreme)

#2

espère	(hope)
décrivît	(described)
poëmes	(poems)
jusqu'à	(up)
arrête	(stop)
l'alcôve	(the alcove)
mûrs	(ripe)
sérénade	(serenade)
châle	(shawl)

#3

crête	(peak)
réfléchi	(rational)
piqûre	(sting, pitting)
là	(there)
albâtre	(alabaster)
déïté	(deity)
grèves	(shores, strikes)
l'hôtel (*e* is [ɛ])	(the hotel)
établît	(established)

#4

l'abîme	(the abyss)
bûtes	(drank)
désastre	(disaster)
rêve	(dream)
prévôt	(provost)
verdâtre	(greenish)
goëlette	(schooner)
à	(at, to, in)
misère	(misery)

WORKSHEET #17: French vowels with accent marks

Provide IPA:

#5

éphémère	(short-lived)
côte	(coast)
pâlir	(to fade)
mêmes	(same)
dîner (*er* is [e])	(dinner)
tête-à-tête	(head-to-head)
naïve	(naive)
fût	(he was)
réside	(reside)

#6

malgré	(despite)
tâche	(task)
dévôts	(devout ones)
chèvre	(goat)
là	(there)
frêle	(frail)
Israël	(Israel)
bûcher (*er* is [e])	(stake)
émîtes	(emitted)

#7

désarme	(disarm)
çà	(that)
fêtes	(parties)
caïque	(narrow boat)
crûs	(believed)
l'épître	(the epistle)
trône	(throne)
mâts	(masts)
élève	(student)

#8

chênes	(oaks)
delà (*e* is [ə])	(beyond)
caractère	(character)
brûlé	(burned)
l'âme	(soul)
poëtes	(poets)
délice	(delight)
tôt	(early)
abîme	(abyss)

WORKSHEET #17: French vowels with accent marks

Provide IPA:

#9

répète	(repeats)
quitté	(left)
prête	(ready)
maïs	(corn)
hâte	(haste)
sitôt	(as soon as)
mûre	(blackberry, ripe)
là-bas (*a* is [ɑ])	(over there)
définîtes	(defined)

#11

blâme	(blame)
être	(be)
qu'à	(x)
îles	(islands)
troëne	(privet)
récit	(story)
dûre	(last)
l'hôpital	(hospital)
crèche	(nativity scene)

#10

zône	(area)
gît	(lies)
révèle	(reveals)
haï	(hated)
méprise	(mistake)
lorsqu'à	(when)
bêtes	(animals)
sûr	(sure, safe)
âpre	(bitter)

#12

arôme	(flavor)
débris	(debris)
préfère	(preferred)
là	(there)
gîte	(cottage)
sût	(knew)
Zaïde	(Zaide)
tête	(head)
bâtir	(to build)

UNIT 18:

French final spellings

RULES FOR TRANSCRIPTION

French final spellings

Spelling	IPA	Sample Words
Final *-as*	[ɑ] Dark [ɑ]	bas [bɑ] (low) pas [pɑ] (step)
Final *-as* verb ending	[a] Bright [a]	seras [səɾa] (will be)
Final *-ed(s)*	[e] Closed Front	pied [pje] pieds [pje]
Final *-er(s)* (silent *r*)	[e] Closed Front	donner [dɔne] archers [aɾʃe]
Final *-ez*	[e] Closed Front	venez [vəne]
Final *-ec(s)*	[ɛk] Open Front	avec [avɛk] becs [bɛk]
Final *-ef(s)*	[ɛf] Open Front	chef [ʃɛf] chefs [ʃɛf]
Final *-el(s)*	[ɛl] Open Front	nouvel [nuvɛl] quels [kɛl]
* Final *-et(s)*	[ɛ] Semi-Open Front	promet [prɔmɛ] oiselets [wazəlɛ]
Final *-e* and *-es*	[ə] Schwa	porte [pɔɾtə] arbres [aɾbɾə]
o + final silent consonant(s)	[o] Closed Back	trop [tɾo] flots [flo]

REVIEW: MER/VER WORDS

Mer/ver spellings are transcribed with an open [ɛ] and a pronounced *r*: *mer(s)* [mɛɾ] *vers* [vɛɾ] *amer(s)* [amɛɾ] *divers* [divɛɾ] *envers* [ɑ̃vɛɾ] *hiver(s)* [ivɛɾ] *travers* [tɾavɛɾ] *univers* [ynivɛɾ]

Other [ɛɾ] words: *cher(s)* [ʃɛɾ] *enfer* [ɑ̃fɛɾ] *éther* [etɛɾ] *fer(s)* [fɛɾ] *fier* [fjɛɾ] *hier* [jɛɾ] *sers* [sɛɾ]

* All spellings that are normally transcribed with a final [ɛ], are pronounced a bit more closed than the fully open [ɛ] indicates. The symbol [ɛ] has been created to accommodate this sound.

CLASSWORK #18: French final spellings

Provide IPA:

1.	dormez	(you sleep)	5.	flot	(stream)
2.	pétales	(petals)	6.	rochers	(rocks)
3.	objet	(object)	7.	avec	(with)
4.	bercer	(to rock)	8.	port	(harbor)

TRANSCRIPTION WITHIN THE PHRASE #18: Articles

The articles *ces, des, les, mes, ses,* and *tes* are transcribed with a semi-closed [(e)] when followed by a word with an [i], [e], or [y] in the first syllable. Otherwise, these words are transcribed with a semi-open [ɛ]. Example: *les lauriers et les cyprès* [lɛ lɔrjez e l(e) siprɛ].

Classwork: *to dry up its vast waves,*
De dessécher ses vastes flots,
(e)

1. *Over there, by the church,*
Là-bas, vers l'église,

2. *break the windowpanes of this curse,*
Brisez les vitres de maléfice,

3. *treasure to me so dear;*
Trésor qui m'est si cher;

4. *and I no longer dare to hope,*
Et je n'ose plus espérer,

5. *floating with my desires,*
Flotter avecque mes désirs,

6. *What a cruel fate!*
Sort cruel!

7. *These waters, tired of the exercise*
Ces flots, lassés de l'exercise
ɑ

8. *as soon as sad winter*
Dès que le triste hiver

9. *Sleep, sleep my beauty,*
Dormez, dormez, ma belle,

10. *you do not know what life is.*
tu ne sais pas ce que c'est que la vie.
sɛ

11. *with its lips half closed,*
De ses lèvres micloses,

12. *like the petals of the roses*
Comme les pétales de roses

WORKSHEET #18: French final spellings

Provide IPA:

#1

clochers [kloʃe]	(bells)
falot [falo]	(lantern)
sonnet [sɔne]	(sonnet)
riches [riʃə]	(rich)
volez [vole]	(you fly)
bref [brɛf]	(brief)
préparer [prepare]	(to prepare)
mort [mɔr]	(dead)

#2

folles [fɔlə]	(crazy)
dîners [dine]	(dinners)
linots [lino]	(linnets)
met [mɛ]	(met)
brûler [bryle]	(to burn)
sec [sɛ]	(dry)
valsez [valse]	(you waltz)
cor [cɔr]	(horn)

#3

donnez [dɔne]	(you give)
misérables [miserablə]	(miserable)
cacher [kaʃe]	(to hide)
vol [vɔl]	(flight)
bel [bɛl]	(beautiful)
quartiers (*i* is [j]) [kartje]	(neighborhoods)
argot [argo]	(slang)
sommet [some]	(top)

#4

étiez (*i* is [j]) [etje]	(you were)
clef [klef]	(key)
lors [lɔrs]	(as, while)
muguet [mygyɛ]	(thrush)
fermer [fɛrme]	(to close)
pavots [pavo]	(poppies)
disperser [dispɛrse]	(to disperse)
taches [taʃe]	(spots)

WORKSHEET #18: French final spellings

Provide IPA:

#5

éternel	(eternal)
sachez	(you know)
discret	(discrete)
mot	(word)
chercher	(to search)
bords	(edges)
archers	(archers)
ténèbres	(darkness)

#6

héros	(hero)
versez	(you pour)
corps	(body)
filet	(net)
séparer	(to separate)
appel	(call)
péchers	(fisheries)
certes	(certainly)

#7

céder	(to give in)
dort	(sleeps)
sujet	(about)
mortel	(fatal)
vergers	(orchards)
pâles	(pale)
brisez	(you break)
cachots	(dungeons)

#8

sonner	(to sound)
chef	(head, chief)
hors	(except, outside)
bergers	(shepherds)
galop	(gallop)
cet	(this)
frères	(brothers)
quittez	(you quit)

WORKSHEET #18: French final spellings

Provide IPA:

#9

l'or [lɔr]	(the gold)
cavaliers (*i* is [j]) [kavalje]	(horsemen)
sommes [sɔmə]	(we are)
bec [b?]	(beak)
garder [garde]	(to keep)
promet [prøme]	(promise)
dispos [dispo]	(rested)
admirez [admire]	(you admire)

#10

cigales [sigales	(cicadas)
abricot [abriko]	(apricot)
répéter	(to repeat)
bonnet	(cap)
effort (*e* is [(e)])	(effort)
partez	(you go)
sel	(salt)
légers	(lights)

#11

flotter	(to float)
brèves	(short)
célébrez	(you celebrate)
jet	(fountain)
ménestrel	(minstrel)
canots	(canoes)
glaciers (*i* is [j])	(glaciers)
sol	(ground)

#12

clos	(closed)
archet	(bow)
résister	(to resist)
halliers (*i* is [j])	(thickets)
tel	(as)
fort	(strong)
marchez	(you walk)
scélérates	(rogues)

UNIT 19:

French vowel clusters: front vowels

RULES FOR TRANSCRIPTION

French vowel clusters: front vowels

Spelling	IPA	Sample Words
Final *-ai* verb ending	[e] Closed Front	dirai [diɾe] (will say)
ai	[ɛ] Open Front	solitaire [sɔlitɛɾə]
aî	[ɛ] Open Front	faîte [fɛtə]
ay	[ɛj] Open Front + Glide	crayon [kɾɛjõ]
ei	[ɛ] Open Front	seigneur [sɛɲœɾ]
All final [ɛ]	[ɛ̝] Semi-Open Front	paix [pɛ̝] donnait [dɔnɛ̝] chantaient [ʃɑ̃tɛ̝]
*Vocalic harmonization of *ai*	[(e)] Semi-Closed Front	laisse [lɛsə] → laisser [l(e)se]
*Vocalic harmonization of *aî*	[(e)] Semi-Closed Front	fraîche [fɾɛʃə] → fraîchir [fɾ(e)ʃiɾ]
*Vocalic harmonization of *ay*	[(e)] Semi-Closed Front	rayon [ɾɛjõ] → rayonner [ɾ(e)jɔne]
*Vocalic harmonization of *ei*	[(e)] Semi-Closed Front	neige [nɛʒə] → neiger [n(e)ʒe]
*Vocalic harmonization of *ê*	[(e)] Semi-Closed Front	mêle [mɛlə] → mêler [m(e)le]
Final *-ie*	[i] Closed Front	choisie [ʃwazi]

EXCEPTION WORDS

The following final *-ai* words are transcribed with a semi-open front [ɛ̝]: *balai* [balɛ̝], *lai* [lɛ̝], *mai* [mɛ̝], *rai* [ɾɛ̝], *vrai* [vɾɛ̝]. All other final *-ai* words are closed [e]: *ai* [e], *gai* [ge], *quai* [ke]. Additional exception words include: *pays* [pei] and *maison* [m(e)zõ].

Dictionary transcription indicates an open [ɛ] pronunciation for the words *sais*, *sait*, and *vais*. Standard texts recommend a closed [e] pronunciation. The [ɛ̝] symbol provides a suitable solution.

* VOCALIC HARMONIZATION

Vocalic harmonization closes a vowel to match the closed [e], [i], or [y] quality of a following syllable. It is applied to *ai, aî, ei, ê, ay,* and *eu* spellings only. Vocalic harmonization of *ai* is the most frequently occurring spelling.

CLASSWORK #19: French vowel clusters: front vowels

Provide IPA:

1. haleine (breath)
2. aimé (liked, loved)
3. parfait (perfect)
4. jolie (nice)
5. chaînette (chain)
6. marchaient (walking)
7. l'aigle (the eagle)
8. célébrai (celebrate)

TRANSCRIPTION WITHIN THE PHRASE #19

Classwork: *I dreamed that you left me;*
J'ai rêvé que tu me quittais;

1. *Ah! how beautiful she was,*
Ah! comme elle était belle,

2. *winged poet of my solitude*
Barde ailé de ma solitude

3. *but your destiny*
Mais votre destinée

4. *and I did not know that I loved you,*
Et je n'ai su que je t'aimais,

5. *Never have you been so lovely,*
Jamais tu ne fus si belle,

6. *The moon was growing sad.*
La lune s'attristait.

7. *Row! Sleep! Love! said the women.*
Ramez! Dormez! | Aimez! disaient-elles.

8. *my dear, what is the storm to me?*
Mignonne, que me fait l'orage?

9. *O the frail and fresh murmur!*
Ô le frêle et frais murmure!

10. *If my verses had wings*
Si mes vers avaient des ailes

11. *in order to await the arrival of the evening,*
Pour laisser arriver le soir,
wa

12. *and how I loved her!*
Et comme je l'aimais!

WORKSHEET #19: French vowel clusters: front vowels

Provide IPA:

#1

connais	(know)	[kɔnɛ]
vaine	(empty)	[vɛnə]
maladie	(disease)	[maladi]
disparaître	(disappear)	[disparɛtrə]
bénirai	(bless)	[benirɛ]
reine	(queen)	[rɛnə]
attiraient	(attracted)	[atirɛ]
prairie	(grassland)	[prɛri]

#2

cherchaient	(looked for)	[ʃɛrʃɛ]
flétrie	(withered)	[fletri]
atteigne	(reaches)	[atɛɲə]
naît	(was born)	[nɛ]
souffrirai	(suffer)	[sufrirɛ]
ait	(have)	[ɛ]
éclairé	(lit)	[eklere]
plaine	(plain)	[plɛnə]

#3

seiche	(cuttlefish)	[s(e)ʃə]
déterminai	(determined)	[determinɛ]
l'aile	(wing)	[l(e)lə]
patrie	(homeland)	[patri]
neiger	(snow)	[neʒə]
finiraient	(eventually)	[finirɛ]
apparaître	(appear)	[aparɛtrə]
épais	(thick)	[epɛ]

#4

avaient	(had)	[avɛ]
plaire	(please)	[plɛrə]
inapaisés	(unappeased)	[inapɛse]
connaître	(know)	[konɛtrə]
guérirai	(heal)	[gerirɛ
lait	(milk)	[lɛ]
finie	(finished)	[fini]
seigle	(rye)	[sɛglə]

WORKSHEET #19: French vowel clusters: front vowels

Provide IPA:

#5

attraits	(attractions)	[atrɛ]
verveine	(verbena)	[vɛrvɛnə]
harmonie	(harmony)	[armɔni]
saisir	(hold, grasp)	[sɛsir]
disaient	(said)	[disɛ]
faible	(feeble, faint)	[fɛblə]
lirai	(I will read)	[lirɛ]
plaît	(please)	[plɛ]

#6

sait	(knows)	[sɛ]
traîne	(drag, train)	[trɛnə]
chérie	(darling)	[ʃeri]
fraise	(strawberry)	[frɛzə]
volaient	(flying)	[vɔlɛ]
estimai	(estimate)	[ɛstime]
délaissée	(abandoned)	[delɛseə]
pleine	(full)	[plinə]

#7

traits	(features)	[trɛ]
peigne	(comb)	[pɛɲə]
frénésie	(frenzy)	[frenezi]
aimable	(friendly)	[ɛmablə]
paraît	(appears)	[parɛ]
baissés	(lowered)	[bɛse]
étaient	(were)	[etɛ]
manifestai	(expressed)	[manifɛstɛ]

#8

flottaient	(floating)	(flotɛ]
chaînes	(chains)	[ʃɛnə]
paisible	(peaceful)	(pɛsiblə]
tait	(keep quiet)	[tɛ]
bénie	(blessed)	[beni]
veines	(veins)	[vinə]
déclarai	(declared)	[deklarɛ]
haine	(hatred)	[ɛnə]

WORKSHEET #19: French vowel clusters: front vowels

Provide IPA:

#9

faits	(facts)
peine	(sorrow)
dormaient	(sleeping)
maître	(master)
vivrai	(will live)
hardie	(bold)
chaise	(chair)
apaiser	(calm down)

#10

treize	(thirteen)
amie	(friend)
claire	(clear)
baiser	(kiss)
murmuraient	(whispering)
pourrai	(could)
vrais	(true)
paraîtra	(published)

#11

brûlai	(burned)
maîtresse	(mistress)
frémissait	(quivering)
seize	(sixteen)
ravie	(delighted)
ailé	(winged)
laine	(wool)
parlaient	(talking)

#12

dédie	(devote)
répétaient	(repeated)
graine	(seed)
palais	(palace)
naître	(to be born)
frémirai	(shudder)
saisit	(grabs)
baleine	(whale)

UNIT 20:

French vowel clusters: back and mixed vowels

RULES FOR TRANSCRIPTION

French vowel clusters: back and mixed vowels

Spelling	IPA	Sample Words
au, eau	[o] Closed Back	pauvre [povɾə] beau [bo]
au + r	[ɔ] Open Back	aurore [ɔɾɔɾə]
eu, œu, œ + pronounced consonant	[œ] Open Mixed	fleur [flœɾ] cœur [kœɾ] œil [œj]
Medial *ue* (rare)	[œ] Open Mixed	cueillir [kœjiɾ] querelle [kœɾɛlə] (except in hiatus: cruel [kryɛl] tendues [tɑ̃dyə])
eu + s + vowel	[ø] Closed Mixed	amoureuse [amuɾøzə]
Final -*eu*	[ø] Closed Mixed	feu [fø]
eu, œu + final silent consonant	[ø] Closed Mixed	glorieux [glɔɾjø] vœux [vø]
Medial *eu* + [ø] (vocalic harmonization)	[(ø)] Closed Mixed	peur [pœɾ] → peureuse [p(ø)ɾøzə]
ou, où, oû	[u] Closed Back	rouge [ɾuʒə] où [u] voûte [vutə]

EXCEPTION WORDS

Conjugated forms of *avoir* (spellings *eu* and *eû*) are transcribed with an [y] symbol: *eu/eus/eut/eût* [y] *eurent* [yɾə] *eusse/eussent* [ysə] *eûtes/eutes* [ytə] *eûmes* [ymə] *eues/eue* [yə]

CLASSWORK #20: French vowel clusters: back and mixed vowels

Provide IPA:

1. sœurs (sisters)
2. auraient (they would have)
3. ténébreuse (dark, gloomy)
4. agneaux (lambs)
5. brumeux (misty)
6. pauvrette (poor thing)
7. farouche (fierce, shy)
8. heure (time, hour)

TRANSCRIPTION WITHIN THE PHRASE #20

Provide IPA:

where the red hibiscus with its scent divine
Classwork: Où l'açoka rouge aux odeurs divines

1. *The spray of water moves its thousand flowers,*
La gerbe d'eau qui berce ses mille fleurs,

2. *happy to stir the clear water,*
Heureux de troubler l'eau claire,

3. *you cannot love me with the same ardor.*
Si tu ne peux m'aimer | avec la même ardeur.

4. *Beside the lilies with purple blossoms,*
Du côté des lilas | aux touffes violettes,
j

5. *I will speak of the rose with graceful pleats.*
Je dirai la rose aux plis gracieux.
j

6. *yellow, wilted, your full flower;*
Jaunir, flétrir, votre épanie fleur;

7. *it is necessary that the saddest heart surrender*
Il faut que le cœur le plus triste cède

8. *to appease troubles, to soothe sorrow,*
Pour apaiser les maux, soulager la douleur,

9. *the loveliest of my days.*
Les plus beaux de mes jours.

10. *by the wind rocking and soft*
Au souffle berceur et doux

11. *There, all is order and beauty,*
Là, tout n'est qu'ordre et beauté,

12. *to talk of our beautiful love,*
Pour parler de nos beaux amours,

WORKSHEET #20: French vowel clusters: back and mixed vowels

Provide IPA:

#1

causes (causes)
[cozə]

pleut (rains)
[plø]

nouveau (new)
[nuvo]

valeur (value)
[valœr]

lauriers (*i* is [j]) (laurels)
[lorje]

bœufs (*fs* is silent) (oxen)
[bø]

anneaux (rings)
[ano]

mœlleuse (soft)
[mœlø]

#2

lumineuse (radiant)
lyminøsə]

aurais (would have)
[orɛ]

chaleureux (warm, welcoming)
[ʃalørø]

eau (water)
[o]

œufs (*fs* is silent) (eggs)
[ø]

autour (around)
[otu]

rigueur (rigor)
[rigyø]

haut (top)
[ˈo]

#3

vœu (vow)
[vø]

ouverte (opened)
[uvɛrtə]

heurte (hits, hurts)
[hørtə]

sauvage (wild)
[sovaʒə]

peux (can)
[pø]

rideaux (curtains)
[rido]

douteuse (doubtful)
[dutøʒə]

auréole (halo)
[oreɔlə]

#4

sœurette (little sister)
[sørɛtə]

morceaux (pieces)
[mɔrso]

creux (hollow)
[krø]

boutique (shop)
[butikə]

vigueur (vigor, strength)
[vigœyr]

auprès (next to, near)
[oprɛ]

pleureuse (mourner)
[plørøsə]

j'aurais (I would)
[ʒorɛ]

WORKSHEET #20: French vowel clusters: back and mixed vowels

Provide IPA:

#5

austère [ostɛrə]	(austere)
pâleur [pɑlø]	(paleness)
veut [vø]	(wants)
saurez [sore]	(you know)
œuvres [øvrə]	(works)
drapeau [drapo]	(flag)
courage [curaʒə]	(courage)
berceuse [bɛrsøsə]	(lullaby)

#6

taureaux [toro]	(bulls)
écœure [ekørə]	(disgust)
jeux [ʒø]	(games)
hameau [amo]	(hamlet)
moqueur [mɔkœr]	(teasing)
pastoureau [pasturo]	(shepherd)
comètes [kɔmetə]	(comets)
rêveuse [rɛvøsə]	(dreamily)

#7

écouter [ekute]	(listen)
veuve [vøvə]	(widow)
beauté [bote]	(beauty)
mœurs [mør]	(manners)
généreux [ʒenerø]	(generous)
chaud [ʃo]	(hot)
peureuse [pørøsə]	(fearful)
aurez [ore]	(will have)

#8

maure [morə]	(moor)
feux [fø]	(fires)
souffrir [sufrir]	(suffer)
cœur [kœr]	(heart)
bateau [bato]	(boat)
charmeuse [ʃarmøsə]	(engaging)
autres [otrə]	(another)
pleure [plørə]	(cries)

WORKSHEET #20: French vowel clusters: back and mixed vowels

Provide IPA:

#9

bouquets	(bouquets)
sauveur	(savior)
aurifère	(gold-bearing)
rameaux	(branches)
heureuse	(happy)
l'aube	(the dawn)
chœur	(chorus)
eux	(them)

#10

aveux	(confessions)
jalousie	(jealousy)
saurais	(would know)
pêcheur	(fisherman)
château	(castle)
œuf	(egg)
épaule	(shoulder)
creuser	(dig)

#11

jaune	(yellow)
queue	(tail)
surtout	(mostly)
orageuse	(stormy)
aurait	(would have)
peuple	(people)
tableaux	(paintings)
vœux	(vows)

#12

manœuvre	(maneuver)
sauras	(will know)
chapeau	(hat)
veu	(seen)
bouches	(mouths)
d'amoureuses	(of lovers)
audace	(bold)
vapeur	(steam)

UNIT 21:

French semivowels

RULES FOR TRANSCRIPTION

French semivowels

Spelling	IPA	Sample Words
i, y + vowel	[j] Prepalatal Glide	lierre [ljɛɾə] yeux [jø]
ou + vowel	[w] Bilabial Glide	jouet [ʒwɛ] oui [wi]
u + vowel	[ɥ] Prepalatal Glide	nuit [nɥi] suave [sɥavə]
* Medial *ill*	[j] Prepalatal Glide	feuille [fœjə] brille [bɾijə]
* Vowel + *il*	[j] Prepalatal Glide	soleil [sɔlɛj] œil [œj]
Consonant + *il*	[il] Dental Lateral	avril [avɾil]
Spelling *oi*	[wa] Bilabial Glide	doigts [dwa] joie [ʒwa]
Spelling *oy*	[waj] Bilabial Glide	voyageur [vwajaʒœɾ]

EXCEPTION WORDS

Medial *ill* exception words: *mille* [milə] *ville* [vilə] *tranquille* [tɾɑ̃kilə] *oscille* [ɔsilə]
Dark [ɑ] exception words: *trois* [tɾwɑ] *bois* [bwɑ] *voix* [vwɑ]

*Medial *ill* and final *il* are transcribed independently from a preceding vowel:
ailleurs [ajœɾ] (not [ɛjœɾ]) *travail* [tɾavaj]

CLASSWORK #21: French semivowels

Provide IPA:

1.	joyeux	(happy)	5.	espoir	(hope)
2.	lumière	(light)	6.	charmille	(arbor)
3.	suis	(am)	7.	oui	(yes)
4.	puéril	(childish)	8.	travail	(work)

TRANSCRIPTION WITHIN THE PHRASE #21

Provide IPA:

Classwork: *the day that shines is the best;*
Le jour qui luit | est le meilleur;

1. *the night to lose its veils,*
   À la nuit de perdre ses voiles,

2. *by Him be my sins absolved:*
   De lui soient mes péchés abolus:
   ə

3. *The playful brooks in the deserted woods*
   Les ruisseaux jaseurs par les bois déserts
   ɑ bwɑ

4. *Night of stars, under your veils,*
   Nuit d'étoiles, sous tes voiles,

5. *O sound soft of the rain,*
   Ô bruit doux de la pluie,

6. *The clouds, grave travelers,*
   Les nuages, graves voyageurs,

7. *To your Son say that I am His;*
   À votre Fils dites que je suis sienne;

8. *but the night, the sky and the waves.*
   Que la nuit, le ciel et les lames.

9. *of these foggy skies*
   De ces ciels brouillés

10. *The last leaf*
    La dernière feuille

11. *The damp suns*
    Les soleils mouillés

12. *Your wild sadness, like unto mine,*
    Ta tristesse sauvage, à la mienne pareille,

WORKSHEET #21: French semivowels

Provide IPA:

#1

nuage	(cloud)
[nwaʒə]	
cils	(eyelashes)
[si]	
pitié	(pity)
[pitje]	
s'épanouit	(blossoms)
[sepanwi]	
gouvernail	(rudder)
[guvɛrnɛ]	
avoir	(have)
[avwa]	
oreille	(ear)
[orilə]	
loyal	(loyal)
[lwajal]	

#2

amitié	(friendship)
[amitje]	
étoiles	(stars)
[etwa]	
réveille	(wake up)
[revilə]	
péril	(risk)
[peri]	
fruit	(fruit)
[frɥi]	
? souhait	(wish)
[su	
accueil	(welcome)
[akɥi]	
croyais	(believed)
[krwajɛ]	

#3

rouet	(spinning wheel)
[rwɛ]	
miel	(honey)
[mjɛl]	
lueurs	(lights)
[lɥɛy]	
effroyable (*e* is [(e)])	(terrible)
[efrwajablə]	
abeilles	(bees)
[abilə]	
profil	(profile)
[profi]	
gloire	(glory)
[glwarə]	
fauteuil	(armchair)
[faytɛɥi]	

#4

soyez	(been)
[swaje]	
perpétuelle	(perpetual)
[pɛrpetɥelə]	
l'œil	(the eye)
[lœi]	
crois	(I believe)
[krwa]	
vieux	(old)
[vjœu]	
ouïr	(hear)
[wi]	
babil	(babble)
[babi]	
meilleur	(best)
[milɛur]	

WORKSHEET #21: French semivowels

Provide IPA:

#5

exil	(exile)
brouillard	(fog)
voyez	(see)
lieu	(place)
mémoire	(memory)
chevreuil	(deer)
persuader	(persuade)
alouette	(lark)

#6

ciel	(sky)
merveilleux	(wonderful)
épanouie	(blossomed)
royaume	(kingdom)
grésil	(fine hail)
autrui	(others)
pourquoi	(why)
sommeil	(sleep)

#7

parfois	(sometimes)
réveil	(awakening)
il	(he)
muable	(changeable)
adieu	(farewell)
voyais	(saw)
cueillir (*ue* is [œ])	(gather)
éblouis	(dazzled)

#8

jouir	(enjoy)
l'écueil	(the reef)
vierge	(blank)
noyer	(walnut tree)
éveille	(awake)
baril	(barrel)
oiseaux	(birds)
muet	(mute)

WORKSHEET #21: French semivowels

Provide IPA:

#9

civil	(civil)
l'alouette	(the lark)
œillets	(carnations)
minuit	(midnight)
foyer	(home)
seuil	(threshold)
victoire	(win, victory)
pierre	(stone)

#10

voyage	(travel)
orgueil	(pride)
milieu	(middle)
pouvoir	(be able, power)
subtil (*b* is [p])	(subtle)
fillette	(little girl)
réjouir	(rejoice)
lui	(him)

#11

fil	(wire)
royal	(royal)
luisaient	(shining)
brillaient	(shining)
savoir	(know, knowledge)
mieux	(more)
jouait	(played)
corail	(coral)

#12

pareil	(same)
boire	(to drink)
soyeux	(silky)
mouette	(seagull)
vils	(vile)
famille	(family)
luire	(shine)
dernier	(last)

UNIT 22:

French schwa

RULES FOR TRANSCRIPTION

French schwa

Spelling	IPA	Sample Words
Final *-e* and *-es*	[ə] Schwa	harpe [aɾpə] petites [pətitə]
consonant + *e* + consonant + vowel	[ə]	chevelure [ʃəvəlyɾə]
re- as a prefix	[ə]	regrets [ɾəgɾɛ] refrain [ɾəfɾɛ̃]
Initial *rest-, resp-*	[ɛ] Open Front	restaient [ɾɛstɛ] resplendir [ɾɛsplɑ̃diɾ]
* Verb ending *-ent*	[ə]	passent [pɑsə]
fais + vowel	[ə]	faisait [fəzɛ] faisons [fəzõ]

EXCEPTION WORDS

dessous [dəsu] *dessus* [dəsy] *monsieur* [məsjø] *ressemble* [ɾəsɑ̃blə] *secret* [səkɾɛ]

* Consonant + final *ent* is [ɑ̃] for all other parts of speech: *moment* [mɔmɑ̃]
Note: verb ending *-ient* is [jɛ̃] and verb ending *-aient* is [ɛ]

CLASSWORK #22: French schwa

Provide IPA:

1. restais (stayed)
2. premier (first)
3. vertige (dizziness)
4. devenu (became)
5. lettre (letter)
6. reflet (reflection)
7. sonnent (sound) v.
8. faiblesse (weakness)

TRANSCRIPTION WITHIN THE PHRASE #22

Provide IPA:

there to be just enough breeze
Classwork: Qu'il fasse justes assez de brise

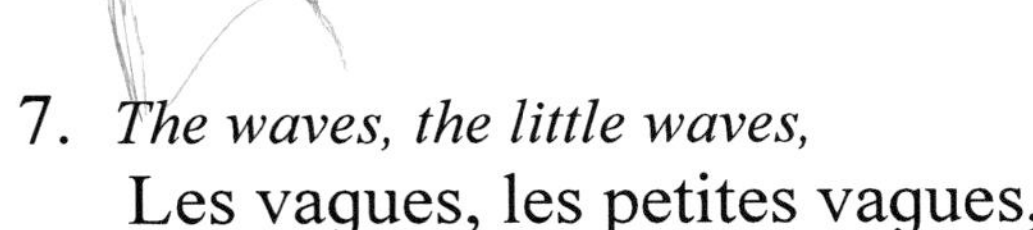

1. *I have strewn it with flowers and herbs*
   je l'ai parsemé de fleurs et d'herbes
   [ʒə le parsɛme də flø ze dɛrbə]

2. *I was walking the other day,*
   Je me promenais l'autre jour,
   [ʒə mə promɛnɛ lotr

3. *The beautiful night flowers, half closed,*
   Les belles de nuit, demi-closes,

4. *do not repulse me*
   Ne me repousse pas

5. *when all charms are reborn;*
   que tout charme renaisse;

6. *Turn toward the poet*
   Tourne devers le poète

7. *The waves, the little waves,*
   Les vagues, les petites vagues,

8. *Won't you return?*
   Ne devez-vous revenir?

9. *how many towns and villages,*
   Que de villes et de hameaux,

10. *moan the turtle doves.*
    Se plaignent les tourterelles.

11. *your moist eyes close again,*
    tes yeux humides se referment (verb),

12. *that I was becoming you,*
    que je devenais toi-même,

WORKSHEET #22: French schwa

Provide IPA:

#1

rebelle	(rebel)
[rəbɛlə]	
mystérieuses	(mysterious)
[misterjœsə]	
genoux	(knees)
[ʒənu]	
prennent	(take)
[prɛnə]	
escaladez	(climb)
[ɛskaladə]	
reste	(remain, stay)
[rɛstə]	
hôtellerie	(hotels)
[hotɛləri]	
retenue	(restraint)
[rətənyə]	

#2

cheval	(horse)
[ʃəval]	
muette	(mute)
[mwɛtə]	
victorieuses	(victorious)
[victorjœsə]	
respirer	(breathe)
[rɛspirə]	
primevères	(primroses)
[primәvɛrə]	
esprits	(spirits)
[ɛspri]	
recevoir	(receive)
[rəzəvwa]	
brillent	(shine) v.
[brilə]	

#3

restera	(will stay)
[rəstɛra]	
leger	(light)
[lɛʒə]	
sienne	(hers)
[sjenə]	
disent	(say)
[dizə]	
préservez	(you preserve)
[prezɛrvə]	
regret	(regret)
[rəgre]	
grenouilles	(frogs)
[grənujə]	
mienne	(mine)
[mjɛnə]	

#4

destinée	(destiny)
[dɛstineə]	
mener	(to lead)
[məne]	
éternelle	(eternal)
[etɛrnɛlə]	
vivent	(live) v.
[vivə]	
retraite	(retreat)
[rətrɛ]	
pleines	(full)
[plɛnə]	
batelier	(boatman)
[batəlje]	
respecté	(respected)
[rəspɛkte]	

WORKSHEET #22: French schwa

Provide IPA:

#5

- éperviers (hawks) [epɛrvie]
- celui (the one) [səlɥi]
- restait (was left, stayed) [rəstɛ]
- troublent (disturb) [trublə]
- demoiselles (young ladies) [dəmwazɛlə]
- revenir (come back) [rəvəni]
- violettes (violet) [vwalɛtə]
- souvenir (memory) [suvənir]

#6

- aigres (sour) [ɛgrə]
- renaître (reborn) [rənɛtrə]
- savent (know) v. [savə]
- fierté (pride) [fjɛrte]
- chevilles (ankles) [ʃevilə]
- restée (stayed) [rəsteə]
- petit (small) [pəti]
- marinier (boatman) [marinjə]

#7

- autrefois (formerly) [otrəfwa]
- ivresse (drunkenness) [ivrɛsə]
- refleurir (bloom again) [rəflœri]
- fermiers (farmers) [fermje]
- soient (were) [swaə]
- respirez (you breathe) [rɛspirə]
- velours (velvet) [vəlu]
- reines (queens) [rɛnə]

#8

- liberté (freedom) [libɛrte]
- reproche (complaint) [rəprɔʃə]
- promener (to walk) [promənə]
- restes (stays) [rɛstə]
- querelles (disputes) [kerɛlə]
- cherchent (seek) [ʃɛrʃə]
- remède (remedy) [rɛmedə]
- venir (come, arrive) [vɛni]

WORKSHEET #22: French schwa

Provide IPA:

#9

viennent	(come)
repos	(rest)
liesse	(jubilation)
sera	(will be)
achever	(to finish)
couverts	(silverware)
propre	(clean)
respect (*c* silent)	(respect)

#10

rester	(to stay)
meurent	(die) v.
tienne	(held, yours)
grenier	(attic)
noble	(noble)
reluit	(shines)
verbal	(verbal)
fenêtres	(windows)

#11

laine	(wool)
revoir	(see again)
peuvent	(can) v.
forteresse	(fortress)
mesures	(measures)
terminer	(finish)
respire	(breathing)
élever	(to raise)

#12

rappeler	(to remind)
furent	(were)
quenouilles	(cattails)
resté	(stayed)
menaces	(threats)
servirez	(you serve)
tourterelles	(doves)
refroidie	(cooled)

UNIT 23:

French [ɑ̃] and [õ]

RULES FOR TRANSCRIPTION

French [ɑ̃] and [õ]

Spelling	IPA	Sample Words
am, em + consonant	[ɑ̃] Nasal Dark [ɑ]	flambeau [flɑ̃bo] temps [tɑ̃]
am, em + *h, m, n,* or vowel	Not nasal	flamme [flɑmə] demeure [dəmœɾə]
an, en + consonant	[ɑ̃] Nasal Dark [ɑ]	romance [ɾɔmɑ̃sə] encore [ɑ̃kɔɾə]
an, en + *h, m, n,* or vowel	Not nasal	année [aneə] tenir [təniɾ]
Final *-an*	[ɑ̃] Nasal Dark [ɑ]	ruban [ɾybɑ̃]
om, on + consonant	[õ] Nasal Closed Back	ombre [õbɾə] hirondelle [iɾõdɛlə]
om, on + *h, m, n,* or vowel	Not nasal	automne [otɔnə] bonheur [bɔnœɾ]
Final *-om, -on*	[õ] Nasal Closed Back	nom [nõ] chanson [ʃɑ̃sõ]

The "n" or "m" that follow a nasal vowel will be silent

Exception words: enivré [ɑ̃nivɾe] enneigé [ɑ̃n(e)ʒe] ennui [ɑ̃nɥi]

Memory aid: the consonants that nullify the nasal rules are in the word *human*

CLASSWORK #23: French [ɑ̃] and [õ]

Provide IPA:

1. trembler (shudder)
   [trɑ̃ble]
2. anneau (ring)
   [ano]
3. plan (map)
   [plɑ̃]
4. hommage (tribute)
   [ɔmaʒə
5. doucement (softly)
   [dusəmɑ̃]
6. mignon (cute)
   [miɲõ]
7. lente (slow)
   [lentə]
8. colombe (dove)
   [kolɤbə]
9. champêtre (rustic)
10. sanglots (sobs)

TRANSCRIPTION WITHIN THE PHRASE #23

Provide IPA:

Classwork: *Carol of the children who have no more houses*
Noël des enfants qui n'ont plus de maisons
(e)

1. *and to hear voices in her heart.*
Et d'entendre en son cœur des voix.
vwɑ

2. *one senses the slow return*
On sent lentement revenir

3. *and full of sorrows without number,*
Et fécond | en peines sans nombre,

4. *admiring his great tilted antlers:*
Admirant son grand bois penché;
bwɑ

5. *and that we are still together*
Et que l'on soit encore ensemble

6. *here is my heart, my trembling heart,*
Voici mon cœur, mon cœur tremblant,

7. *and your heart will hear silent words.*
Et ton coeur entendra des mots silencieux.

8. *his name I will speak, dreaming*
Je dirai son nom, | en rêvant

9. *and, when the winds are insane,*
Et, quand les vents sont en démence,

10. *I tremble in seeing your face*
Je tremble en voyant ton visage

11. *that go up in the pure air for an adventure.*
Qui s'en vont dans l'air pur à l'aventure.

12. *One hears the knocking of bones of the dancers;*
On entend claquer les os̲ des danseurs;

WORKSHEET #23: French [ã] and [õ]

Provide IPA:

#1

blanche	(white)
amis	(friends)
vallon	(small valley)
envie	(longing)
nombre	(number)
champagne	(champagne)
divan	(couch)
fromage	(cheese)
tendrement	(tenderly)
membres	(members)

#2

penche	(tilts)
granit	(granite)
remplit	(fills)
étonné	(surprised)
branches	(branches)
frisson	(shudder)
cadran	(dial)
chambre	(bedroom)
allons	(let's go)
tristement	(sadly)

#3

seulement	(only)
violon	(violin)
ouragan	(hurricane)
emplit	(fills)
familles	(families)
pensée	(thought)
nomme	(names)
lampe	(lamp)
trompe	(trumpet)
avant	(before)

#4

océan	(ocean)
balcon	(balcony)
voyant	(seeing)
l'humanité	(humanity)
empire	(empire)
monde	(world)
entre	(between)
promesse	(promise)
comment	(how)
rampe	(handrail)

WORKSHEET #23: French [ɑ̃] and [õ]

Provide IPA:

#5

firmament	(firmament)
harmonie	(harmony)
embaumée	(embalmed)
chameau	(camel)
Pan	(Pan)
lambeaux	(shreds)
aimons	(love)
silence	(silence)
raison	(reason)
couchant	(sunset)

#6

commence	(starts)
l'onde	(the water)
simplement	(simply)
ans	(years)
bannir	(to ban)
élan	(momentum)
donnent	(give)
novembre	(November)
prison	(prison)
jambe	(leg)

#7

selon	(according to)
camps	(camps)
remord	(remorse)
ensemble	(ensemble)
profond	(deep)
an	(year)
dame	(lady)
l'empire	(the empire)
abandonné	(abandoned)
tourment	(torment) n.

#8

lamente	(laments)
pommes	(apples)
contre	(against)
tyran	(tyrant)
semble	(seems)
buisson	(bush)
enflammé (a is [ɑ])	(inflamed)
ramures	(branches)
présent	(present) n.
étrange	(strange)

WORKSHEET #23: French [ɑ̃] and [õ]

Provide IPA:

#9

cent	(hundred)
manoir	(mansion)
langueur	(languor)
élan	(momentum)
sombre	(dark)
tempête	(storm)
frissonne	(shudders)
d'ambre	(of amber)
pardon	(forgiveness)
vêtement	(clothing)

#10

emporte	(takes away)
saison	(season)
campagnards	(rustic)
j'entends	(I understand)
pavane	(struts)
espérance	(hope)
domaine	(domain)
vraiment	(really)
fontaine	(fountain)
maman	(mom)

#11

souvent	(often)
agonie	(agony)
charmant	(charming)
avons	(we have)
pampre	(vine)
vienne	(come)
lentement	(slowly)
clan	(group)
sinon	(otherwise)
ramier	(pigeon)

#12

moment	(moment)
poison	(poison)
devant	(in front)
ironique	(ironically)
exemple	(example)
vanité	(vanity)
en	(in)
splendeur	(splendor)
compagne	(companion)
tambour	(drum)

UNIT 24:

French [ɛ̃] and [œ̃]

RULES FOR TRANSCRIPTION

French [ɛ̃] and [œ̃]

Spelling	IPA	Sample Words
aim, ain, ein + consonant	[ɛ̃] Nasal Open Front	ainsi [ɛ̃si] empreinte [ɑ̃pɾɛ̃tə]
Final *-aim, -ain, -ein*	[ɛ̃] Nasal Open Front	certain [sɛɾtɛ̃] plein [plɛ̃]
ai, ei + *m, n* + *h, m, n,* or vowel	Not nasal	aime [ɛmə] sereine [səɾɛnə]
i, y + *m, n* + consonant	[ɛ̃] Nasal Open Front	printemps [pɾɛ̃tɑ̃] sympathie [sɛ̃pati]
Final *i* or *y* + *m* or *n*	[ɛ̃] Nasal Open Front	matin [matɛ̃] thym [tɛ̃]
i, y + *n, m* + *h, m, n,* or vowel	Not nasal	immortel [immɔɾtɛl] dynamo [dinamo]
Verb ending *-ient*	[jɛ̃] Nasal Open Front	vient [vjɛ̃] tient [tjɛ̃]
Final *-en(s)*	[ɛ̃] Nasal Open Front	bien [bjɛ̃] moyens [mwajɛ̃]
oin + consonant or final	[wɛ̃] Nasal Open Front	point [pwɛ̃] loin [lwɛ̃]
um, un + consonant or final	[œ̃] Nasal Open Mixed	humble [œ̃blə] un [œ̃] parfum [paɾfœ̃]
um, un + *h, m, n,* or vowel	Not nasal	lune [lynə] humaine [ymɛnə]

Note: the "n" or "m" that follow a nasal vowel will be silent

Exception words: *Amen* [amɛn] *Carmen* [kaɾmɛn] *en* [ɑ̃] encens [ɑ̃sɑ̃] *gens* [ʒɑ̃] *Poulenc* [pulɛ̃k] *album* [albɔm] *aquarium* [akaɾjɔm] *géranium* [ʒeɾanjɔm]

Memory aid: the consonants that nullify the nasal rules are in the word *human*

CLASSWORK #24: French [ɛ̃] and [œ̃]

Provide IPA:

1.	jardin	(garden)	5.	hautaine	(haughty)
2.	lundi	(Monday)	6.	maintenant	(now)
3.	étincelle	(spark)	7.	cymbales	(cymbals)
4.	pointe	(tip, peak)	8.	demain	(tomorrow)

TRANSCRIPTION WITHIN THE PHRASE #24

Provide IPA:

you would take, one day, the path to the sacred place.
Classwork: Tu porterais un jour tes pas dans le saint lieu.

1. *like a grain of incense, it may inflame it.*
Comme un grain d'encens, il l'enflamme.
ɑ

2. *enveloped in a sleep full of mystery,*
Ensevelie en un sommeil plein de mystère,

3. *like a long shroud trailing to the East,*
comme un long linceul traînant à l'Orient,

4. *O vows! O perfumes! O kisses infinite!*
Ô serments! | ô parfums! | ô baisers infinis!

5. *A spring envelopes us with its smile,*
Un printemps nous enveloppe de son sourire

6. *my heart, like a lily fully blooming, overflows,*
Mon cœur comme un lys plein s'épanche,

7. *with that slow rhythm that silence interrupts.*
Avec ce rythme lent qu'un silence interrompt.
(e)

8. *from a horn in the distant woods,*
Un cor dans le lointain des bois,
bwɑ

9. *calls out a song plaintive, eternal and distant.*
Appelle un chant plaintif, | éternel et lointain.

10. *place a kiss, and from an angel become a woman,*
Pose un baiser, | et d'ange deviens femme,

11. *as a tree by a kingfisher.*
pour un arbre par un martin-pêcheur.

12. *I have had, for a year, spring in my soul*
J'ai depuis un an le printemps dans l'âme

WORKSHEET #24: French [ɛ̃] and [œ̃]

Provide IPA:

#1

destin	(destiny)
quelqu'un	(someone)
peint	(painted)
inutile	(useless)
nimbe	(halo)
gardien	(guardian)
vingt	(twenty)
joint	(attached)

#2

foin	(hay)
atteint	(suffering)
parfums	(perfumes)
implore	(beg)
humain	(human)
afin	(in order to)
amertume	(bitterness)
chrétiens	(Christians)

#3

printemps	(spring)
mains	(hands)
triumphant (*i* [ij])	(triumphant)
combien	(how many)
impossible	(impossible)
groin	(snout)
cuisine	(kitchen)
festin	(feast)

#4

symphonie	(symphony)
témoins	(witnesses)
innocence (*nn* [nn])	(innocence)
vint	(came)
marin	(marine)
commun	(common)
plaintes	(complaints)
lendemain	(next day)

WORKSHEET #24: French [ɛ̃] and [œ̃]

Provide IPA:

#5

sphynx	(sphinx)
parisien	(Parisian)
humeur	(mood)
ceinture	(belt)
chacun	(each)
déclin	(decline)
impétueux	(impetuous)
besoin	(need)

#6

pain	(bread)
symbole	(symbol)
hymne	(hymn)
moindres	(less)
liens	(links)
brun	(brown)
chemin	(path)
teint	(dyed, complexion)

#7

devinrent	(became)
tien	(yours)
jungle	(jungle)
ceint	(encircled)
immense ([mm])	(huge)
chagrin	(grief)
limpides	(clear)
poing	(fist)

#8

voisin	(neighbor)
tribuns	(tribunes)
serein	(serene)
étreinte	(hugged)
rime	(rhyme)
musicien	(musician)
pourpoint	(doublet)
faim	(hunger)

WORKSHEET #24: French [ɛ̃] and [œ̃]

Provide IPA:

#9

feinte	(craftiness)
coin	(corner)
prochaine	(next)
train	(train)
impérieux	(imperative)
matins	(mornings)
humble	(humble)
divin	(divine)

#10

sien	(his, hers)
fortunées	(fortunate)
tintent	(jingle) v.
crains	(fear)
aucun	(none)
poindre	(dawn)
imprudent	(unwise)
jasmin	(jasmine)

#11

reviens	(comes back)
jacynthes	(hyacinths)
importun	(unwelcome)
chien	(dog)
lointains	(distant)
emprunté	(borrowed)
satin	(satin)
ultime	(ultimate)

#12

enfin	(finally)
un	(a)
timbres	(tones)
soin	(care)
vainqueur	(winner)
quotidien	(daily)
l’instant	(the moment)
graines	(seeds)

Provide IPA:

1. laisser (leave)
2. reconnaître (recognize)
3. très (very)
4. vœux (vows)
5. l'avenue (avenue)
6. maintient (maintains, holds)
7. tranquille (quiet)
8. oui (yes)
9. marguerites (daisies)
10. dîners (dinners)
11. voyaient (saw)
12. apaisent (calm) v.
13. moineau (sparrow)
14. infinie (infinite)
15. miel (honey)
16. en (in)
17. aurai (will have)
18. tourterelle (dove)
19. subtil (subtle)
20. comprendre (understand)
21. regard (look)
22. je (I)
23. plutôt (rather)
24. œil (eye)
25. humble (humble)
26. avec (with)
27. rien (nothing)
28. vaisselle (tableware)
29. élégie (elegy)
30. rêvais (dreaming)
31. femme (woman)
32. bruns (brown)
33. les lèvres (the lips)
34. deuil (mourning)
35. poëte (poet)
36. suivez (follow)

37. flots (waves)
[flo]

38. point (point)
[pwɛ̃]

39. neiges (snow)
[niʒə]

40. bâtiras (will build)
[batira]

41. explique (explain)
[ɛksplikə]

42. restai (remained)
[rəstɛ]

43. chose (thing)
[ʃozə]

44. là-bas (over there)
[labɑ]

45. harmonieuse (harmonious)
[armɔnjɛyzə]

46. parfum (perfume)
[parfœ̃]

47. grenouille (frog)
[grənyilə]

48. paix (peace)
[pɛ]

49. océan (ocean)
[ɔseɑ̃]

50. limpide (clear)
[lɛ̃pidə]

51. aucun (none)
[okœ̃]

52. frayeur (fright)
[frajœ]

53. tes pieds (your feet)
[tɛz pjɛ]

54. chanson (song)
[ʃɑ̃sɔ̃]

55. pâquerette (daisy)
[pakərɛtə]

56. thym (thyme)
[tim]

57. longtemps (for a long time)
[lɔngtɛ̃]

58. immortelle (immortal)
[immɔrtɛlə]

59. faisons (do)
[fɛsɔ̃]

60. travers (through)
[travɛr]

61. cieux (heavens)
[sjø]

62. dévotion (devotion)
[devɔtwɛ̃]

63. exactement (exactly)
[ɛgzaktəmɑ̃]

64. mériter (merit)
[merite]

65. prince (prince)
[prɛ̃sə]

66. roitelet (wren)
[rwatəle]

67. demeures (mansions)
[dəmœrə]

68. berçait (rocking)
[bɛrsɛ]

69. déïté (deity)
[deite]

70. cygne (swan)
[siŋə]

Provide IPA for the following phrase:

La perle est aux ondes (The pearl is in the waves)

[la pɛrlə e ɑ ɔndə]

UNIT 25:

Latin classification of symbols

GENERAL TERMS

IPA. The *International Phonetic Alphabet* was established by the International Phonetic Association around 1888. Each symbol stands for one phonetic sound and is enclosed in brackets. Authentic pronunciation, accurate formation, and precise resonance must be defined for each symbol within the respective language.

Dialect: a form of pronunciation belonging to a specific geographic location and time period. The appropriate pronunciation for Latin lyric diction is dictated by its formal usage in the Roman Catholic Church. Guidelines for Liturgical Latin pronunciation were established by the Gregorian Chant scholars.

PHONETIC TERMS (additional terms on pages 165 and 166)

Articulation and enunciation: the act of speaking or singing phonetic sounds.
Aspirate: a consonant that is articulated with an audible release of breath (English and German *p, t, k*)
Continuant: a consonant that maintains a continuous and even flow of sound (*l, n, m, r, s, z*)
Dental: a consonant that is articulated with the tongue tip touching the upper row of teeth (Latin *d, n, t, l*)

WORD STRUCTURE

Monosyllable: a word that contains one syllable. A polysyllabic word contains two or more syllables.
Monophthong: a word with one vowel sound per syllable. A diphthong contains two vowel sounds per syllable and a triphthong contains three vowel sounds per syllable.
Rising Diphthong: two vowel sounds in the same syllable with a lengthening of the second vowel
Falling Diphthong: two vowel sounds in the same syllable with a lengthening of the first vowel
Hiatus: adjacent vowel sounds that occupy consecutive syllables
Prevocalic: a consonant that precedes a vowel sound
Intervocalic: a consonant or vowel that stands between vowel sounds
Postvocalic: a consonant that follows a vowel sound
Initial: the first letter or sound of a word
Medial: a letter or sound in the middle of a word
Final: the last letter or sound of a word

SCHOLARLY AUTHORITY

The rules outlined in the following units are based upon Robert S. Hines' *Singer's Manual of Latin Diction and Phonetics* published by Schirmer Books, copyright 1975. Dr. Daniel Solomon, professor of Latin and Director of Undergraduate Studies in Classical Studies at Vanderbilt University, is the Latin text and translation editor. English translations of the Holy Scriptures are Douay-Rheims translations (see www.vulgate.org).

CHARACTERISTICS OF THE LATIN LANGUAGE AND IPA

1) Purity of the vowel line is the glue of the legato and the defining characteristic of the Latin language. Legato is movement from consonant to vowel and from pitch to pitch in a smooth and connected flow of sound. There are no glottal stops in Latin.
2) Syllabic stress is formed by a weighted accentuation of the stressed syllable.
3) Primary stress is on the first syllable in two syllable words. An advanced knowledge of Latin grammar is required in order to identify the stressed syllable in words that contain three or more syllables. For these words, the stressed syllable is indicated within the text by an underlined vowel.
4) Vowels are precise, neat, pure, and frontal in placement. They maintain their formation throughout vocalization.
5) Consonants are quick, crisp, and clean. Do not allow consonant articulation to be pressed. Consonants should not interrupt the flow of vowels nor should they disrupt the legato line.
6) Dental consonants: the tongue tip contacts the back of the upper front teeth for consonants *d, n, t,* and *l.*
7) Plosive consonants: a non-aspirate quality is required for consonants *b, d, g, p, t,* and *k.*
8) Latin IPA symbols are identical to English symbols. Do not assume that the sounds are identical. English vowels are medial in placement while the Latin vowels are more forward and highly resonated.
9) Accent marks are used in many Latin texts to indicate the stressed syllable.
10) The schwa does not exist in Latin. The schwa represents a weakening of the vowel in English. Do not weaken the quality of Latin vowels in unstressed syllables.

PRONUNCIATION GUIDE

FRONT VOWELS

IPA	ENGLISH (approximation)	LATIN
[i]	eat, greet	pie, spiritu [ˈpi-ɛ] [ˈspiɾitu]
[ɛ]	met, friend	vere, excelsis [ˈvɛɾɛ] [ɛkˈʃɛlsis]

BACK VOWELS

[u]	food, blue	Jesu, unum [ˈjɛzu] [ˈunum]
[ɔ]	talk, ought	nobis, dolor [ˈnɔbis] [ˈdɔlɔɾ]

CENTRAL VOWEL

[ɑ]	father, robin	patris, anima [ˈpɑtɾis] [ˈanimɑ]

GLIDE

[j]	yet, year	ejus, justi [ˈɛ-jus] [ˈjusti]
[w]	winter, web	qui, requiem [kwi] [ˈrɛ-kwi-ɛm]

HIATUS (adjacent vowel sounds that occupy consecutive syllables)

ENGLISH: poem, create, naive
[ˈpoʊ-ɛm][kɹi-ˈɛɪt][nɑɪ-ˈiv]

LATIN: poema, die, filius
[pɔ-ˈɛ-mɑ][ˈdi-ɛ][ˈfi-li-us]

STRESS MARK

[ˈ]	remember, above [ɹɪˈmɛmbə][ʔʌˈbʌv]	hominibus, culpa [ɔˈminibus] [ˈkulpɑ]

DENTAL CONSONANTS The following consonants are classified as dental in Latin but alveolar in English (Latin consonants *d* and *t* are both dental and plosive)

IPA	ENGLISH (approximation)	LATIN
[d]	dance, decide	domine, defende [ˈdɔminɛ] [dɛˈfɛndɛ]
[n]	novel, news	nobis, nomini [ˈnɔbis] [ˈnɔmini]
[t]	table, bitter	tuo, trinitate [ˈtu-ɔ] [tɾiniˈtɑtɛ]
[l]	life, little	libera, tollis [ˈlibɛɾɑ] [ˈtɔllis]
[ɾ]/[r]	thread, throne	gloria, terra, rex [ˈglɔ-ɾi-ɑ][ˈtɛɾɾɑ][rɛx]

PLOSIVE CONSONANTS (articulation in Latin is non-aspirate)

IPA	ENGLISH (approximation)	LATIN
[b]	beauty, abide	bonæ, bibite [ˈbɔnɛ] [ˈbibitɛ]
[g]	grace, agree	gratia, synagoga [ˈgɾɑ-tsi-ɑ][sinɑˈgɔgɑ]
[p]	pity, approve	pacem, populi [ˈpɑtʃɛm] [ˈpɔpuli]
[k]	candle, lack	Christi, cantica [ˈkɾisti] [ˈkɑntikɑ]

NASAL CONSONANTS

IPA	ENGLISH (approximation)	LATIN
[ɲ]		agnus, magnam [ˈɑɲus] [ˈmɑɲɑm]
[ŋ]	song, young	sanctus, sanguis [ˈsɑŋktus] [ˈsɑŋgwis]

AFFRICATE CONSONANTS

IPA	ENGLISH (approximation)	LATIN
[dʒ]/[tʃ]	judge, church	gentes, cæli [ˈdʒɛntɛs] [ˈtʃɛli]

:lassification of Symbols: Consonants

Voicing: A voiced consonant engages vocal cords. A voiceless consonant does not employ the vocal cords.

Points of Articulation	Latin	English
Bilabial [bɑɪˈleɪbɪəl] Refers to the lips	[b] [p] [m] [w]	[b] [p] [m] [w] [ʍ]
Labiodental [leɪbɪoˈdɛntəl] Involves the lower lip and the upper row of teeth	[v] [f]	[v] [f]
Dental [ˈdɛntəl] Involves the tip of the tongue and the back of the upper row of teeth	[d] [t] [z] [s] [l] [n] [ɾ] [r]	[ð] [θ]
Alveolar [ʔælˈviələ] Involves the tip of the tongue and the ridge behind the upper teeth		[d] [t] [z] [s] [l] [n] [ɾ] [ɹ]
Prepalatal [pɹɪˈpælətəl] Involves the tip of tongue and the area between the alveolar ridge and hard palate	[ʃ] [dʒ] [tʃ] [j] [ɲ]	[ʒ] [ʃ] [dʒ] [tʃ]
Palatal [ˈpælətəl] Involves a front arch of the tongue and the hard palate		[j]
Velar [ˈvilə] Involves the back of the tongue and the soft palate	[g] [k] [ŋ]	[g] [k] [ŋ]
Glottal [ˈglɑtəl] Involves the air flow and the opening between the vocal cords		[ʔ] [h]

Manner of Articulation	Latin	English
Plosive [ˈploʊsɪv] or **Stop** [stɑp] A momentary closure of the air flow passage	[b] [p] [d] [t] [g] [k]	[b] [p] [d] [t] [g] [k] [ʔ]
Fricative [ˈfɹɪkətɪv] Produced by directing the air flow past a set of articulators	[v] [f] [z] [s] [ʃ]	[v] [f] [z] [s] [ʍ] [ʒ] [ʃ] [h] [ð] [θ]
Affricate [ˈʔæfɹɪkət] A stop that is followed by a fricative	[dʒ] [tʃ]	[dʒ] [tʃ]
Nasal [ˈneɪzəl] Produced by directing vocalized tone through the nasal passages	[m] [n] [ɲ] [ŋ]	[m] [n] [ŋ]
Lateral [ˈlætəɾəl] Produced by directing vocalized tone over the sides of the tongue	[l]	[l]
Glide [glɑɪd] Produced by directing vocalized tone past a set of articulators without friction	[j] [w]	[j] [w]
Trill [tɹɪl] Formed by taps with the tip of the tongue against the alveolar ridge	[ɾ] [r]	[ɾ]
Retroflex [ˈɹɛtɹoʊflɛks] Produced with tongue tip curled up		[ɹ]

Classification of Vowels

Quality	**Latin**	**English**
Closed Implies a closer proximity between the tongue and roof of the mouth	[i] [u]	[i] [u] [o]
Open Implies more space between the tongue and roof of the mouth	[ɛ] [ɔ]	[ɪ] [ɛ] [ʊ] [ɔ]

Peak of tongue arch	**Latin**	**English**
Front (tongue vowel) The arch of the tongue is forward with tip down during enunciation	[i] [ɛ]	[i] [ɪ] [ɛ]
Back (lip vowel) The arch of the tongue is back with tip down during enunciation	[u] [ɔ]	[u] [ʊ] [o] [ɔ]
Central The tongue maintains a low position during enunciation	dark [ɑ]	[æ] [ɑ] [ʌ] [ɜ]

Provide IPA to complete the following chart for Latin consonants:

	Bilabial	Labiodental	Dental	Alveolar	Prepalatal	Palatal	Velar	Glottal
Plosive voiced voiceless								
Fricative voiced voiceless								
Affricate voiced voiceless								
Nasal voiced								
Lateral voiced								
Trill voiced								
Glide voiced								

Provide vowel descriptions for the following symbols:

Latin Vowels

IPA	Quality	Peak tongue arch
[i]		
[ɛ]		
[u]		
[ɔ]		
[ɑ]		

See vowel chart on page 234

English Vowels

	IPA	Quality	Peak tongue arch
greet	[i]		
bit	[ɪ]		
said	[ɛ]		
blue	[u]		
look	[ʊ]		
obey	[o]		
ought	[ɔ]		
sat	[æ]		
father	[ɑ]		
up	[ʌ]		
bird	[ɜ]		

UNIT 26:

Latin vowels

RULES FOR TRANSCRIPTION

Latin vowels

Spelling	IPA	Sample Words
a	[ɑ] Dark [ɑ]	amara [ɑ'mɑɾɑ] laudate [lɑu-'dɑ-tɛ]
ae and *œ*	[ɛ] Open Front	saecula ['sɛkulɑ] cœli ['tʃɛli]
e	[ɛ] Open Front	miserere [mizɛ'ɾɛɾɛ] leonis [lɛ-'ɔ-nis]
i (as a single vowel in the syllable)	[i] Closed Front	mitis ['mitis] pietate [pi-ɛ-'tɑ-tɛ]
y	[i] Closed Front	Kyrie ['ki-ɾi-ɛ]
o	[ɔ] Open Back	oculos ['ɔkulɔs] introire [in-tɾɔ-'i-ɾɛ]
u (as a single vowel in the syllable)	[u] Closed Back	numerus ['numɛɾus] tuum ['tu-um]

DOUBLE CONSONANTS

Consonants that are doubled in spelling are also doubled in transcription.

VOWEL CLUSTERS

The *au* spelling is the only vowel cluster that functions as a falling diphthong: *auris* ['ɑːu-ɾis]. Spellings *a, e,* and *o* + vowel are always in hiatus (hiatus occurs when consecutive vowels occupy separate syllables). Spellings *i* and *u* + vowel are in hiatus in this unit (rules for *i* and *u* in a rising diphthong are introduced in unit 28).

STRESSED SYLLABLES

The first syllable is always stressed in two syllable words. A dictionary is required in order to identify the stressed syllable of words with three or more syllables. The vowel of the stressed syllable is underlined in words with three or more syllables.

The stress mark is placed:

1) before a single consonant: *dulcis* ['dultʃis]
2) between double consonants: *annuntio* [ɑn'nuntsiɔ]
3) after the first consonant in a consonant cluster: *portare* [pɔɾ'tɑɾɛ]

Exceptions: Do not divide consonant clusters that belong with a prefix: *excuso* [ɛks'kuzɔ]
Do not divide consonant blends: *repleta* [rɛ'plɛtɑ]

CLASSWORK #26: Latin vowels

Provide IPA:

1.	debita	(debts)	5.	platea	(street)
2.	æternam	(eternal)	6.	ludendo	(playing)
3.	apparuit	(he appeared)	7.	invidia	(envy)
4.	oblivio	(forgetfulness)	8.	vota	(prayers)

TRANSCRIPTION WITHIN THE PHRASE #26

Note: *c* is [k] and *r* is [ɾ] for this exercise only. Provide IPA:

and forgive us our trespasses, as we forgive those who trespass against us.
Classwork: Et dimitte nobis debita nostra, sicut et nos dimittimus debitoribus nostris. (*Matthaeum 6:12*)

1. *All scripture is divinely inspired*
   Timotheum II - 3:16
   omnis scriptura divinitus inspirata

2. *The name of the Lord is a strong tower*
   Proverbia 18:10
   turris fortissima nomen Domini

3. *Thou alone art the most High over all the earth.*
   Psalmi 82:19
   tu solus Altissimus in omni terra.

4. *Praise ye the Lord, and call upon His name*
   Paralipomenon I - 16:8
   confitemini Domino invocate nomen

5. *He cares about you.*
   Peter I - 5:7
   ipsi cura est de vobis

6. *Christ died for our sins;*
   Corinthios I - 15:3
   Christus mortuus est pro peccatis nostris
   k

7. *love covereth a multitude of sins*
   Proverbia 10:12, b
   universa delicta operit caritas

8. *I am not come to destroy, but to fulfill.*
   Matthaeum 5:17 (words of Christ)
   non veni solvere, sed adimplere.

9. *And the truth of the Lord remaineth forever.*
   Psalmi 116:2
   et veritas Domini manet in æternum.

10. *For unto us a Child is born,*
    Isaias 9:6
    Parvulus enim natus est nobis,

11. *and the Word was made flesh,*
    Ioannis 1:14 (referring to Christ)
    et verbum caro factum est,

12. *Thou shalt wash me, and I shall be whiter than snow.*
    Psalmi 50:9
    lavabis me, et super nivem dealbabor.

WORKSHEET #26: Latin vowels

Provide IPA:

#1

nivem	(snow)
favilla	(ash)
admoneo	(I admonish)
moniti	(warned)
duo	(two)
tantum	(only)
insidiæ	(treason)
paulo	(a little)

#2

medelam	(healing)
pluit	(it's raining)
nauta	(sailor)
dolentem	(grieving)
lilia	(lilies)
fidei	(faith)
illumina	(shine)
tædium	(weariness)

#3

paulatim	(gradually)
attendite	(look)
ægrus	(ill)
fletu	(weeping)
templo	(temple)
meum	(my)
intima	(innermost)
nolui	(I refused)

#4

ave	(hail)
doleo	(I suffer pain)
litteræ	(letters)
viduata	(widowed)
nomini	(name)
multitudine	(multitude)
veniet	(he will come)
pietate	(piety)

WORKSHEET #26: Latin vowels

Provide IPA:

#5

æneus	(bronze)
votum	(prayer/vow)
optime	(best)
plena	(full)
beatum	(happy)
mallui	(I preferred)
anima	(soul)
dubium	(doubt)

#6

immolatum	(sacrificed)
gloriæ	(glory)
fidelium	(believers)
videte	(see)
adnuo	(I promise)
milia	(thousands)
linteum	(linen)
dona	(grant)

#7

mea	(my)
tuum	(your)
defendat	(he defends)
illa	(she)
æstas	(summer)
voluntate	(will)
animalia	(animals)
omnipotenti	(almighty)

#8

tanto	(so much)
eum	(him)
tabellæ	(documents)
infinita	(infinite)
familia	(family)
alui	(I cherished)
bibite	(drink)
mundi	(world)

WORKSHEET #26: Latin vowels

Provide IPA:

#9

omnium	(all)
bona	(goods)
deinde	(next)
puella	(girl)
manet	(he remains)
lumine	(light)
æris	(air)
vita	(life)

#10

animæ	(souls)
montem	(mountain)
unitate	(unity)
fleo	(I weep)
vale	(farewell)
tui	(your)
autem	(but)
divina	(divine)

#11

Dominum	(Lord)
tympano	(drum)
illibata	(unspoiled)
beato	(blessed)
manuum	(hands)
æstimator	(weighing)
filio	(son)
panem	(bread)

#12

veniæ	(forgiveness)
pedum	(feet)
amen	(amen)
emitte	(send)
Deum	(God)
medio	(middle)
olim	(formerly)
tuo	(yours)

UNIT 27:

Latin consonants *s, c, r,* and *g*

RULES FOR TRANSCRIPTION

Latin consonants *s, c, r,* and *g*

Spelling	IPA	Sample Words
c or *g* + *a, o, u,* consonant, or final	[k] [g] Velar Plosive (Stop)	glorificamus [glɔɾifiˈkɑmus] tunc [tunk]
c + front vowel	[tʃ] Prepalatal Affricate	preces [ˈpɾɛtʃɛs] speciosa [spɛ-tʃi-ˈɔ-zɑ]
g + front vowel	[dʒ] Prepalatal Affricate	agens [ˈɑdʒɛnz]
Initial *r*	[r] Rolled r	rubet [ˈrubɛt] recordor [rɛˈkɔɾdɔɾ]
All other *r*	[ɾ] Flipped r	propter [ˈpɾɔptɛɾ] terris [ˈtɛɾɾis]
Intervocalic *s*	[z] Dental Fricative	visita [ˈvizitɑ]
Voiced consonant + final *s*	[z]	potens [ˈpɔtɛnz]
All other *s*	[s] Dental Fricative	solus [ˈsɔlus] passionis [pɑs-si-ˈɔ-nis]

CLASSWORK #27: Latin consonants *s, c, r,* and *g*

Provide IPA:

1. accipite (take)
2. peccatis (sins)
3. laboriose (laboriously)
4. sapiens (wise)
5. reus (defendant)
6. imago (image)
7. cui (to which)
8. gravitas (seriousness)
9. incensum (incense)
10. fregit (he broke)

TRANSCRIPTION WITHIN THE PHRASE #27

Provide IPA:

In all thy ways think on Him, and He will direct thy steps.
Classwork: in omnibus viis tuis cogita illum et ipse diriget gressus tuos (*Proverbia 3:6*)

1. *In the beginning was the Word,*
   Ioannis 1:1, a
   In principio erat Verbum,

2. *and the Word was with God*
   Ioannis 1:1, a
   et Verbum erat apud Deum,

3. *And the Word was God.*
   Ioannis 1:1, b
   et Deus erat Verbum.

4. *The same was in the beginning with God.*
   Ioannis 1:1, b (Referring to Christ)
   Hoc erat in principio apud Deum. (*h* is silent)

5. *He came unto His own and His own received Him not*
   Ioannis 1:11 (Referring to Christ)
   In propria venit, et sui eum non receperunt.

6. *For all have sinned and do need the glory of God.*
   Romanos 3:23
   omnes enim peccaverunt et egent gloriam Dei

7. *No man cometh to the Father, but by me.*
   Ioannis 14:6 (words of Christ)
   nemo venit ad Patrem nisi per me

8. *With the heart man believeth unto righteousness;*
   Romanos 10:10, a
   Corde enim creditur ad iustitiam

9. *with the mouth confession is made unto salvation*
   Romanos 10:10, b
   ore autem confessio fit in salutem

10. *And he said: Let us make man*
    Genesis 1:26, a
    et ait faciamus hominem (*h* is silent)

11. *in our image and likeness:*
    Genesis 1:26, b
    ad imaginem et similitudinem nostram

12. *Rejoice in the Lord always: again, I say, rejoice.*
    Ioannis 1:29
    gaudete in Domino semper iterum dico gaudete

WORKSHEET #27: Latin consonants *s, c, r,* and *g*

Provide IPA:

#1

dirigatur	(it is directed)
sincera	(honest)
reformasti	(you restored)
prudens	(prudent)
benedictus	(blessed)
confiteor	(confess)
visibilium	(visible)
largitor	(giver)
invocabo	(I will call)

#2

argumentum	(proof)
supplicio	(penalty)
divites	(rich)
factum	(deed)
exclamans	(crying)
gente	(nation)
ridentem	(laughing)
vigor	(vigor)
prolusio	(prelude)

#3

præclaræ	(excellent)
gaude	(rejoice)
radium	(radius)
abundans	(abundant)
cithara	(harp)
indulgere	(to pardon)
delicta	(offenses)
ecclesiæ	(church)
secundum	(second)

#4

asperges	(you will sprinkle)
fugo	(I chase away)
clementis	(favorable)
declinet	(he declines)
malens	(preferring)
remissionem	(forgiveness)
ingratus	(ungrateful)
luceat	(it shines)
thesaurus	(treasure)

WORKSHEET #27: Latin consonants *s, c, r,* and *g*

Provide IPA:

#5

perpetuæ	(perpetual)
altissimi	(highest)
valens	(strong)
litigo	(I quarrel)
nunc	(now)
unigenite	(only child)
fugaces	(fleeting)
promisisti	(you promised)
redime	(redeem)

#6

desidero	(I long for)
innocentia	(innocence)
pagi	(villages)
caritas	(charity)
ego	(I)
silens	(silent)
inclino	(I bend)
ipsum	(very)
redemptor	(redeemer)

#7

elemosina	(alms)
laudamus	(we praise)
guberna	(guide)
dolens	(painful)
accepta	(acceptable)
igitur	(so)
sæcula	(ages)
fatigo	(I worry)
repleta	(full)

#8

immaculatam	(stainless)
affligit	(it afflicts)
rei	(thing)
misereatur	(he is gracious)
conspectu	(sight)
statuens	(setting)
digressio	(separation)
pacem	(peace)
lætare	(to rejoice)

WORKSHEET #27: Latin consonants *s, c, r,* and *g*

Provide IPA:

#9

calicem	(cup)
navigo	(I sail)
benedictum	(blessed)
gladius	(sword)
sæculorum	(centuries)
archangelo	(archangel)
robur	(strength)
propositum	(design)
ditans	(enriching)

#10

cælis	(heaven)
inclyti	(glorious)
peccatorum	(sins)
manibus	(hands)
revelante	(revealing)
degusto	(I taste)
ventosus	(windy)
genitum	(generated)
adulescens	(young man)

#11

quærens	(seeking)
gaudium	(joy)
restituo	(I restore)
custodiat	(he guards)
angeli	(angels)
progressus	(advance)
amica	(friend)
doloso	(deceitful)
sacrificium	(sacrifice)

#12

invisibilium	(unseen)
dicere	(to say)
laganum	(cake)
aureus	(golden)
testamenti	(testament)
canticum	(song)
nutrimens	(nourishment)
repleamur	(we are filled)
evangelium	(news)

UNIT 28:

Latin consonants
[ɲ], [ŋ], [j], [ʃ], *h, qu,* and *x*

RULES FOR TRANSCRIPTION

Latin consonants [ɲ], [ŋ], [j], [ʃ], *h, qu,* and *x*

Spelling	IPA	Sample Words
gn	[ɲ] Prepalatal Nasal	regnum ['rɛɲum]
Spellings with *h*: *ch*	[k] Velar Plosive (Stop)	chorus ['kɔɾus]
Spellings with *h*: *ihi*	[iki]	mihi ['miki]
Spellings with *h*: *ph*	[f] Bilabial Fricative	seraphim ['sɛɾafim]
Spellings with *h*: *th*	[t] Dental Stop	sabaoth ['sɑ-bɑ-ɔt]
All other *h*	Silent *h*	hosanna [ɔ'zɑnnɑ]
Intervocalic *i*	[j]	cuius ['ku-jus]
Initial *i* + vowel	[j]	iudico ['judikɔ]
j	[j] Prepalatal Glide	jubilate [jubi'lɑtɛ]
ngu + vowel	[ŋgw]	distinguo [dis'tiŋgwɔ]
nct	[ŋkt]	punctum ['puŋktum]
ps	[ps]	psalterio [psɑl-'tɛ-ɾi-ɔ]
qu	[kw]	quoque ['kwɔ-kwɛ] quia ['kwi-ɑ]
sc + front vowel	[ʃ] Prepalatal Fricative	ascendat [ɑ'ʃɛndɑt] conscius ['kɔn-ʃi-us]
* *t* + *i* + vowel	[ts]	viventium [vi-'vɛn-tsi-um]
Initial *ex* + vowel	[gz]	exemplar [ɛgz'ɛmplɑɾ]
Initial *ex* + s + vowel	[gz]	exsultate [ɛgzul'tɑtɛ]
Initial *ex* + *h*	[gz]	exhilaro [ɛgz'ilɑɾɔ]
Initial *ex* + *c* + front vowel	[kʃ]	excellentia [ɛk-ʃɛl-'lɛn-tsi-ɑ]
Initial *ex* + consonant	[ks]	excolo ['ɛkskɔlɔ]
All other *x*	[ks]	dilexit [di'lɛksit] calix ['kɑliks]
z	[dz]	Lazarus ['lɑdzɑɾus]

* Except when preceded by *s*: *ostium* ['ɔstium]

CLASSWORK #28: Latin consonants [ɲ], [ŋ], [j], [ʃ], *h, qu,* and *x*

Provide IPA:

1. discerne (distinguish)
2. magnam (large)
3. excipio (I take out)
4. iurandum (oath)
5. neque (nor)
6. exemplar (model)
7. sanguis (blood)
8. dexteram (right)
9. homine (man)
10. potentiam (power)

TRANSCRIPTION WITHIN THE PHRASE #28

He that believeth in me, though he were dead, yet shall he live

Classwork: qui credit in me et si mortuus fuerit vivet (*Ioannem 11:25, b - words of Christ*)

1. *As it is written: There is none righteous, no not one*
   Romanos 3:11
   sicut scriptum est quia non est iustus quisquam

2. *Believe in the Lord Jesus and thou shalt be saved*
   Actus 16:31
   crede in Domino Iesu et salvus eris tu

3. *Christ Jesus came into the world to save sinners*
   Timotheum I - 1:15
   Christus Iesus venit in mundum peccatores salvos

4. *and He dwelt among us, and we saw His glory*
   Ioannis 1:14 (referring to Christ)
   et habitavit in nobis: et vidimus gloriam ejus,

5. *The Lord hath laid on Him the iniquity of us all.*
   Isaias 53:6
   Dominus posuit in eo iniquitatem omnium nostrum

6. *Surely He hath borne our infirmities*
   Isaias 53:4
   vere languores nostros ipse tulit

7. *in Him was life, and the Life was the light of men*
   Ioannis 1:4
   in ipso vita erat, et vita erat lux hominum:

8. *With the heart man believeth unto righteousness;*
   Romanos 10:10, a
   Corde enim creditur ad iustitiam

9. *He, who knew no sin, hath become sin for us*
   Corinthios II - 5:21
   eum qui non noverat peccatum pro nobis peccatum fecit

10. *Thou hast given me the protection of Thy salvation:*
    Psalmi 17:36
    et dedisti mihi protectionem salutis tuæ:

11. *I will not fear what man can do unto me.*
    Psalmi 117:6
    non timebo quid faciat mihi homo.

12. *I can do all things in Him who strengtheneth me.*
    Philippenses 4:13
    omnia possum in eo qui me confortat

WORKSHEET #28: Latin consonants [ɲ], [ŋ], [j], [ʃ], *h, qu,* and *x*

Provide IPA:

#1

etiam	(even so)
quia	(because)
exertus	(tested)
scio	(I know)
majestate	(majesty)
distinguo	(I distinguish)
chordis	(string)
proximus	(nearest)
agnosco	(I acknowledge)

#2

institutione	(institution)
peior	(worse)
derelinquo	(I forsake)
perscitus	(very clever)
exclamavit	(he cried)
sanctificas	(you sanctify)
ignito	(set on fire)
hymnus	(hymn)
exsequor	(I maintain)

#3

adjutorium	(help)
pharetra	(quiver)
descendit	(he went down)
benigne	(kindly)
nunquam	(never)
sanguine	(blood)
exhilaro	(I make cheerful)
tentationem	(temptation)
maxima	(maximum)

#4

dignatus	(pleased)
scelerum	(crimes)
hiems	(winter)
orationem	(prayer)
felix	(happy)
percunctor	(I hesitate)
examino	(I examine)
conqueror	(I complain loudly)
ejus	(his)

WORKSHEET #28: Latin consonants [ɲ], [ŋ], [j], [ʃ], *h, qu,* and *x*

Provide IPA:

#5

maligno	(malignant)
cuius	(whose)
suscipe	(receive)
exspecto	(I expect)
anguis	(snake)
resurrectionis	(resurrection)
postquam	(after)
exsules	(refugees)
antiphon	(sequence)

#6

dignæ	(worthy)
iudico	(I judge)
audax	(bold)
excessum	(departure)
habitavit	(he dwelt)
benedictione	(blessing)
exercitus	(army)
sacrosanctum	(sacred)
propinquo	(I approach)

#7

discipulis	(students)
crux	(the cross)
mihi	(to me)
quoniam	(for)
excusationes	(excuses)
iube	(bid)
exultatione	(joy)
pugna	(fight)
languore	(disease)

#8

cognita	(learned)
ascensionis	(ascension)
oblationem	(offering)
tibique	(and to you)
honorem	(honor)
explicando	(explaining)
sanctimonia	(purity)
jubilate	(shout)
exhibeo	(I show)

WORKSHEET #28: Latin consonants [ɲ], [ŋ], [j], [ʃ], *h, qu,* and *x*

Provide IPA:

#9

sancto	(holy)
thema	(theme)
agnus	(lamb)
luxuria	(luxury)
devotio	(devotion)
iniquitates	(transgressions)
excedo	(I exceed)
juvenis	(youth)
eximo	(I free)

#10

consecratio	(consecration)
regni	(kingdom)
iucunditas	(pleasure)
excito	(I call forth)
hilaris	(cheerful)
dilexi	(I loved)
punctum	(point)
exaudi	(listen)
quorum	(whose)

#11

exitus	(exit)
cherubim	(cherubs)
substantiæ	(substance)
lingua	(language)
justis	(just)
resurrexit	(he rose)
excelsis	(highest)
deditque	(and he gave)
ignis	(fire)

#12

iocus	(joke)
exsultant	(they delight)
hodie	(today)
relinquo	(I leave)
annuntiem	(I announce)
excellentia	(excellence)
frux	(fruit)
magna	(great)
sanctorum	(saints)

Provide IPA:

1. exaudi (listen)
2. chordarum (strings)
3. diesque (and days)
4. cœli (heavens)
5. exclamo (I shout)
6. ideo (therefore)
7. concupisco (I covet)
8. aggredior (I go to)
9. maiestas (majesty)
10. gloriosæ (glorious)
11. essentia (essence)
12. sanctum (holy)
13. crucem (cross)
14. agimus (we act)
15. fugere (to escape)
16. lætans (rejoicing)
17. exilium (exile)
18. piscis (fish)
19. nihil (nothing)
20. exsultate (sing)
21. theatrum (theater)
22. repellas (you repel)
23. martyres (martyrs)
24. iucundus (agreeable)
25. exhorresco (I dread)
26. habere (to have)
27. velox (quick)
28. plebs (folk)
29. excelsis (highest)
30. adstringo (I tighten)
31. justi (just)
32. sanguinis (blood)
33. regnum (kingdom)
34. triumphus (triumph)

UNIT 29:

English classification of symbols

INTRODUCTORY NOTES

GENERAL TERMS

IPA. The *International Phonetic Alphabet* was established by the International Phonetic Association around 1888. Each symbol stands for one phonetic sound and is enclosed in brackets. Authentic pronunciation, accurate formation, and precise resonance must be defined for each symbol within the respective language.
Pronunciation: conversion of letters into the proper choice of speech sounds as represented by IPA
Enunciation and Articulation: the act of speaking or singing phonetic sounds
Expression: the act of conveying mood, color and sentiment of lyric texts
Monosyllable: a word with one syllable – polysyllabic words contain two or more syllables
Monophthong: a vowel sound that maintains one articulatory position throughout the course of the syllable
Rising Diphthong: two vowel sounds in the same syllable with a lengthening of the second vowel
Falling Diphthong: two vowel sounds in the same syllable with a lengthening of the first vowel
Triphthong: three vowel sounds within the same syllable
Hiatus: adjacent vowel sounds that occupy consecutive syllables
Prevocalic: a consonant preceding a vowel
Intervocalic: a consonant that stands between vowels
Postvocalic: a consonant following a vowel
Initial: the first letter or sound of a word
Medial: a letter or sound in the middle of a word
Final: the last letter or sound of a word
Apocopation or truncation: a vowel or group of letters omitted from the end of a word
Aspirate: a consonant that is sounded with an audible release of breath (English *p, t, k*)

SCHOLARLY AUTHORITY

The exercises in this text were designed to follow rules established by Madeleine Marshall, author of the *Singer's Manual of English Diction.* Marshall promotes a standardized pronunciation of the English language and provides transcription rules based on spelling. Her approach to lyric diction enhances ease of production for the soloist and encourages vocalic blend within the choral group.

CHOICE OF SYMBOLS

There are approximately 15 vowel sounds in English. This text follows Marshall by introducing only those that are most favorable for lyric diction. For the sake of uniformity, clarity, and ease of production, bright [a] and back [ɒ] are replaced with dark [ɑ]. Words like *night* [naɪt], *song* [sɒŋ] and *father* [ˈfɑðə] all contain a dark [ɑ] in lyric transcription. Due to similarities in sound between [i] and [e], the closed [e] is replaced with open [ɛ].

CHARACTERISTICS OF THE ENGLISH LANGUAGE AND IPA

1) There are eleven primary vowel sounds in English: [i ɪ ɛ æ ɑ u ʊ o ɔ ɜ ʌ]. There are four secondary vowel sounds in between the primary vowels: bright [a] is between [æ] and [ɑ], back [ɒ] is between [ɑ] and [ɔ], closed front [e] is between [i] and [ɛ], and semi-open front [ɨ] is between [i] and [ɪ]. Transcription of secondary vowels is not recommended for lyric diction.
2) English vowels in unstressed syllables are short in speech but extended for singing. The pronunciation of the schwa may be defined as a weakened version of a primary vowel sound. Pronunciation follows spelling and is often determined by the composer's setting (see page 19 of *IPA Handbook for Singers*).
3) Syllabic stress is formed by a weighted accentuation and a rise in pitch of the stressed syllable.
4) A dictionary or fluency in the language is required in order to identify the stressed syllable.
5) English speech is medial in placement. Vowels must be clear and resonant for lyric diction.
6) Consonants clusters are prevalent. Each pronounced consonant must be articulated in a quick, crisp, and clean manner. Do not allow the contact between articulators to be pressed.
7) An aspirated articulation is required for plosive consonants *p, t,* and *k.*

PRONUNCIATION GUIDE

FRONT VOWELS

IPA	ENGLISH
[i]	greet, heat, field
[ɪ]	hill, win, build, been
[ɛ]	help, bread, friend, many

BACK VOWELS

IPA	ENGLISH
[u]	food, through, blue, grew
[ʊ]	book, should, put
[o]	obey, protect, melody
[ɔ]	talk, saw, ought, cause

CENTRAL VOWELS

IPA	ENGLISH
[æ]	fact, hat, shadow, carry
[ɑ]	father, heart, sorrow

CENTRAL VOWELS

[ɜ]	bird, hurt, word, earth
[ʌ]	dove, sun, young

SCHWA (See page 19 of the *IPA Handbook for Singers* for the English pronunciation of schwa)

[ə]	sofa, angel, petal

SEMICONSONANTS

[j]	yet, year, dew, lute
[w]	winter, web, sweet

DIPHTHONGS

[ɑɪ]	kind, my, guide, height
[ɛɪ]	shade, aid, they, break
[ɔɪ]	voice, boy, rejoice
[ɑʊ]	sound, crown, vow
[oʊ]	glow, hope, so, road

CONSONANTS

Bilabial	[b]	ball	Alveolar		
	[p]	paper		[l]	live
	[m]	mammoth		[ɾ]	three
	[w]	wind		[ɹ]	train
	[ʍ]	when	Prepalatal	[ʒ]	vision
Labiodental	[v]	vine		[ʃ]	sheep
	[f]	fair		[dʒ]	judge
Dental	[ð]	feather		[tʃ]	chair
	[θ]	thin	Palatal	[j]	yes
Alveolar	[d]	deed	Velar	[g]	go
	[t]	tea		[k]	keep
	[z]	zoo		[ŋ]	sing
	[s]	since	Glottal	[h]	house
	[n]	nice		[ʔ]	I, alert

DIACRITICAL MARKS

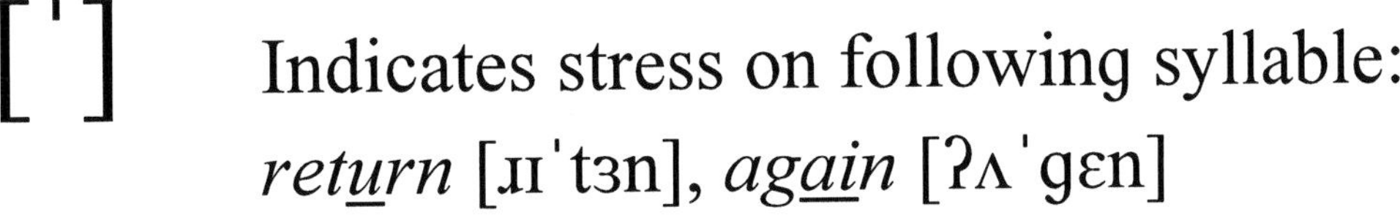
[ˈ] Indicates stress on following syllable:
return [ɹɪˈtɜn], *again* [ʔʌˈgɛn]

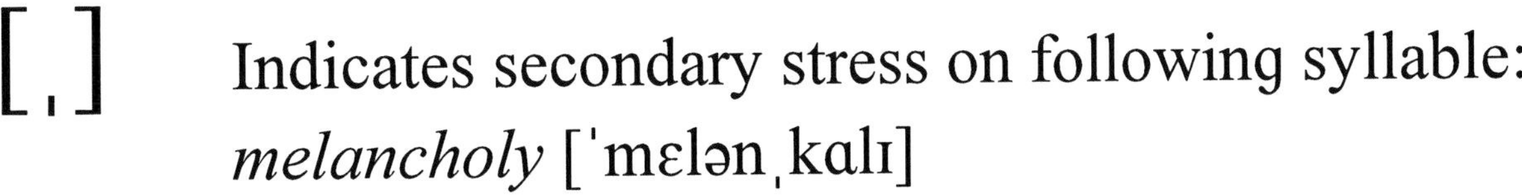
[ˌ] Indicates secondary stress on following syllable:
melancholy [ˈmɛlənˌkɑlɪ]

UNIT 29: Classification of Consonants

Voicing
Voiced Consonant: The voice is engaged during the articulation of a consonant **Voiceless Consonant:** The voice is not engaged during the articulation of a consonant

Points of Articulation	English
Bilabial [bɑɪ'lɛɪbɪəl] Refers to the lips	[p] [b] [m] [ʍ][w]
Labiodental [lɛɪbɪo'dɛntəl] Involves the lower lip and the upper row of teeth	[f] [v]
Dental ['dɛntəl] Involves the tip of the tongue and the back of the upper row of teeth	[θ] [ð]
Alveolar [ʔæl'viələ] Involves the tip of the tongue and the ridge behind the upper teeth	[t] [d] [s] [z] [l] [n] [ɾ] [ɹ]
Prepalatal [pɹɪ'pælətəl] The tip of tongue touches area between the alveolar ridge and hard palate	[ʃ] [ʒ] [tʃ] [dʒ]
Palatal ['pælətəl] The middle of the tongue contacts the hard palate	[j]
Velar ['vilə] The back of the tongue contacts the soft palate	[k] [g] [ŋ]
Glottal ['glɑtəl] Involves the air flow and the opening between the vocal cords	[ʔ] [h]

Manner of Articulation	English
Stop [stɑp] A momentary closure of the air flow passage	[p] [b] [t] [d] [k] [g] [ʔ]
Fricative ['fɹɪkətɪv] Produced by directing the air flow past a set of articulators	[f] [v] [s] [z] [ʍ] [ʃ] [ʒ] [h] [θ] [ð]
Affricate ['ʔæfɹɪkət] A stop that is followed by a fricative	[tʃ] [dʒ]
Nasal ['nɛɪzəl] Produced by directing vocalized tone through the nasal passages	[m] [n] [ŋ]
Lateral ['lætərəl] Produced by directing vocalized tone over the sides of the tongue	[l]
Glide [glɑɪd] Produced by directing vocalized tone past a set of articulators without friction	[j] [w]
Trill [tɹɪl] Formed by taps with the tip of the tongue against the alveolar ridge	[ɾ]
Retroflex ['ɹɛtɹoʊflɛks] Produced with lips rounded and tongue tip curled up	[ɹ]

WORKSHEET #29: Classification of Consonants

I. Identify the following points of articulation:

1. Bilabial
2. Labiodental
3. Dental
4. Alveolar
5. Prepalatal
6. Palatal
7. Velar
8. Glottal

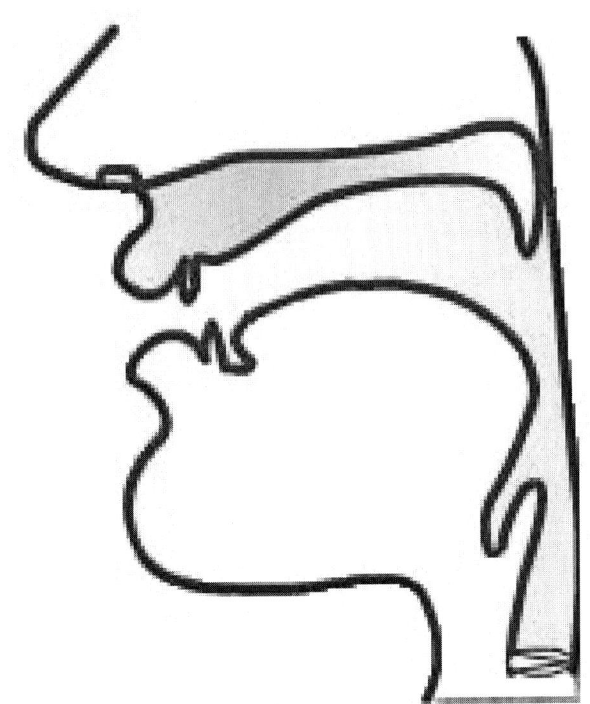

II. Provide IPA to complete the following chart for English consonants:

	Bilabial	Labiodental	Dental	Alveolar	Prepalatal	Palatal	Velar	Glottal
Stop voiced voiceless								
Fricative voiced voiceless								
Affricate voiced voiceless								
Nasal voiced								
Lateral voiced								
Glide voiced								
Trill voiced								
Retroflex voiced								

UNIT 29: Classification of Vowels

Quality	English
Closed Requires a rounding or spreading of the lips and a closer proximity between the articulators during enunciation	[i] [u] [o]
Open Also defined as lax, the open vowels require more space between the articulators than their closed counterparts	[ɪ] [ɛ] [ʊ] [ɔ]

Peak of tongue arch	English
Front (tongue vowel) The arch of the tongue is forward with tip down during enunciation	[i] [ɪ] [ɛ]
Back (lip vowel) The arch of the tongue is back with tip down during enunciation	[u] [ʊ] [o] [ɔ]
Central Tongue maintains a central position during enunciation	[ɑ] [æ] [ɜ] [ʌ]

See vowel chart on page 234

WORKSHEET #29: Classification of Vowels

Provide vowel descriptions for the following symbols:

IPA	Quality	Peak tongue arch
[i]		
[ɪ]		
[ɛ]		
[u]		
[ʊ]		
[o]		
[ɔ]		
[æ]		
[ɑ]		
[ɜ]		
[ʌ]		

UNIT 30:

English flipped [ɾ], retroflex [ɹ], and silent *r*

RULES FOR TRANSCRIPTION

English rules for art song: flipped [ɾ], retroflex [ɹ], and silent *r*

Spelling	IPA	Sample Words
**r* + pronounced vowel	[ɹ] Alveolar Retroflex	spring [spɹɪŋ] rhythm ['ɹɪðəm] every ['ʔɛvɹɪ]
Intervocalic *r*	[ɾ] Alveolar Flipped	merry ['mɛɾɪ] spirit ['spɪɾɪt]
thr	[ɾ] Alveolar Flipped	thread [θɾɛd] throne [θɾoʊn] three [θɾi]
Initial *gr* and *cr* of dramatic words	[ɾ] Alveolar Flipped	cruel ['kɾuəl] grim [gɾɪm]
Initial *r* + [u]	[ɾɾ] Alveolar Flipped	ruby ['ɾɾubɪ] room [ɾɾum]
Consonant + *r* + [u]	[ɾ] Alveolar Flipped	fruit [fɾut] approve [ʔʌ'pɾuv]
r + consonant	Silent *r*	heart [hɑ:t] sword [sɔ:d]
r + breath, rest, or final silent *e*	Silent *r*	dear [dɪə] ever ['ʔɛvə] star [stɑ:]

* The retroflex *r* has less carrying power than the flipped *r*. Oratorio and operatic literature require a flipped articulation of *r* except in words with the consonant clusters *dr* and *tr*.

Transcription of *r* within the phrase

Intervocalic *r* within the phrase is flipped [ɾ]. Two exceptions apply:

1. Light flipped [ɾ]: Articulate a lightly flipped *r* when a final *r* word is followed by an unaccented initial vowel word or syllable. Purpose: the flipped *r* connects elements that are unstressed within the phrase.

   I weep for wonder wand'ring far alone [ʔɑɪ wip fɔ: 'wʌndə 'wɑndɹɪŋ fɑ:(ɾ) ʌ'loʊn]

   Sure on this Shining Night by Agee/Barber

2. Silent *r*: A final *r* should remain silent when followed by an initial vowel word that is stressed within the phrase. The *r* is not considered intervocalic since the glottal stop clearly functions as a consonant.

   Your eyes, your mien, your tongue declare [jɔə ʔɑɪz jɔə min jɔə tʌŋ dɪ'klɛə]

   If Music be the Food of Love by Heveningham/Purcell

Note: A flipped *r* may sound too formal for American art song lyrics. In this case, the flipped *r* may be replaced with a rapidly articulated vowel *r*. The German vowel [ʁ] provides a suitable lyric replacement since it is formed with the tongue tip touching the lower row of teeth. It is helpful to retain the flipped [ɾ] transcription as a reminder that enunciated *r* must never alter the formation of a preceding vowel.

Worksheet #30: English flipped [ɾ], retroflex [ɹ], and silent *r*

Provide IPA:

Classwork

1. throne [θ_oʊn]
2. warm [wɔ_m]
3. silvery ['sɪlvə_ɪ]
4. mercy ['mɜ_sɪ]
5. brave [b_ɛɪv]
6. grief [g_if]
7. tower [taʊə_]
8. rich [_ɪtʃ]
9. prudent ['p_udənt]
10. rule [_ul]

#1

1. another [ʔʌ'nʌðə_]
2. grieve [g_iv]
3. fresh [f_ɛʃ]
4. room [_um]
5. turn [tɜ_n]
6. starry ['stɑ_ɪ]
7. brethren ['bɹɛð_ən]
8. wrong [_ɑŋ]
9. crude [k_ud]
10. form [fɔ_m]

#2

1. tarry ['tæ_ɪ]
2. mourn [mɔ_n]
3. through [θ_u]
4. letter ['lɛtə_]
5. girl [gɜ_l]
6. wraps [_æps]
7. rumor ['_umə_]
8. cradle ['k_ɛɪdəl]
9. approve [ʔʌ'p_uv]
10. stream [st_im]

#3

1. hearing ['hɪə_ɪŋ]
2. bird [bɜ_d]
3. winter ['wɪntə_]
4. threshold ['θ_ɛʃhoʊld]
5. fortune ['fɔ_tʃən]
6. ruby ['_ubɪ]
7. springs [sp_ɪŋz]
8. crush [k_ʌʃ]
9. river ['_ɪvə_]
10. improve [ʔɪm'p_uv]

#4

1. hark [hɑ_k]
2. rock [_ɑk]
3. fruitless ['f_utləs]
4. clover ['kloʊvə_]
5. root [_ut]
6. early ['ʔɜ_lɪ]
7. greater ['g_ɛɪtə_]
8. throw [θ_oʊ]
9. serene [sɪ'_in]
10. pray [p_ɛɪ]

#5

1. thread [θ_ɛd]
2. brought [b_ɔt]
3. proved [p_uvd]
4. linger ['lɪŋgə_]
5. rough [_ʌf]
6. garden [gɑ_dən]
7. eternal [ʔɪ'tɜ_nəl]
8. roof [_uf]
9. whispering ['ʍɪspə_ɪŋ]
10. cringe [k_ɪndʒ]

#6

1. rosy ['_oʊzɪ]
2. nearer ['nɪə_ə_]
3. growl [g_aʊl]
4. charms [tʃɑ_mz]
5. true [t_u]
6. work [wɜ_k]
7. threat [θ_ɛt]
8. slender ['slɛndə_]
9. rubies ['_ubɪz]
10. fragrant ['f_ɛɪg_ənt]

#7

1. forth [fɔ_θ]
2. crown [k_aʊn]
3. ruin ['_uɪn]
4. silver ['sɪlvə_]
5. throat [θ_oʊt]
6. right [_ɑɪt]
7. heard [hɜ_d]
8. croon [k_un]
9. trees [t_iz]
10. glittering ['glɪtə_ɪŋ]

#8

1. grace [g_ɛɪs]
2. water ['wɔtə_]
3. broom [b_um]
4. purple ['pɜ_pəl]
5. roost [_ust]
6. forget [fɔ_'gɛt]
7. horizon [hɔ'_ɑɪzən]
8. drop [d_ɑp]
9. throng [θ_ɑŋ]
10. race [_ɛɪs]

Worksheet #30: English flipped [ɾ], retroflex [ɹ], and silent *r*

Provide IPA:

#9

1.	tender	['tɛndə_]
2.	cry	[k_ɑɪ]
3.	raise	[_ɛɪz]
4.	born	[bɔ_n]
5.	horrid	['hɔ_ɪd]
6.	three	[θ_i]
7.	pretty	['p_ɪtɪ]
8.	rooms	[_umz]
9.	first	[fɜ_st]
10.	groom	[g_um]

#10

1.	part	[pɑ_t]
2.	grass	[g_ɑs]
3.	curious	['kjʊə_ɪəs]
4.	better	['bɛtə_]
5.	routine	[_u'tin]
6.	ring	[_ɪŋ]
7.	truth	[t_uθ]
8.	word	[wɜ_d]
9.	drink	[d_ɪŋk]
10.	thrift	[θ_ɪft]

#11

1.	breeze	[b_iz]
2.	cruel	['k_uəl]
3.	scorn	[skɔ_n]
4.	thrill	[θ_ɪl]
5.	over	['ʔoʊvə_]
6.	rude	[_ud]
7.	paradise	['pæ_ədɑɪs]
8.	burn	[bɜ_n]
9.	grave	[g_ɛɪv]
10.	ready	['_ɛdɪ]

#12

1.	bitter	['bɪtə_]
2.	crumble	['k_ʌmbəl]
3.	mirth	[mɜ_θ]
4.	rue	[_u]
5.	thrice	[θ_ɑɪs]
6.	reach	[_itʃ]
7.	darkness	['dɑ_knəs]
8.	sorrows	['sɑ_oʊz]
9.	praise	[p_ɛɪz]
10.	fruit	[f_ut]

#13

1.	thrive	[θ_ɑɪv]
2.	wonder	['wʌndə_]
3.	murmuring	['mɜ_mə_ɪŋ]
4.	friend	[f_ɛnd]
5.	ruthless	['_uθləs]
6.	crystal	['k_ɪstəl]
7.	broods	[b_udz]
8.	perish	['pɛ_ɪʃ]
9.	arms	[ʔɑ_mz]
10.	rhyme	[_ɑɪm]

#14

1.	later	['lɛɪtə_]
2.	green	[g_in]
3.	ruler	['_ulə_]
4.	reason	['_izən]
5.	hard	[hɑ_d]
6.	world	[wɜ_ld]
7.	enthrall	[ʔɪn'θ_ɔl]
8.	prove	[p_uv]
9.	breath	[b_ɛθ]
10.	misery	['mɪzə_ɪ]

Transcription within the phrase: enunciate the following verses from classical literature

Adoration:

[ðɑʊ ʔɑ:t ʔoʊ gɑd ðə lɑɪf ənd lɑɪt]
[əv ʔɔl ðɪs 'wʌndɹəs wɜld wi si]
[ɪts gloʊ bɑɪ dɛɪ ɪts smɑɪl bɑɪ nɑɪt]
[ɑ: bət ɹɪ'flɛkʃənz kɔt fɹəm ði]
[ʍɛə'ʔɛə wi tɜn ðɑɪ 'glɔɾɪz ʃɑɪn]
[ənd ɔl θɪŋz 'fɛə(ɾ) ənd bɹɑɪt ɑ: ðɑɪn]

Sacred Songs Moore.

Spirited Action:

[nɑʊ 'stɔ:mɪŋ 'fjʊəɾɪ ɾoʊz]
[ənd 'klæmə sʌtʃ əz hɜd ɪn 'hɛvən tɪl nɑʊ]
[wɑz 'nɛvə ʔɑ:mz ɑn 'ʔɑ:mə 'klæʃɪŋ bɹɛɪd]
['hɔɾɪbəl 'dɪskɔ:d ənd ðə 'mædənɪŋ ʍilz]
[əv 'bɹɛɪzən 'tʃæɾɪəts dɑɪə wɑz ðə nɔɪz]
[əv 'kɑnflɪkt ʔoʊvə'hɛd ðə 'dɪzməl hɪs]
[əv 'fɑɪəɾɪ dɑ:ts ɪn 'flɛɪmɪŋ 'vɑlɪz flu]
[ənd 'flɑɪɪŋ 'vɔltəd 'ɑɪðə hoʊst wɪð fɑɪə]

Paradise Lost, Book VI. Milton.

UNIT 31:

English fricatives [θ], [ð], [ʃ], [ʒ] and affricates [tʃ] and [dʒ]

RULES FOR TRANSCRIPTION

English fricatives [θ], [ð], [ʃ], [ʒ] and affricates [tʃ] and [dʒ]

Spelling	IPA	Sample Words
th	[θ] Voiceless Dental Fricative	*thing, three, breath*
th	[ð] Voiced Dental Fricative	*breathe, father, this,*with*
c, s, sh, tion	[ʃ] Voiceless Prepalatal Fricative	*precious, sure, share, devotion*
s, z	[ʒ] Voiced Prepalatal Fricative	*vision, treasure, azure*
c + front vowel / *ch*	[tʃ] Voiceless Prepalatal Affricate	*ancient, choose, search*
g + front vowel / *j, dg*	[dʒ] Voiced Prepalatal Affricate	*gentle, age, judge*
Initial vowel words	[ʔ] Voiceless Glottal Stop	*honor* [ˈʔɑnə], *awake*

* Marshall recommends a voiced pronunciation of *th* for the word *with*

Transcription of final *ths*

Final voiceless *th* is voiced in the plural form of specified words:

SINGULAR FORM VOICELESS [θ]		PLURAL FORM VOICED [ð]	
bath	[bɑθ]	baths	[bɑðz]
cloth	[klɑθ]	cloths	[klɑðz]
moth	[mɑθ]	moths	[mɑðz]
mouth	[mɑʊθ]	mouths	[mɑʊðz]
oath	[ʔoʊθ]	oaths	[ʔoʊðz]
path	[pɑθ]	paths	[pɑðz]
truth	[tɾuθ]	truths	[tɾuðz]

Worksheet #31: English fricatives [θ], [ð], [ʃ], [ʒ], affricates [tʃ] and [dʒ]

Provide IPA:

Classwork

1. marriage ['mæ_ɪ_]
2. gracious ['g_eɪ_əs]
3. paths [pa_z]
4. thirst [_ɜ_st]
5. charming ['_a_mɪŋ]
6. rhythm ['_ɪ_əm]
7. treasure ['t_ɛ_ə_]
8. angel ['_eɪn_əl]

#1

1. stretch [st_ɛ_]
2. enthroned [_ɪn'__oʊnd]
3. large [la_]
4. withered ['wɪ_ə_d]
5. shroud [__aʊd]
6. anxious ['_æŋk_əs]
7. pleasure ['plɛ_ə_]
8. truths [t_u_z]

#2

1. chamber ['_eɪmbə_]
2. derision [dɪ'_ɪ_ən]
3. strength [st_ɛŋ_]
4. northern ['nɔ__ə_n]
5. range [_eɪn_]
6. approach [_ʌ'p_oʊ_]
7. cloths [kla_z]
8. precious ['p_ɛ_əs]

#3

1. charge [_a_]
2. dangerous ['deɪn_ə_əs]
3. months [mʌn_s]
4. short [_ɔ_t]
5. revision [_ɪ'vɪ_ən]
6. feather ['fɛ_ə_]
7. breathless ['b_ɛ_ləs]
8. ancient ['_eɪn_ənt]

#4

1. generation [_ɛnə'_eɪ_ən]
2. diversion [dɪ'vɜ_ən]
3. father ['fa_ə_]
4. exposure [_ɪks'poʊ_ə_]
5. shore [_ɔə_]
6. wretched ['_ɛ_əd]
7. thorough ['_ɔə_oʊ]
8. paths [pa_z]

#5

1. neither ['naɪ_ə_]
2. depths [dɛp_s]
3. fortunes ['fɔ__ənz]
4. cringing ['k_ɪn_ɪŋ]
5. provision [p_o'vɪ_ən]
6. raineth ['_eɪnə_]
7. shrine [__aɪn]
8. excursions [_ɪks'kɜ__ənz]

#6

1. persuasion [pɜ_'sweɪ_ən]
2. reached [_i_t]
3. forge [fɔ_]
4. shriek [__ik]
5. azure ['_æ_ə_]
6. earthly ['_ɜ_lɪ]
7. hither ['hɪ_ə_]
8. lengths [lɛŋ_s]

#7

1. revenge [_ɪ'vɛn_]
2. leisure ['li_ə_]
3. mouths [maʊ_z]
4. everything ['_ɛv_ɪ_ɪŋ]
5. thither ['_ɪ_ə_]
6. sharp [_a_p]
7. aversion [_ʌ'vɜ_ən]
8. future ['fju_ə_]

#8

1. rage [_eɪ_]
2. friendship ['f_ɛnd_ɪp]
3. measures ['mɛ_ə_z]
4. thorn [_ɔ_n]
5. soothe [su_]
6. cheer [_ɪə_]
7. enclosure [_ɪn'kloʊ_ə_]
8. baths [ba_z]

Worksheet #31: English fricatives [θ], [ð], [ʃ], [ʒ], affricates [tʃ] and [dʒ]

Provide IPA:

#9			#10			#11		
1.	farther	['fa___ə_]	1.	worthy	['wɜ___ɪ]	1.	shear	[_ɪə_]
2.	gentler	['__ɛntlə_]	2.	rushes	['_ʌ_əz]	2.	rapture	['_æp__ə_]
3.	church	[__ɜ___]	3.	intrusion	[_ɪn't_u_ən]	3.	moths	[mɑ_z]
4.	shepherds	['_ɛpə_dz]	4.	cherish	['__ɛ_ɪ_]	4.	stranger	[st_ɛɪn__ə_]
5.	hearth	[hɑ___]	5.	oaths	[_oʊ_z]	5.	leather	['lɛ_ə_]
6.	either	['_ɑɪ_ə_]	6.	north	[nɔ___]	6.	wreath	[_i_]
7.	precision	[p_ɪ'sɪ_ən]	7.	measureless	['mɛ_ə_ləs]	7.	closure	['kloʊ_ə_]
8.	breathes	[b_i_z]	8.	journey	['__ɜ_nɪ]	8.	underneath	[_ʌndə_'ni_]

#12			#13			#14		
1.	others	['_ʌ_ə_z]	1.	brush	[b_ʌ_]	1.	warmth	[wɔ__m__]
2.	faiths	[fɛɪ_s]	2.	injure	['_ɪn__ə_]	2.	composure	[kʌm'poʊ_ə_]
3.	region	['_i__ən]	3.	further	['fɜ_ə_]	3.	wreaths	[_i_z]
4.	thunder	['_ʌndə_]	4.	henceforth	['hɛnsfɔ___]	4.	share	[_ɛə_]
5.	showers	[_ɑʊə_z]	5.	version	['vɜ___ən]	5.	venture	['vɛn__ə_]
6.	disclosure	[dɪs'kloʊ_ə_]	6.	marching	['mɑ___ɪŋ]	6.	bridge	[b_ɪ__]
7.	weather	['wɛ_ə_]	7.	soldiers	['soʊl__ə_z]	7.	unmeasured	[_ʌn'mɛ_ə_d]
8.	search	[sɜ___]	8.	clothes	[kloʊ_z]	8.	gathered	['gæ_ə_d]

Transcription within the phrase: enunciate the following verses from classical literature

Solemnity:
[ʔɔl ðət bɹið]
[wɪl ʃɛə ðɑɪ 'dɛstɪnɪ ðə gɛɪ wɪl lɑf]
[ʍɛn ðɑʊ ɑːt gɑn ðə 'sɑləm bɾud əv kɛə]
[plɑd ɑn ənd ʔitʃ wʌn æz bɪ'fɔə wɪl tʃɛɪs]
[hɪz 'fɛɪvoɾɪt 'fæntəm jɛt ɔl ðiz ʃæl liv]
[ðɛə mɜθ ənd ðɛə(ɾ) ɪm'plɔɪmənts ənd ʃæl kʌm]
[ənd mɛɪk ðɛə bɛd wɪð ði æz ðə lɑŋ tɹɛɪn]
[əv 'ʔɛɪdʒəs glɑɪdz ʌ'wɛɪ ðə sʌnz əv mɛn]
[ðə juθ ɪn lɑɪfs gɹin spɹɪŋ ənd hi hu goʊz]
[ɪn ðə fʊl stɹɛŋθ əv jɪəz 'mɛɪtɹən ənd mɛɪd]
[ənd ðə swit bɛɪb ənd ðə gɹɛɪ 'hɛdəd mæn]
[ʃæl wʌn bɑɪ wʌn bi 'gæðəd tə ðɑɪ sɑɪd]
[bɑɪ ðoʊz hu ɪn ðɛə tɜn ʃæl 'fɑloʊ ðɛm]

Thanatopsis. Bryant.

Perplexity:
[gɑd noʊz ʔɑɪm nɔt mɑɪ'sɛlf]
[ʔɑɪm 'sʌmbɑdɪ ɛls]
[ðæts mi 'jɑndə]
[noʊ ðæts 'sʌmbɑdɪ ɛls gɑt 'ɪntə mɑɪ ʃuz]
[ʔɑɪ wɑz mɑɪ'sɛlf lɑst nɑɪt]
[bət ɑɪ fɛl ʌ'slip ɑn ðə 'mɑʊntən]
[ənd ðɛɪv tʃɛɪndʒd mɑɪ gʌn]
[ənd 'ʔɛvɹɪθɪŋz tʃɛɪndʒd ənd ɑɪm tʃɛɪndʒd]
[ənd ɑɪ kɑnt tɛl ʍɑts mɑɪ nɛɪm ɔː hu ɑɪ ʔæm]

Rip Van Winkle. Irving.

UNIT 32:

English front vowels [i], [ɪ], [ɛ], central [æ], consonants [ŋ], final *d, s*

RULES FOR TRANSCRIPTION

English front vowels [i], [ɪ], [ɛ], central [æ], consonants [ŋ], final *d, s*

Spelling	IPA	Sample Words
e, ea, ee, ei, i, ie, eo	[i] Closed Front	*we, heat, breeze, receive, ski, field, people*
ee, i, ui, y	[ɪ] Open Front	*been, give, build, myth*
Unstressed *i, ie, ing, y*	[ɪ] Open Front	*divine, prairie, stories, pitied, ringing, mercy*
a, ai, e, ea, ie, u	[ɛ] Open Front	*many, said, help, bread, friend, bury*
a	[æ] Central Vowel	*glad, lamb, man, plaid, thank*
a + flipped [ɾ]	[æ] Central Vowel	*arrow, carol, carry, marry, tarry*
ng or *n* + [k]	[ŋ] Velar Nasal	*sing* [sɪŋ] *singer* [ˈsɪŋə] *drink* [dɹɪŋk]
Comparative and superlative forms	[ŋg] Velar Nasal	*young* [ˈjʌŋ] *younger* [ˈjʌŋgə] *youngest* [ˈjʌŋgəst]
Voiced consonant + final *ed*	[d] Alveolar Stop	*pleased* [d], *loved* [d], *seemed* [d]
Voiceless consonant + final *ed*	[t] Alveolar Stop	*sipped* [t], *missed* [t], *looked* [t]
Voiced consonant + final *s*	[z] Alveolar Fricative	*leaves* [z], *birds* [z], *things* [z]
Voiceless consonant + final *s*	[s] Alveolar Fricative	*notes* [s], *works* [s], *griefs* [s]

Worksheet #32: Front vowels [i], [ɪ], [ɛ], central [æ], consonants [ŋ], final *d, s*

Provide IPA:

Classwork

1. beaming ________________
2. valleys ________________
3. wish ________________
4. dreamed ________________
5. cherish ________________
6. thinks ________________
7. streams ________________
8. perished ________________
9. carried ________________
10. quickly ________________

#1

1. marry ________________
2. being ________________
3. fenced ________________
4. this ________________
5. tarries ________________
6. deemed ________________
7. pitied ________________
8. shells ________________
9. vanish ________________
10. weeks ________________

#2

1. arr<u>ow</u> [oʊ] ________________
2. sleeps ________________
3. heavily ________________
4. winged ________________
5. relish ________________
6. lambs ________________
7. shrink ________________
8. nannies ________________
9. feeling ________________
10. wrapped ________________

#3

1. evening ________________
2. freshly ________________
3. carries ________________
4. brink ________________
5. tarry ________________
6. dreams ________________
7. pensive ________________
8. streets ________________
9. weaved ________________
10. lashed ________________

#4

1. ranks ________________
2. evil ________________
3. angry ________________
4. grim ________________
5. cherries ________________
6. bees ________________
7. fixed ________________
8. wedding ________________
9. seethed ________________
10. carrying ________________

#5

1. bridge ________________
2. attic ________________
3. seemed ________________
4. depths ________________
5. reeds ________________
6. charity ________________
7. easy ________________
8. fancied ________________
9. breathing ________________
10. wished ________________

#6

1. breathed ________________
2. parish ________________
3. stretched ________________
4. married ________________
5. lips ________________
6. seeing ________________
7. captive ________________
8. trees ________________
9. drink ________________
10. any ________________

#7

1. banish ________________
2. lived ________________
3. emptied ________________
4. weaving ________________
5. knees ________________
6. chilly ________________
7. fish ________________
8. carriage ________________
9. meets ________________
10. vanished ________________

#8

1. splendid ________________
2. filled ________________
3. stepped ________________
4. charity ________________
5. rich ________________
6. berries ________________
7. thanks ________________
8. leaving ________________
9. many ________________
10. shields ________________

Worksheet #32: Front vowels [i], [ɪ], [ɛ], central [æ], consonants [ŋ], final *d, s*

Provide IPA:

#9

1. cherished ____________
2. creeps ____________
3. fancies ____________
4. ease ____________
5. hanging ____________
6. sinned ____________
7. really ____________
8. languish ____________
9. thin ____________
10. buried ____________

#10

1. pleased ____________
2. carry ____________
3. thrill ____________
4. sweets ____________
5. anguish ____________
6. reached ____________
7. frenzied ____________
8. hangs ____________
9. everything ____________
10. briefly ____________

#11

1. pretty ____________
2. grieved ____________
3. tarried ____________
4. these ____________
5. banks ____________
6. cities ____________
7. leaped ____________
8. friendship ____________
9. chill ____________
10. speaking ____________

#12

1. yielding ____________
2. carol [ə] ____________
3. perish ____________
4. beamed ____________
5. lilies ____________
6. deaths ____________
7. sink ____________
8. eaves ____________
9. ready ____________
10. ceased ____________

#13

1. shrieked ____________
2. gems ____________
3. clink ____________
4. speaks ____________
5. busy ____________
6. magic ____________
7. sealed ____________
8. pities ____________
9. fleeting ____________
10. marriage ____________

#14

1. ships ____________
2. sensed ____________
3. rapid ____________
4. freely ____________
5. pleasing ____________
6. marries ____________
7. begged ____________
8. weeps ____________
9. parish ____________
10. thieves ____________

Transcription within the phrase: enunciate the following verses from classical literature

Admiration:
[ʍɑt ə pis əv wɜk ɪz mæn]
[haʊ ˈnoʊbel ɪn ˈɹizən]
[haʊ ˈʔɪnfɪnɪt ɪn ˈfækəltɪ]
[ɪn fɔːm ənd ˈmuvɪŋ haʊ ɪksˈpɹɛs ənd ˈʔædmɪɾəbəl]
[ɪn ˈʔækʃən haʊ laɪk ən ˈʔɛɪndʒəl]
[ɪn æpɹɪˈhɛnʃən haʊ laɪk ə gɑd]
[ðə ˈbjutɪ əv ðə wɜld]
[ðə ˈpæɾəgɑn əv ˈʔænɪməlz]

Hamlet, Act II., Sc. 2. Shakespeare.

Joy:
[ðɛn sɪŋ ji bɜdz sɪŋ sɪŋ ə ˈdʒɔɪəs sɑŋ]
[ənd lɛt ðə jʌŋ læmz baʊnd]
[əz tə ðə ˈtɛɪbəz saʊnd]
[wi ɪn θɔt wɪl dʒɔɪn jɔə θɾɑŋ]
[ji ðət pɑɪp ənd ji ðət plɛɪ]
[ji ðət θɾu jɔə hɑːts tʌˈdɛɪ]
[fil ðə ˈglædnəs əv ðə mɛɪ]

Intimations of Immortality. Wordsworth.

UNIT 33:

English back vowels [ɔ], [u], [ʊ], central [ɑ], consonant [ʍ], semiconsonants [w], [j]

RULES FOR TRANSCRIPTION

Spelling	IPA	Sample Words
al	[ɔ] Open Back	***all***, *call, halt, salt* **Silent *l*:** *stalk, talk, walk*
aw	[ɔ] Open Back	***fawns***, *awe, dawn, draw, law, saw, thaw*
or	[ɔː] Open Back	***born***, *form, forth, Lord, morn, short, storm*
au	[ɔ] Open Back	***August***, *cause, daughter, laurel, pause, taught*
ou	[ɔ] Open Back	***fought***, *brought, ought, sought, thought*
war	[ɔː] Open Back	***war***, *swarm, warm, warn, warrior*
Exceptions	[ɔ] Open Back	*broad, broth, moss, water, wharf*
Single *o*	[ɑ] Dark Central	*drop, fond, got, lost, monarch, off, strong*
ar	[ɑː] Dark Central	*art, charms, darling, far, garden, heart*
w/wh + a	[ɑ] Dark Central	*wander, want, was, wash, watch, what*
Final *-alm* (the *l* is silent)	[ɑ] Dark Central	*alms, balm, calm, palm, psalm*
Exceptions	[ɑ] Dark Central	*Ah, father, swallow, borrow, sorrow, tomorrow*
o, oo, ou, u	[u] Closed Back	*lose, soon, through, truth*
**l, ll, s, t, n, d, th + u, ew* Memory aid: *E<u>ll</u>a <u>St</u>a<u>nd</u>e<u>th</u>*	[ju] Rising Diphthong	*lute* [ljut], *illude, suit, tune, new, dew, enthuse*
o, oo, ou, u	[ʊ] Open Back	*wolf, woman, book, could, full*
wh	[ʍ] Bilabial Fricative	*what, wheat, when, where* (except: *who* and *whole*)
w	[w] Bilabial Glide	*wave, win, wind* (Old English: *wind* [waɪnd])
y	[j] Palatal Glide	*yes, year, yellow*

* The *Ella Standeth* rule does not apply to consonant blends with *l*: *flew* [flu], *blue* [blu]. Additional note: the consonants in the memory aid include the Italian dental consonants and the English dental *th.*

Worksheet #33: Back [ɔ], [u], [ʊ], central [ɑ], consonant [ʍ], semiconsonants [w], [j]

Provide IPA:

Classwork

1. charms ______
2. draws ______
3. promised ______
4. taught ______
5. solitude ______
6. waltz ______
7. should ______
8. courtly ______
9. flew ______
10. Lord ______
11. whence ______
12. balm ______

#1

1. jaw ______
2. march ______
3. taunt ______
4. knew ______
5. rocks ______
6. course ______
7. which ______
8. swords ______
9. shook ______
10. falls ______
11. lose ______
12. broad ______

#2

1. walled ______
2. yarn ______
3. suit ______
4. courts ______
5. oft ______
6. scorch ______
7. gnaws ______
8. whistling ______
9. foot ______
10. haunt ______
11. blooming ______
12. wroth ______

#3

1. bought ______
2. foggy ______
3. lute ______
4. haul ______
5. watched ______
6. claw ______
7. two ______
8. thorny ______
9. starts ______
10. calls ______
11. put ______
12. swarm ______

#4

1. torn ______
2. arms ______
3. r<u>e</u>sume [ɪ] ______
4. want ______
5. goods ______
6. clause ______
7. slew ______
8. laws ______
9. shot ______
10. balked ______
11. calms ______
12. fought ______

#5

1. warn ______
2. whose ______
3. cross ______
4. thought ______
5. stud<u>e</u>nt [ə] ______
6. forth ______
7. hearts ______
8. plausibly ______
9. fluid ______
10. salt ______
11. took ______
12. yawning ______

#6

1. wat<u>e</u>r [ə] ______
2. whom ______
3. talked ______
4. stars ______
5. law ______
6. dews ______
7. thoughts ______
8. soon ______
9. clock ______
10. pausing ______
11. brook ______
12. forced ______

#7

1. harm ______
2. thawed ______
3. when ______
4. stood ______
5. cause ______
6. news ______
7. knock ______
8. forge ______
9. loose ______
10. sought ______
11. palm ______
12. walls ______

#8

1. laud ______
2. hardly ______
3. stalks ______
4. flute ______
5. dawning ______
6. what ______
7. tunes ______
8. coughing ______
9. books ______
10. chords ______
11. sobs ______
12. warning ______

Worksheet #33: Back [ɔ], [u], [ʊ], central [ɑ], consonant [ʍ], semiconsonants [w], [j]

Provide IPA:

#9

1. halls ____________
2. robin ____________
3. faulty ____________
4. duke ____________
5. gorge ____________
6. could ____________
7. warms ____________
8. who ____________
9. wrought ____________
10. barn ____________
11. June ____________
12. straw ____________

#10

1. fawn ____________
2. warmth ____________
3. dewy ____________
4. holly ____________
5. scalds ____________
6. choose ____________
7. naught ____________
8. looking ____________
9. yard ____________
10. coughs ____________
11. wheels ____________
12. shortly ____________

#11

1. doom ____________
2. jolly ____________
3. ought ____________
4. pull ____________
5. torch ____________
6. cart ____________
7. flaunt ____________
8. qualms ____________
9. walks ____________
10. sue ____________
11. whisking ____________
12. hawk ____________

#12

1. mourning ____________
2. dew ____________
3. full ____________
4. horn ____________
5. lodge ____________
6. crawl ____________
7. swoon ____________
8. warm ____________
9. wheat ____________
10. draught ____________
11. charge ____________
12. hall ____________

#13

1. watching ____________
2. north ____________
3. push ____________
4. court ____________
5. tossed ____________
6. ball ____________
7. smart ____________
8. haughty ____________
9. soothe ____________
10. duty ____________
11. awe ____________
12. calmly ____________

#14

1. porch ____________
2. new ____________
3. crop ____________
4. woods ____________
5. blue ____________
6. shawls ____________
7. hark ____________
8. daunt ____________
9. washed ____________
10. stall ____________
11. alms ____________
12. brought ____________

Transcription within the phrase: enunciate the following verses from classical literature

Defiant Reply:
[bæk tə ðɑɪ ˈpʌnɪʃmənt]
[fɔls ˈfjudʒɪtɪv ənd tu ðɑɪ spid æd wɪŋz]
[lɛst wɪð ə ʍɪp əv ˈskɔːpɪənz ɑɪ pɜˈsju]
[ðɑɪ ˈlɪŋgərɪŋ ɔː wɪð wʌn stɹoʊk əv ðɪs dɑːt]
[stɹɛɪndʒ ˈhɔrəz sidʒ ði ənd pæŋz ʌnˈfɛlt bɪˈfɔə]

Paradise Lost, Book II. Milton.

Disdain:
[ʔɑɪ wɪl bɑɪ wɪð ju sɛl wɪð ju tɔk wɪð ju]
[wɔk wɪð ju ənd soʊ ˈfɑloʊɪŋ bət ʔɑɪ wɪl nɔt]
[ʔit wɪð ju dɹɪŋk wɪð ju nɔː pɹɛɪ wɪð ju]

Merchant of Venice, Act I., Sc.3. Shakespeare.

Authority:
[mɑːk ʍɛə ʃi stændz ʌˈɾaʊnd hɜ fɔːm ɑɪ dɹɔ]
[ði ˈʔɔfəl ˈsɜkəl əv ɑʊə ˈsɑləm tʃɜtʃ]
[sɛt bət ə fʊt wɪðˈɪn ðæt ˈhoʊlɪ gɾaʊnd]
[ənd ɑn ðə hɛd jɛɪ ðoʊ ɪt wɔə(ɾ) ə kɹɑʊn]
[ʔɑɪ lɔntʃ ðə kɜs əv ɹoʊm]

Richelieu, Act IV., Sc 2. Bulwer.

Affection:
[ɹɑɪz mɑɪ ˈtʃɪldɹən fɔː ji ʔɑː mɑɪn]
[mɑɪn boʊθ ənd ɪn jɔə swit ənd jʌŋ dɪˈlɑɪt]
[mɑɪ ʔoʊn lɑst juθ bɹiðz ˈmjuzɪkəl]

Richelieu, Act 1., Sc. 2. Bulwer.

UNIT 34:

English central vowels [ɜ], [ʌ], unstressed [o], and the schwa

RULES FOR TRANSCRIPTION

English central vowels [ɜ], [ʌ], unstressed [o], and the schwa

Spelling	IPA	Sample Words
e, ea, i, o, u + r	[ɜ] Central	*her, search, bird, word, hurt*
o, oo, ou, u	[ʌ] Central	*love, blood, young, dusk*
o in unstressed syllable (except final syllable: *purpose* [ˈpɜpəs])	[o] Closed Back	*obey* [ʔoˈbɛɪ], *provide, melody, victory*
*Unstressed syllables	[ə] Schwa	*noble* [ˈnoʊbəl], *angel, autumn, fountain, reason*

* Defining the pronunciation of the schwa is based on spelling. See page 19 of the *IPA Handbook for Singers*.

Articles *the* and *a* have two pronunciations

the [ðə] and *a* [ə] precede initial consonant words
the [ði] and *an* [æn]/[ən] precede initial vowel words

Specified monosyllables have a strong and weak form

Pronunciation is based upon context, interpretation, and duration of the pitch.

Monosyllables	Strong Form	Weak Form	Monosyllables	Strong Form	Weak Form
am	[ʔæm]	[əm]	have	[hæv]	[həv]
and	[ʔænd]	[ənd]	of	[ʔʌv]	[əv]
as	[ʔæz]	[əz]	some	[sʌm]	[səm]
at	[ʔæt]	[ət]	than	[ðæn]	[ðən]
but	[bʌt]	[bət]	that	[ðæt]	[ðət]
can	[kæn]	[kən]	them	[ðɛm]	[ðəm]
come	[kʌm]	[kəm]	then	[ðɛn]	[ðən]
does	[dʌz]	[dəz]	to	[tu]	[tə]
from	[fɹʌm]	[fɹəm]	was	[wɑz]	[wəz]
had	[hæd]	[həd]	what	[ʍɑt]	[ʍət]
has	[hæz]	[həz]	when	[ʍɛn]	[ʍən]

Strong and weak forms within the phrase

am		***can***	
strong [ʔæm] *Am I welcome?*	weak [əm] *Here am I*	strong [kæn] *if they can,*	weak [kən] *who can tell*
has		***had***	
strong [hæz] *All that he has, is lost*	weak [həz] *The night has come*	strong [hæd] *She gave what she had*	weak [həd] *if we had known*
that		***them***	
strong [ðæt] *Enough of that*	weak [ðət] *Think not that I forget*	strong [ðɛm] *In them my hopes do carry*	weak [ðəm] *Let them sing*
to		***was***	
strong [tu] *Sway to and fro*	weak [tə] *from dawn to dusk*	strong [wɑz] *blind though I was,*	weak [wəz] *my aim was sure*

Worksheet #34: English central vowels [ɜ], [ʌ], unstressed [o], and the schwa

Provide IPA:

Classwork

1. thankfulness ____________
2. blushing ____________
3. listen ____________
4. chariot ____________
5. pearly ____________
6. captain ____________
7. humble ____________
8. good ____________
9. wonders ____________
10. victory ____________

#1

1. happiness ____________
2. under ____________
3. polite [ɑɪ] ____________
4. women ____________
5. yearning ____________
6. autumn ____________
7. pull ____________
8. delicate ____________
9. cup ____________
10. turtles ____________

#2

1. crimson ____________
2. melodies ____________
3. just ____________
4. sequence ____________
5. would ____________
6. human ____________
7. turning ____________
8. fallen ____________
9. summer ____________
10. little ____________

#3

1. single ____________
2. worthy ____________
3. garland ____________
4. suddenly ____________
5. possess ____________
6. visions ____________
7. rook ____________
8. honest ____________
9. dusty ____________
10. thunder ____________

#4

1. flourish ____________
2. countries ____________
3. jungle ____________
4. woman ____________
5. tedious ____________
6. looks ____________
7. garden ____________
8. peacefulness ____________
9. daffodils ____________
10. hunger ____________

#5

1. number ____________
2. sullen ____________
3. could ____________
4. passions ____________
5. dusk ____________
6. tenderness ____________
7. certainly ____________
8. mandolin ____________
9. lurking ____________
10. equal ____________

#6

1. sweetness ____________
2. hovers ____________
3. memories ____________
4. purpose ____________
5. loved ____________
6. written ____________
7. crystal ____________
8. put ____________
9. distant ____________
10. circling ____________

#7

1. mercy ____________
2. village ____________
3. justice ____________
4. people ____________
5. agony ____________
6. stood ____________
7. phantom ____________
8. hearken ____________
9. brother ____________
10. darkness ____________

#8

1. project ____________
2. constant ____________
3. brooks ____________
4. hermit ____________
5. drums ____________
6. even ____________
7. further ____________
8. mingle ____________
9. judgment ____________
10. reason ____________

Worksheet #34: English central vowels [ɜ], [ʌ], unstressed [o], and the schwa

Provide IPA:

#9

1. offence ____________
2. curtain ____________
3. dozen ____________
4. journey ____________
5. puts ____________
6. marble ____________
7. suffer ____________
8. portion ____________
9. young ____________
10. earliest ____________

#10

1. fluttering ____________
2. soften ____________
3. worlds ____________
4. present ____________
5. nothing ____________
6. jealousy ____________
7. book ____________
8. harmonies ____________
9. infant ____________
10. double ____________

#11

1. whispering ____________
2. loveliest ____________
3. person ____________
4. opposite ____________
5. husband ____________
6. fully ____________
7. doves ____________
8. children ____________
9. service ____________
10. troubles ____________

#12

1. purple ____________
2. cover ____________
3. majesty ____________
4. servant ____________
5. honey ____________
6. burden ____________
7. echoing ____________
8. wondrous ____________
9. looked ____________
10. chirping ____________

#13

1. poetic ____________
2. earthly ____________
3. slumbering ____________
4. hushed ____________
5. often ____________
6. image ____________
7. cautious ____________
8. senses ____________
9. took ____________
10. circle ____________

#14

1. early ____________
2. possession ____________
3. others ____________
4. foot ____________
5. bashfulness ____________
6. pleasant ____________
7. awful ____________
8. cunning ____________
9. heaven ____________
10. kingdom ____________

Transcription within the phrase: enunciate the following verses from classical literature

Sarcasm:

[fɛə sɜ ju spæt ɑn mi ɑn ˈwɛnzdɛɪ lɑst]
[ju spɜnd mi sʌtʃ ə dɛɪ ʌˈnʌðə tɑɪm]
[ju kɔld mi dɑg ənd fɔ: ðiz ˈkɜtəsɪz]
[ʔɑɪl lɛnd ju ðʌs mʌtʃ ˈmʌnɪz]

Merchant of Venice, Act I., Sc. 3. Shakespeare.

Suspicion:

[lɛt mi hæv mɛn ʌˈbɑʊt mi ðət ɑ: fæt]
[slik ˈhɛdəd mɛn ənd sʌtʃ əz slip oˈnɑɪts]
[jɑnd ˈkɑsɪəs həz ə lin ənd ˈhʌŋgɹɪ lʊk]
[hi θɪŋks tu mʌtʃ sʌtʃ mɛn ɑ: ˈdɛɪndʒərəs]

Julius Caesar, Act I., Sc. 2. Shakespeare.

Exclamation:

[ji ˈʔigəlz ˈplɛɪmɛɪts əv ðə ˈmɑʊntən stɔ:m]
[ji ˈlɑɪtnɪŋz ðə dɹɛd ˈʔærouz əv ðə klɑʊdz]
[ji sɑɪnz ənd ˈwʌndəz əv ði ˈʔɛləmənts]
[ˈʔʌtə fɔ:θ gɑd ənd fɪl ðə hɪlz wɪð pɹɛɪz]

Hymn before Sunrise. Coleridge.

UNIT 35:

Primary vowels in unstressed syllables

RULES FOR TRANSCRIPTION

English prefixes are transcribed with [ʌ], [ɪ], [ɔ], [ɜ], or [ʊ]

Spelling	IPA	Sample Words
Prefix spelling *a*	[ʌ] Central	*agree, cathedral, lament*
Prefix spelling *com*	[ʌ] Central	*commitment, compassion, complete*
Prefix spelling *con*	[ʌ] Central	*concern, condemn, conflicting*
Prefix spelling *u*	[ʌ] Central	*uncertain, uplifting*
Prefix spelling *e*	[ɪ] Open Front	*belief, depend, enrich, presume, review, select*
Prefix spelling *or*	[ɔː] Open Back	*forgive, horizon, tormented*
Prefix spelling *per*	[ɜ] Central	*perceive, perfection, persistent*
Prefix spelling *sur*	[ɜ] Central	*surprise, surround, survive*
Prefix spelling *ful*	[ʊ] Open Back	*fulfill*

Additional Notes

Primary vowels in unstressed syllables are required in the following cases:

I. Unstressed syllables with diphthongs: *always* [ˈʔɔlwɛɪz] *paradise* [ˈpærədɑɪs] *meadow* [ˈmɛdoʊ]

II. Words with secondary stress: *melancholy* [ˈmɛlənˌkɑlɪ]

III. Unstressed syllables of compound words: *waterfall* [ˈwɔtəfɔl]
Exception: a schwa [ə] is used for the following final elements:
-some: winsome [ˈwɪnsəm]
-man: gentleman [ˈdʒɛntəlmən]
-ward: wayward [ˈwɛɪwəd]
-land: highland [ˈhɑɪlənd]

Exception: *homeland* [ˈhoʊmlænd]

Defining the pronunciation of schwa is important since the schwa is extended for singing. Rules for prefixes are outlined above. Rules for other unstressed syllables are based on spelling. Refer to page 19 of the *IPA Handbook for Singers* for more details.

Worksheet #35: Primary vowels in unstressed syllables

Provide IPA:

Classwork

1. compassion ________
2. forgive ________
3. protect ________
4. believe ________
5. unworthy ________
6. elegant ________
7. assemble ________
8. perhaps ________
9. intrigue ________
10. essential ________

#1

1. prolongs ________
2. abroad ________
3. enemies ________
4. forbidden ________
5. exquisite ________
6. consumed ________
7. perfection ________
8. indefinite ________
9. unless ________
10. celestial ________

#2

1. release ________
2. envious ________
3. astonishment ________
4. produce ________
5. forgiven ________
6. increase ________
7. uncertain ________
8. persistent ________
9. convincing ________
10. esteem ________

#3

1. permissible ________
2. ingratitude ________
3. errand ________
4. rewards ________
5. uneasy ________
6. enrich ________
7. adorned ________
8. forgotten ________
9. concluding ________
10. opinion ________

#4

1. productions ________
2. across ________
3. immortal ________
4. forsook ________
5. exalt ________
6. companions ________
7. embers ________
8. perceptive ________
9. unjust ________
10. determine ________

#5

1. procedure ________
2. confirm ________
3. fulfills ________
4. enough ________
5. unthinkable ________
6. indwell ________
7. enter ________
8. abundance ________
9. permissive ________
10. repentance ________

#6

1. inherit ________
2. confusion ________
3. pretend ________
4. survival [ɑɪ] ________
5. edges ________
6. forlorn ________
7. unequal ________
8. existence ________
9. approve ________
10. proficient ________

#7

1. forbid ________
2. endlessly ________
3. concealed ________
4. exclusive ________
5. perpetual ________
6. informed ________
7. unhappy ________
8. beloved ________
9. profuse ________
10. asleep ________

#8

1. surrender ________
2. tormented ________
3. redemption ________
4. entrance ________
5. consider ________
6. protection ________
7. entrusted ________
8. cathedral ________
9. iniquities ________
10. unending ________

Worksheet #35: Primary vowels in unstressed syllables

Provide IPA:

#9

1. serenity ______________
2. forget ______________
3. complexity ______________
4. endeavors ______________
5. permission ______________
6. indeed ______________
7. obedience ______________
8. unleashed ______________
9. envies ______________
10. another ______________

#10

1. perceive ______________
2. deserves ______________
3. fulfilled ______________
4. essence ______________
5. concerned ______________
6. intrinsic ______________
7. lament ______________
8. emerged ______________
9. oppressed ______________
10. undeserving ______________

#11

1. emerald ______________
2. description ______________
3. perplexed ______________
4. extremely ______________
5. upheld ______________
6. invisible ______________
7. propelled ______________
8. contentment ______________
9. fulfill ______________
10. assistance ______________

#12

1. attendance ______________
2. omitted ______________
3. inevitable ______________
4. untrue ______________
5. beyond ______________
6. conspiracy ______________
7. tormenting ______________
8. elegy ______________
9. perception ______________
10. entangled ______________

#13

1. ascending ______________
2. perfume ______________
3. incessantly ______________
4. excellent ______________
5. eternity ______________
6. procession ______________
7. untouched ______________
8. deliberate ______________
9. forever ______________
10. commitments ______________

#14

1. compelled ______________
2. rehearse ______________
3. unspotted ______________
4. encourage ______________
5. pursue ______________
6. indulgent ______________
7. obedient ______________
8. fulfilling ______________
9. amid ______________
10. element ______________

Transcription within the phrase: enunciate the following verses from classical literature

Despair:

[hi ɪz ɪn ðə ˈmaɪtɪ dip]
[mɛn ɑ: noʊ mɔə]
[hɛlp hɛlp hi ʃaʊts ɪnˈsɛsəntlɪ]
[ˈnʌθɪŋ ɪn ðə hɔˈɾaɪzən ˈnʌθɪŋ ɪn ðə skaɪ]
[hi ɪmˈplɔ:z ðə blu vɔlt ðə wɛɪvz ðə ɾaks ɔl ɑ: dɛf]
[hi ˈsʌplɪkɛɪts ðə ˈtɛmpəst]
[ði ʔɪmˈpɛnətɹəbəl ˈtɛmpəst oˈbɛɪz]
[ˈoʊnlɪ ði ˈʔɪnfɪnɪt hi jildz tə dɪsˈpɛə]
[ənd hi ɪz ɹoʊld ʌˈwɛɪ]
[ˈɪntə ðə ˈdɪzməl dɛpθs əv ði ʌˈbɪs fɔɾˈɛvə]

Despair. Victor Hugo.

Anger:

[ɪf ðaʊ dʌst ˈslændə hɜ ənd ˈtɔ:tʃə mi]
[ˈnɛvə pɹɛɪ mɔə ʔʌˈbændən ɔl ɹɪˈmɔ:s]
[ɑn ˈhɔɾəz hɛd ˈhɔɾəz ʌˈkjumjulɛɪt]
[du didz tə mɛɪk ˈhɛvən wip ɔl ʔɜθ ʌˈmɛɪzd]
[fɔ: ˈnʌθɪŋ kɑnst ðaʊ tə dæmˈnɛɪʃən ʔæd]
[ˈgɹɛɪtə ðən ðæt]

Othello, Act III. Shakespeare.

UNIT 36:

English diphthongs

RULES FOR TRANSCRIPTION

English Diphthongs

Spelling	IPA	Sample Words
ei, i, ui, y	[ɑɪ]	*either, neither, chime, guide, sky*
ai, ay, ea, ei, ey	[ɛɪ]	*plain, day, great, feint, they*
oi, oy	[ɔɪ]	*voice, joy*
ou, ow	[ɑʊ]	*cloud, town*
o, oa, ow	[oʊ]	*hope, coast, show*

Comparative Study

The transcription of diphthongs varies from source to source. Madeleine Marshall's recommendations reflect an elegant and formal pronunciation of the English language.

SAMPLE WORD	DICTIONARY	*SOUTHERN	MARSHALL
why	[aɪ]/[ɑɪ]	[a]	[ɑɪ]
say	[eɪ]	[e]	[ɛɪ]
joy	[ɔɪ]	[ɔj]	[ɔɪ]
now	[aʊ]/[ɑʊ]	[aw]	[ɑʊ]
go	[oʊ]/[əʊ]	[ow]	[oʊ]

*Southern English is included to point out the omission or weakening of the second vowel sound. Monophthongs are pronounced with an added on-glide or off-glide of the vowel in certain dialects.

Online Dictionary Resources

Cambridge Dictionary provides IPA and audio for American and British English: www.dictionary.cambridge.org

Pons Dictionary provides IPA and audio for English, Italian, German, and French: www.en.pons.com

Word Reference provides IPA for English, Italian, and French with audio for all languages: www.wordreference.com

Worksheet #36: English diphthongs

Provide IPA:

Classwork

1. sparrow ________
2. choice ________
3. shine ________
4. grown ________
5. mountains ________
6. royalty ________
7. hail ________
8. nightingale ________
9. angels ________
10. proud ________

#1

1. shows [ʃoʊs]
2. fame [feɪm]
3. lies [laɪs]
4. yellow [jɛloʊ]
5. boil [bɔɪl]
6. towns [taʊns]
7. voiceless [vɔɪslɛs]
8. pray [pɾeɪ]
9. crowded [kɾaʊdəd]
10. meanwhile [minʍaɪl]

#2

1. forsake [fɔɾseɪk]
2. cry [kɾaɪ]
3. toilsome [tɔɪlsʌm]
4. hold [hoʊld]
5. downward [daʊnwaɾd]
6. silence [saɪlɛns]
7. name [neɪm]
8. oil [ɔɪl]
9. arrow [aɾoʊ]
10. mouth [maʊθ]

#3

1. maiden [meɪdən]
2. poise [pɔɪz]
3. closed [kloʊsd]
4. shout [ʃaʊt]
5. flame [fleɪm]
6. times [taɪms]
7. doubtful [doʊtfʊl]
8. idle [aɪdəl]
9. swallow [swɔloʊ]
10. joyous [ʤɔious]

#4

1. lightly [laɪtli]
2. brown [bɾaʊn]
3. spoil [spɔɪl]
4. fold [foʊld]
5. shame [ʃeɪm]
6. pine [paɪn]
7. disallow [dɪsalaʊ]
8. ocean [oʊʃə]
9. native [neɪtɪv]
10. enjoyment [ɪndʒɔimɪnt]

#5

1. island [aɪland]
2. shroud [ʃɾaʊd]
3. voiced [vɔɪsd]
4. save [seɪv]
5. float [floʊt]
6. howl [haʊl]
7. loyalty [lɔɪjalti]
8. countenance [kaʊntɪnans]
9. nigh [naɪ]
10. wayward [weɪwaɾd]

#6

1. daylight [deɪlaɪt]
2. holy [hoʊli]
3. clouded [klaʊdəd]
4. rainbow [ɾeɪnboʊ]
5. noise [nɔɪz]
6. sign [saɪn]
7. flows [floʊs]
8. waiting [weɪtɪŋ]
9. avoid [ʌvɔɪd]
10. brave [bɾeɪv]

#7

1. right ________
2. joy ________
3. echoes ________
4. sighing ________
5. fountains ________
6. voyage ________
7. praise ________
8. crowned ________
9. daybreak ________
10. ghost ________

#8

1. joining ________
2. boat ________
3. faithful ________
4. arise ________
5. rain ________
6. hoist ________
7. count ________
8. sigh ________
9. willow ________
10. drowsy ________

Worksheet #36: English diphthongs

Provide IPA:

#9

1. poised ________________
2. cloudless ________________
3. faith ________________
4. noises ________________
5. owl ________________
6. snowy ________________
7. height ________________
8. gold ________________
9. beside ________________
10. remain ________________

#10

1. butterfly ________________
2. fading ________________
3. narrow ________________
4. thine ________________
5. sounds ________________
6. rejoice ________________
7. plain ________________
8. outward ________________
9. hopes ________________
10. coin ________________

#11

1. bright ________________
2. sake ________________
3. allow ________________
4. known ________________
5. points ________________
6. kindly ________________
7. employs ________________
8. lady ________________
9. growing ________________
10. crowd ________________

#12

1. bounds ________________
2. days ________________
3. goodbye ________________
4. nature ________________
5. powder ________________
6. roses ________________
7. toy ________________
8. flown ________________
9. might ________________
10. appointed ________________

#13

1. sorrows ________________
2. however ________________
3. destroy ________________
4. taste ________________
5. mighty ________________
6. both ________________
7. child ________________
8. vowed ________________
9. coy ________________
10. places ________________

#14

1. notes ________________
2. wild ________________
3. void ________________
4. sacred ________________
5. mouse ________________
6. flying ________________
7. throughout ________________
8. pale ________________
9. boyish ________________
10. shadow ________________

Transcription within the phrase: enunciate the following verses from classical literature

Fear:

[ʔɑ ˈmɜsɪ ɑn mɑɪ soʊl ʍɑt ɪz ðæt]
[mɑɪ ʔoʊld fɹɛndz goʊst]
[ðɛɪ sɛɪ nʌn bət ˈwɪkəd foʊks wɔk]
[ʔɑɪ wɪʃ ɑɪ wɜ(ɾ) ət ðə ˈbɑtəm əv ə koʊl pɪt]
[si hɑʊ lɑŋ ənd pɛɪl hɪz fɛɪs həz gɾoʊn sɪns hɪz dɛθ]
[hi ˈnɛvə wəz ˈhændsəm]
[ənd dɛθ həz ɪmˈpɾuvd hɪm ˈvɛɾɪ mʌtʃ ðə ɾɑŋ wɛɪ]
[pɹɛɪ du nɔt kʌm nɪə mi]
[ʔɑɪ wɪʃt ju ˈvɛɾɪ wɛl ʍɛn ju wɜ(ɾ) ʌˈlɑɪv]
[bət ɑɪ kʊd ˈnɛvə(ɾ) ʌˈbɑɪd ə dɛd mæn]
[tʃik bɑɪ dʒɑʊl wɪð mi]
[ʔɑ ʔɑ ˈmɜsɪ ɑn ʌs noʊ ˈnɪəɾə pɹɛɪ ʔɑ ʔɑ]

Moliere.

Graphic Description:

[ənd nɑʊ wɪð ʃɑʊts ðə ˈʃɑkɪŋ ˈɑːmɪz kloʊzd]
[tə ˈlɑnsəz ˈlɑnsəz ʃildz tə ʃildz ʌˈpoʊzd]
[hoʊst ʌˈgɛnst hoʊst ðə ˈʃædoʊɪ ˈlidʒənz dɾu]
[ðə ˈsɑʊndɪŋ dɑːts ən ˈʔɑɪən ˈtɛmpəst flu]
[ˈvɪktəz ənd ˈvæŋkwɪʃt dʒɔɪn pɹoˈmɪskjuəs kɾɑɪz]
[tɹɑɪˈʌmfɪŋ ʃɑʊts ənd ˈdɑɪɪŋ gɾoʊnz ʌˈɾɑɪz]
[wɪð ˈstɹimɪŋ blʌd ðə ˈslɪpəɾɪ fild ɪz dɑɪd]
[ənd ˈslɔtəd ˈhɪɾoʊz swɛl ðə ˈdɹɛdfəl tɑɪd]

Iliad, V. Homer.

UNIT 37:

English schwa replacement of *r*

RULES FOR TRANSCRIPTION

Schwa replacement of *r* in monosyllables and stressed syllables

Spelling	IPA	Sample Words
air, are, ayer, ear, ere	[ɛə]	*air, share, prayer, bear, where*
ear, eer, ere, ier	[ɪə]	*dear, cheer, here, fierce*
oar, ore, our	[ɔə]	*soar, adore, your, pour*
oor, our	[ʊə]	*poor, tour*
ior, ire, yre	[ɑɪə]	*prior, fire, lyre*
our, ower	[ɑʊə]	*our, power*
ure	[jʊə]	*cure, sure*

Additional Notes

1) A flipped *r* is added following the schwa when *r* is intervocalic: *purest* [ˈpjʊəɾəst].
2) The spelling *ure* has two pronunciations. It is transcribed as [jʊə] when it occurs in a stressed syllable: *endure* [ʔɪnˈdjʊə]. It is transcribed with a schwa when it occurs in an unstressed syllable: *leisure* [ˈliʒə]. The triphthong transcription may be used if the unstressed syllable is set on a sustained pitch.
3) A schwa is not recommended for unstressed words *or* [ʔɔː], *for* [fɔː], and *nor* [nɔː]. Note: final *-for* of words with multiple elements is [fɔə]: *before* [bɪˈfɔə]

Comparative Study

The transcription of diphthongs and triphthongs varies from source to source. Madeleine Marshall's recommendations reflect an elegant and formal pronunciation of the English language that elevates and simplifies the delivery of the text.

SAMPLE WORD	*AMERICAN ENGLISH	BRITISH ENGLISH	MARSHALL
there	[ɛɚ]	[ɛə]	[ɛə]
near	[ɪɚ]	[ɪə]	[ɪə]
more	[ɔɚ]	[ɔː]	[ɔə]
poor	[ʊɚ]	[ʊə]	[ʊə]
choir	[ɑɪɚ]	[aɪə]	[ɑɪə]
power	[ɑʊɚ]	[aʊə]	[ɑʊə]
pure	[jʊɚ]	[jʊə]	[jʊə]

*Dictionary transcription provides an [ɚ] symbol. This symbol reflects spoken practice but is not appropriate for lyric diction since it merges a schwa with an *r*-colored vowel. In speech, these sounds occur simultaneously. For singing, the schwa is sustained. According to the rules established by Madeleine Marshall, an *r*-colored vowel would never occur in an unstressed syllable. Vowel *r* is a characteristic sound of the English language but it should be reserved for stressed syllables and monophthongs: *prefer* [pɹɪˈfɜ] *bird* [bɜd] *word* [wɜd].

Worksheet #37: English schwa replacement of *r*

Provide IPA:

Classwork

1. tearful ______
2. or ______
3. cheer ______
4. somewhere ______
5. leisure ______
6. demure ______
7. adore ______
8. entirely ______
9. flowery ______
10. share ______

#1

1. jeer ______
2. admiring ______
3. pleasure ______
4. unaware ______
5. dreary ______
6. cures ______
7. scarce ______
8. for ______
9. hour ______
10. implore ______

#2

1. revere ______
2. your ______
3. venture ______
4. powerfully ______
5. nor ______
6. snare ______
7. empire ______
8. drear ______
9. fairest ______
10. <u>o</u>bscure [ʌ] ______

#3

1. creatures ______
2. wear ______
3. hearing ______
4. procure ______
5. sphere ______
6. or ______
7. fairly ______
8. yourself ______
9. bowers ______
10. desiring ______

#4

1. tired ______
2. cares ______
3. measured ______
4. sincerely ______
5. pierced ______
6. beware ______
7. for ______
8. security ______
9. deploring ______
10. ours ______

#5

1. nor ______
2. flares ______
3. devour ______
4. prairie ______
5. gesture ______
6. merely ______
7. surely ______
8. evermore ______
9. spear ______
10. inspired ______

#6

1. soars ______
2. rapture ______
3. fierceness ______
4. tiresome ______
5. glare ______
6. powers ______
7. or ______
8. insure ______
9. declared ______
10. shear ______

#7

1. carelessly ______
2. sunflower ______
3. exploring ______
4. dire ______
5. appearance ______
6. future ______
7. purity ______
8. beard ______
9. for ______
10. tare ______

#8

1. endureth ______
2. despairing ______
3. rare ______
4. structure ______
5. nor ______
6. tower ______
7. wearied ______
8. before ______
9. years ______
10. fiery ______

Worksheet #37: English schwa replacement of *r*

Provide IPA:

#9

1. fears ______________
2. farewell ______________
3. or ______________
4. treasures ______________
5. desires ______________
6. storing ______________
7. showering ______________
8. lures ______________
9. clearly ______________
10. chair ______________

#10

1. aspire ______________
2. hear ______________
3. towering ______________
4. for ______________
5. endure ______________
6. square ______________
7. door ______________
8. figure ______________
9. nearly ______________
10. prepare ______________

#11

1. pastures ______________
2. dears ______________
3. sorely ______________
4. firelight ______________
5. severe ______________
6. hourly ______________
7. ere ______________
8. nor ______________
9. allures ______________
10. compare ______________

#12

1. cheerfully ______________
2. choir ______________
3. feature ______________
4. neared ______________
5. stair ______________
6. or ______________
7. during ______________
8. ensnare ______________
9. flowering ______________
10. therefore ______________

#13

1. sapphire ______________
2. threadbare ______________
3. endearing ______________
4. powerful ______________
5. displeasure ______________
6. fair ______________
7. clear ______________
8. restoreth ______________
9. for ______________
10. assure ______________

#14

1. pair ______________
2. fierce ______________
3. lovelier ______________
4. demurely ______________
5. wherever ______________
6. shores ______________
7. nor ______________
8. azure ______________
9. sour ______________
10. require ______________

Transcription within the phrase: enunciate the following verses from classical literature

Sorrow:

[ʔoʊ ˈʔɛvə ðʌs fɹəm ˈtʃaɪldhʊdz ʔaʊə]
[ʔaɪv sin maɪ ˈfandəst hoʊps dɪˈkɛɪ]
[ʔaɪ ˈnɛvə lʌvd ə tɹi ɔ: flaʊə]
[bət twaz ðə fɜst tə fɛɪd ʌˈwɛɪ]
[ʔaɪ ˈnɛvə nɜst ə dɪə gʌˈzɛl]
[tə glæd mi wɪð ɪts saft blæk ʔaɪ]
[bət ʍɛn ɪt kɛɪm tə noʊ mi wɛl]
[ənd lʌv mi ʔɪt wəz ʃjʊə tə daɪ]

The Fire-Worshipers. Moore.

Defiant Address:

[ʍɛns ənd ʍat ɑ:t ðaʊ ˈʔɛksəkɹəbəl ʃɛɪp]
[ðæt ˈdɛərəst ðoʊ gɾɪm ənd ˈtɛɾɪbəl ʌdˈvans]
[ðaɪ ˈmɪskɾiɛɪtəd fɹʌnt ʌˈθwɔ:t maɪ wɛɪ]
[tə ˈjandə gɛɪts θɾu ðəm aɪ min tə pas]
[ðət bi ʌˈʃjʊəd wɪðˈaʊt liv askt əv ði]
[ɹɪˈtaɪə(ɾ) ʔɔ: tɛɪst ðaɪ ˈfalɪ ənd lɜn baɪ pɾuf]
[hɛl bɔ:n nɔt tə kʌnˈtɛnd wɪð ˈspɪɾɪts əv ˈhɛvən]

Paradise Lost, Book II. Milton.

UNIT 38:

When to sing [ɑ]

RULES FOR TRANSCRIPTION

I. Certain words that are pronounced with [æ] in American speech are pronounced with a dark [ɑ] for British English

Spelling	IPA	Sample Words
a + [f]	[ɑ] Dark Central	*after, laugh, staff*
a + [s]	[ɑ] Dark Central	*ask, fast, glass, last, pass, vast*
a + [ntʃ]	[ɑ] Dark Central	*blanch, branch*
a + [ns]	[ɑ] Dark Central	*advance, chance, dance, *trance*
a + *th*	[ɑ] Dark Central	*bath, path, rather, wrath*

* Prefix *trans-* is transcribed with [æ]: *transcend* [tɹæn'sɛnd]

MEMORY AID: *After class Blanch danced rather fast.*
['ʔɑftə klɑs blɑntʃ dɑnst 'ɹɑðə fɑst]

II. Spellings -*and*, -*ant* and -*ample* are [ɑ] for the following words only

-*and* [ɑnd]: *command, demand, reprimand*
-*ant* [ɑnt]: *can't, shan't, aunt, advantage, chant, enchant, grant, plant, slant*
-*ample* [ɑmpəl]: *sample, example*

III. Exceptions to section I: words with an [æ] pronunciation

a + *f*	*a* + *s*		*a* + *ns*	*a* + *th*	may be [æ] or [ɑ]	
baffle	aspect	fantastic	cancel	fathom	alas	contrast
daffodil	aspiration	hast	circumstance	gather	ant	enhance
graphic	cascade	passage	expanse	hath	asp	lass
scaffold	chastise	passenger	fancy	math	aspen	mass
riffraff	classic	passive	romance		ass	pasture
traffic	classify	sarcastic	stance		blaspheme	ranch

Worksheet #38: When to sing [ɑ]

Provide IPA:

Classwork

1. glances ______________
2. castle ______________
3. wrath ______________
4. passion ______________
5. demand ______________
6. laughter ______________
7. satin ______________
8. enchanting ______________

#1

1. afternoon ______________
2. candles ______________
3. reprimand ______________
4. plant ______________
5. tasks ______________
6. France ______________
7. chalice ______________
8. baths ______________

#2

1. enhances ______________
2. path ______________
3. lamp ______________
4. class ______________
5. hereafter ______________
6. strand ______________
7. demand ______________
8. chant ______________

#3

1. dancing ______________
2. random ______________
3. pasture ______________
4. commanded ______________
5. enchanted ______________
6. language ______________
7. sample ______________
8. half ______________

#4

1. vastly ______________
2. expanse ______________
3. understand ______________
4. commander ______________
5. palace ______________
6. staffs ______________
7. enchantments ______________
8. blanch ______________

#5

1. reprimanded ______________
2. fantasy ______________
3. example ______________
4. shan't ______________
5. cabin ______________
6. laughed ______________
7. answer ______________
8. passage ______________

#6

1. amber ______________
2. commandment ______________
3. everlasting ______________
4. chancel ______________
5. paths ______________
6. grant ______________
7. flash ______________
8. laughing ______________

#7

1. aunt ______________
2. slander ______________
3. master ______________
4. draft ______________
5. valor ______________
6. command ______________
7. prances ______________
8. branch ______________

#8

1. land ______________
2. trance ______________
3. grafted ______________
4. clasp ______________
5. path ______________
6. flattering ______________
7. plants ______________
8. demanding ______________

Worksheet #38: When to sing [ɑ]

Provide IPA:

#9

1. disaster ______________
2. commands ______________
3. malice ______________
4. slant ______________
5. chaff ______________
6. ample ______________
7. gather ______________
8. lance ______________

#10

1. rafters ______________
2. chance ______________
3. jasper ______________
4. vanity ______________
5. command ______________
6. brand ______________
7. advantage ______________
8. pathway ______________

#11

1. after ______________
2. grasp ______________
3. famished ______________
4. demanded ______________
5. perchance ______________
6. can't ______________
7. branches ______________
8. sand ______________

#12

1. staff ______________
2. planting ______________
3. trample ______________
4. chances ______________
5. rather ______________
6. commanding ______________
7. absent ______________
8. basket ______________

#13

1. grandeur ______________
2. planted ______________
3. faster ______________
4. chancellor ______________
5. demanding ______________
6. languish ______________
7. afterward ______________
8. bath ______________

#14

1. advancing ______________
2. reprimand ______________
3. grand ______________
4. pastel ______________
5. fathomed ______________
6. calf ______________
7. blanket ______________
8. enchant ______________

Transcription within the phrase: enunciate the following verses from classical literature

Mirth:

[hɛɪst ði nɪmf ənd bɹɪŋ wɪð ði]
[dʒɛst ənd ˈjuθfəl ˈdʒɑlɪtɪ]
[kwɪps ənd kɹæŋks ənd ˈwɑntən wɑɪlz]
[nɑdz ənd bɛks ənd ɹiðd smɑɪlz]
[sʌtʃ əz hæŋ ɑn ˈhibɪz tʃik]
[ənd lʌv tə lɪv ɪn ˈdɪmpəl slik]
[spɔːt ðət ˈɹɪŋkəld kɛə dɪˈɾɑɪdz]
[ənd ˈlɑftə ˈhoʊldɪŋ boʊθ hɪz sɑɪdz]
[kʌm ənd tɹɪp ɪt æz ju goʊ]
[ɑn ðə lɑɪt fænˈtæstɪk toʊ]

L'Allegro, I. Milton.

Advice:

[ˈkɹɑmwɛl ʔɑɪ tʃɑːdʒ ði flɪŋ ʌˈwɛɪ æmˈbɪʃən]
[lʌv ðɑɪˈsɛlf lɑst ˈtʃɛɾɪʃ ðoʊz hɑːts ðət hɛɪt ði]
[bi dʒʌst ənd fɪə nɔt]
[lɛt ɔl ði ʔɛndz ðɑʊ ʔɛɪmst æt bi ðɑɪ ˈkʌntɹɪz]
[ðɑɪ gɑdz ənd tɾuθs] (*truth's*)

Henry VIII., Act III., Sc. 2. Shakespeare.

I. Monosyllabic words: Provide IPA

serve	crash	new	whose	put
leaped	waltz	niece	goods	seemed
should	fringe	drench	awe	haunt
bruise	then	flew	threats	group
chill	birch	ceased	judge	calm
you	myths	smooth	warmth	sword
pond	knack	wings	wheat	wrong
spins	ought	scourge	lamps	rouge

II. Unaccented Syllables: Provide IPA

persistent	blissful	petit	lament	prefer
thunder	protect	music	unjust	darkness
studies	humble	complete	fervor	jealous
beyond	remove	listed	attempt	elusive
thirsty	consume	cathedral	surpass	crystal
obey	entrust	select	treasure	forever
uproot	defend	captain	brilliant	effortless
talking	crucial	beggar	servant	fulfill

III. Diphthongs and triphthongs: Provide IPA

pure	meadow	door	fair	dear
I	coy	know	guide	road
now	here	train	eight	hour
inspire	voice	poor	tour	pour
jade	ghost	shy	shout	your

IV. Pronunciation of *r*: Provide IPA

ART SONG			DRAMATIC	OPERA/ORATORIO
far away	cypress	ever	cry	dream
sort	reign	farewell	crude	river
their hearts	carol	charm	grieve	last rain
parlor	starry	throne		

V. Define the *Ella Standeth* rule and provide examples:

VI. When to sing [ɑ]: Provide British pronunciation

fact	calf	rapture	can't
vast	*gather	sand	*lass
paths	ash	branch	answer

* Exceptions

VOWEL CHART

Vowel Chart

CHART DESCRIPTION: The front vowels are on the left side of the chart, the back vowels are on the right, and the mixed vowels are at the top and bottom (the arrows indicate vowel mixing). The schwa is not included since its pronunciation varies from language to language. The points indicate closed vowels, the broader spaces indicate open vowels, and the center space is reserved for central vowels.

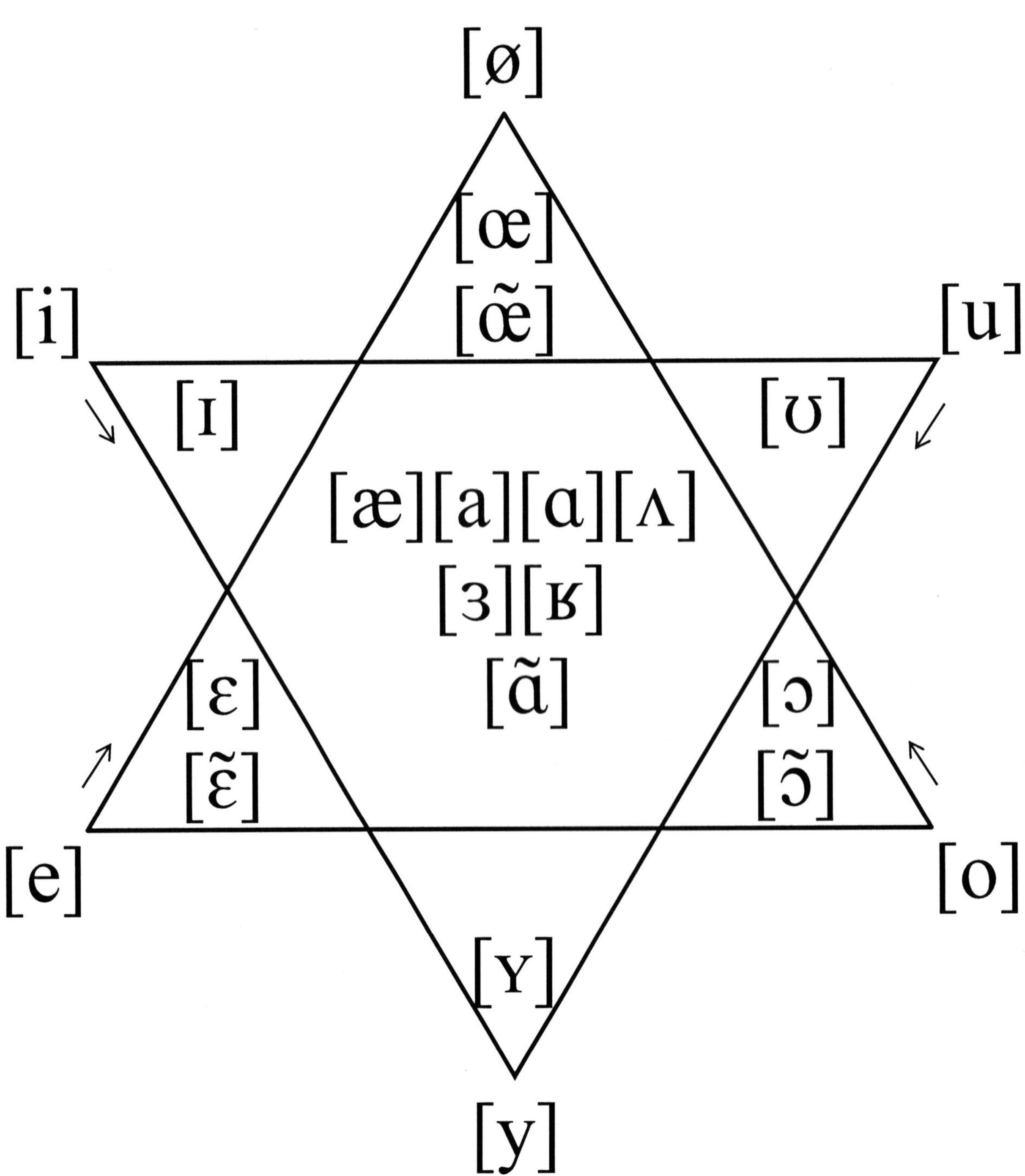

REVIEW OF ITALIAN TRANSCRIPTION RULES

A summary of the rules for frequently occurring words

Review of Italian Transcription Rules

CONSONANTS

[ɾ]	Intervocalic *r* within the word or phrase: *amore* [aˈmoɾe]	[r]	Spelling *r* in other positions: *rose* [ˈrɔze] *aprile* [aˈprile]
[s]	Spelling *s* & *s* + voiceless consonant: *speranza* [speˈɾantsa]	[z]	Spelling *s* + voiced consonant: *sventura* [zvenˈtuɾa]
	Intervocalic *s* with prefix *ri-*: *risuonare* [riswoˈnaɾe]		Other intervocalic single *s*: *tesoro* [teˈzɔɾo] *mese* [ˈmeze]
	Intervocalic *s* with prefixes *tra-* and *pre-*		*Note: Intervocalic pronunciation of "s" is* [s] *in*
	Intervocalic *s* with pronoun *-si*: *dicesi* [ˈditʃesi]		*numerous Italian words. Intervocalic* [z] *is a lyric*
	Intervocalic *s* in compound words: *stasera* [staˈseɾa]		*rule, an elegant manner of pronunciation for singing.*
[dz]	Dictionary required for *z* spelling: *mezzo* [ˈmɛddzo]	[ts]	Dictionary required for *z* spelling: *danza* [ˈdantsa]
[ɲɲ]	Spelling *gn*: *signore* [siɲˈɲoɾe]	[ŋ]	*n* when followed by [g] or [k] sounds: *pianga* [ˈpjaŋga]
[k]	*c* + back vowel or consonant: *core* [ˈkɔɾe] *perché* [perˈke]	[g]	*g* + back vowel or consonant: *lago* [ˈlago] *grato* [ˈgrato]
[tʃ]	*c* + front vowel: *pace* [ˈpatʃe] *cielo* [ˈtʃɛlo] (*i* is silent)	[dʒ]	*g* + front vowel: *gente* [ˈdʒɛnte] *giorno* [ˈdʒorno] (silent *i*
[ʃʃ]	*sc* + front vowel: *esce* [ˈɛʃʃe] *sciarpa* [ˈʃʃarpa] (*i* is silent)	[sk]	*sc* + back vowel or consonant: *scherzo* [ˈskertso] (silent *h*
[ʎʎ]	Spelling *gli* + vowel: *foglio* [ˈfɔʎʎo] (*i* is silent)	[ʎʎi]	Spelling *gli* + consonant or final: *toglimi* [ˈtɔʎʎimi] *gli* [ʎʎi]
[h]	Spelling *h* is silent (there is no [h] sound in Italian)	[ʔ]	There are no glottal stops in Italian

Consonants that are doubled in spelling are also doubled in transcription. The symbols [ʃ] [ɲ] [ʎ] are always doubled in transcription.

VOWELS

[i]	Single *i*: *primi* [ˈprimi] *divino* [diˈvino]	[j]	Spelling *i* + vowel (*i* becomes [j]): *lieto* [ˈljɛto]
	Spelling *ì* (always): *finì* [fiˈni]		(Except when stressed or in hiatus: *Lucia* [luˈtʃiːa])
[u]	Single *u*: *luce* [ˈlutʃe] *futuro* [fuˈtuɾo]	[w]	*u* + vowel: *uomo* [ˈwɔmo] *suora* [ˈswɔɾa]
	Spelling *ù* (always): *virtù* [virˈtu]		(Except in hiatus: *usuale* [uzuˈale]) *qu* is [kw] *gu* is [gw]
[e] closed	Dictionary required for *e, è, é* of stressed syllables Spelling *e* of unstressed syllables: *vivere* [ˈviveɾe]	[ɛ] open	Dictionary required for *e, è, é* of stressed syllables
[o] closed	Dictionary required for *o, ò, ó* of stressed syllables Spelling *o* of unstressed syllables: *giocondo* [dʒoˈkondo]	[ɔ] open	Dictionary required for *o, ò, ó* of stressed syllables Final *ò* is always open [ɔ]: *adorerò* [adoɾeˈɾɔ]
[a]	Spelling *a, à*: *farfalla* [farˈfalla] *carità* [kaɾiˈta]	[ɑ]	All *a* spellings are bright [a]
[ˈ]	Dictionary required to determine primary stressed syllable	[ˌ]	Dictionary required to determine secondary stress

Grave and acute marks indicate the stressed syllable in polysyllabic words. They do not indicate the open or closed quality of *e* and *o*.

Syllabic vowel in vowel clusters within the word

[ː] long	Final stressed *i*, *u* + vowel: tuo [tuːo] *armonia* [armoˈniːa] The first *a, e, o* + vowel within the syllable: *Laura* [ˈlaːuɾa]	[j w] glide	The first *i, u* + vowel within the syllable: *grazia* [ˈgratsja Spelling *i, u* + final stressed vowel: *può* [pwɔ] *più* [pju]

The stressed syllable is characterized by vowel length in Italian, not by a weighted accentuation of the stressed syllable as in English.

Syllabic vowel in vowel clusters within the phrase

A syllabic vowel must be selected when the vowels of separate words share one note. Syllabic vowels are found in the following cases:

- The stressed syllable of a polysyllabic word is syllabic in vowel groups within the phrase: *dolce anima mia* [ˈdoltʃeˈaːnima miːa]
- The first *a, e, o* of an unstressed vowel group within the phrase is syllabic: *alma infiammata* [ˈalmaːinfjamˈmata]
- Final unstressed *i* becomes a [j] glide when followed by an initial vowel word: *begli occhi ardenti* [ˈbɛʎʎjˈɔkkjarˈdɛnti]
- The long vowel of diphthongs or triphthongs is syllabic: *non può andare* [non pwɔːanˈdaɾe]
- The following monosyllabic words are strong and syllabic in vowel groups within the phrase: *a, ah, blu, che, ché, chi, da, dà, deh, dì, do, e, è, ed, fa, fé, fo, fra, fu, già, giù, ha, ho, là, lì, ma, me, né, no, o, oh, re, sa, se, sé, sì, so, sta, sto, su, te, tè, tra, tre, tu, va, vo*

Phrasal doubling

Considerations for phrasal doubling must be made within the context of the musical setting

Initial consonants of *Dio, dei, dea, dee* and *Maria (Virgin Mary)* are doubled when preceded by a final vowel: *Ave Maria* [ˈave *maˈriːa

An initial single consonant is doubled when preceded by a stressed vowel or a strong monosyllable: *una beltà divina* [ˈuna belˈta *diˈvin

Consonant blends with *l* and *r* are doubled when preceded by a stressed vowel or a strong monosyllabic monophthong (refer to the stron monosyllabic words listed above): *la vita è breve* [la ˈvita ɛ ˈ*brɛve]

Sources

These rules are based on Evelina Colorni's *Singers' Italian* with transcription finalized by Dr. Corradina Caporello, Professor of Italian Diction at the *Juilliard School of Music*. Recommended pronunciation dictionary: *Dizionario di ortografia e pronuncia* (dizionario.rai.i

REVIEW OF GERMAN TRANSCRIPTION RULES

A summary of the rules for frequently occurring words

Review of German Transcription Rules

VOWELS

Spelling	Closed Vowels	Open Vowels	Spelling
i + single consonant *i + h* *ie*	[iː]	[ɪ]	*i* + two or more consonants Except: *bin, in, bis, hin, im, mit* final *-ig*, *-in* and unstressed *-ik*
e + single consonant *e + h* *ee*	[eː]	[ɛ]	*e* + two or more consonants Except: *es, des, weg* *ä* is [ɛ] (*ä* + single consonant is [ɛː])
u + single consonant/final *u + h*	[uː]	[ʊ]	*u* + two or more consonants Except: *um, zum, drum*
o + single consonant/final *o + h* *oo*	[oː]	[ɔ]	*o* + two or more consonants Except: *ob, von, vom*
a + single consonant/final *a + h* *aa*	[ɑː]	[a]	*a* + two or more consonants Except: *das, hat, was, an* *man, am, ab*
ü, y + single consonant *ü + h*	[yː]	[ʏ]	*ü, y* + two or more consonants
ö + single consonant *ö + h*	[øː]	[œ]	*ö* + two or more consonants

Schwa [ə]: unstressed *e* / Diphthongs: *ei* and *ai* are [ae], *au* is [ɑo], *eu* and *äu* are [ɔø]

CONSONANTS

IPA	Spelling	IPA	Spelling
[ɾ]	*r* except those listed under [ʁ] Prevocalic *r*	[ʁ]	der, mir, dir, er, ihr wir, wer, für, vor, schwa + *r* + cons. or final
[x]	Back vowel + *ch* *a + ch*	[ç]	Front/mixed vowel + *ch* Initial *ch* + front vowel *-ig* + consonant or final (prevocalic *-ig* is [ɪg])
[h]	Initial *h* of word or element (postvocalic *h* is silent)	[ʔ]	Precedes a word or element that begins with a vowel and is stressed within the phrase
[v]	Spelling: *w*, medial *v*, *v* in words of foreign origin	[f]	Spelling: *f, ph*, initial and final *v* of word or element
[ʃ]	Spelling: *sch* Initial *sp* is [ʃp] Initial *st* is [ʃt]	[s]	Spelling: *s*, *ß* is [ss] and prevocalic *ss* is [ss] Medial and final *s/st/sp* of element is [s]/[st]/[sp]
[z]	Prevocalic *s* is [z] Exceptions: *Rätsel* [ɾɛːtsəl] unsre [ˈʔʊnzɾə]	[ts]	Spelling: *z* is [ts], *tz* is [tts], *-tion* is [tsioːn] Initial *c* + front vowel
[j]	Spelling: *j* (except in words of French origin) Unstressed final *-ie* is [jə]/stressed final *-ie* is [iː]	[p]	*pf* is [pf] *ps* is [ps]
[ŋ]	Spelling: *ng* is [ŋ] Spelling: *nk* is [ŋk]	[k]	Spelling: *k* is [k], *ck* is [kk] *-ig* + *lich* or *reich* is [ɪk] Initial *ch/c* + back vowel or consonant *kn* is [kn] *qu* is [kv] *x* is [ks]

b, d, g + consonant or final become voiceless [p], [t], [k] (except when followed by *l, r* or *n*)
All double consonants are doubled in transcription

REVIEW OF FRENCH TRANSCRIPTION RULES

A summary of the rules for frequently occurring words

Review of French Transcription Rules

CLOSED VOWELS			OPEN VOWELS AND SEMIVOWELS
Single *i, y,* circumflex *î*: *triste* [tristə] *lys* [lis] *île* [ilə] Diæresis *ï: naïf* [naif] Final *-ie*: *amie* [ami] *vie* [vi] (may be [iə] in lyrics)	[i]	[j]	*i, y, ï* + vowel: *lierre* [ljɛɾə], *yeux* [jø] (may be [i] in lyrics) Medial *ill: fille* [fijə] (except: *mille, ville, tranquille, oscille*) Vowel + *il*: *soleil* [sɔlɛj] (consonant + *il*: *avril* [avɾil])
Acute *é*: *étoiles* [etwalə] [e] words: *ai* [e] *et* [e] *gai* [ge] *pays* [pei] *maison* [m(e)zõ] *e* + final *r, rs, z, d, ds*: *chanter* [ʃɑ̃te] (except *mer/ver* words) *-ai* verb ending: *vivrai* [vivɾe]	[e]	[ɛ]	Grave *è, circumflex ê, ë*: *mère* [mɛɾə] *forêt* [fɔɾɛ] *Noël* [nɔɛl] *e* + two or more consonants: *belle* [bɛlə] / *e* + final *c, f, l, t* *a/e* + front vowel combinations: *ai, aî, aie, aies, aient, ay, ei* All final [ɛ] are semi-open [ɛ] (except final *-ai* verb ending) [ɛɾ]: *amer, cher, diver, fier, hier, hiver, mer, traver, ver* Final *e* + double consonant + schwa: *telle* [tɛlə]
Vocalic harmonization of *ai, aî, ei, ay, ê*: *laisser* [l(e)se] *e* + double cons. or *sc*: *essor* [(e)ɔɾ] (not before schwa or *ier*)	[(e)]		
ou, où, oû: *amour* [amuɾ] *où* [u] *voûte* [vutə] Note rare spelling: *août* [u]	[u]	[w]	*ou* + vowel: *alouette* [alwɛtə] (may be [u] in lyrics) *oi* is [wa]: *voici* [vwasi] / *oy* is [waj]: *joyeux* [ʒwajø]
ô: *trône* [tɾonə] / *au* and *eau*: *pauvre* [povɾə] Final [o]: *trop* [tɾo] / *o* + [z] or *-tion*: *rose* [ɾozə] *dévotion* Closed [o] words: *o, oh, fosse, grosse*	[o]	[ɔ]	*o* + pronounced consonant(s): *parole* [paɾɔlə] *au* + *r*: *laurier* [lɔɾje] Open [ɔ] words: *album* [albɔm] *géranium* [ʒeɾanjɔm]
Single *u, û: lune* [lynə] *brûle* [bɾylə] Conjugations of avoir: *eu* [y], *eut* [y], *eût* [y]	[y]	[ɥ]	*u* + vowel: *nuit* [nɥi] *suave* [sɥavə] (may be [y] in lyrics) (except in hiatus: *tendues* [tɑ̃dyə])
Final *-eu: feu* [fø] / *eu, œu* + final silent consonant Spelling *eu* + *s* + vowel: *berceuse* [bɛɾsøzə] Vocalic harmonization: *heureux* [(ø)ɾø]	[ø]	[œ]	*eu, œu* + pronounced consonant: *fleur* [flœɾ] (except *-euse* ending) *œ*: *œil* [œj], *œillet* [œjɛ]
â (always): *âme* [ɑmə] / some medial *ass*: *passer* [pɑse] Some *a* + [z]: *vase* [vɑzə] / final *-as*: *bas* [bɑ] [ɑ]: *ah, diable, flamme, gars, jadis, sable, sabre, taille, bois, voix*	[ɑ]	[a]	Single *a*: *matin* [matɛ̃] / spelling *à*: *déjà* [deʒa] Final *-as* verb ending is [a]: *boiras* [bwaɾa] Medial *emm*: *femme* [famə] / the word: *solennel* [sɔlanɛl]
e, a + *n, m* + consonant: *vent* [vɑ̃] / final *-an*: *océan* [ɔseɑ̃] (except when *e, a* + *n, m* is followed *n, m, h*, or a vowel) Except: *enivré* [ɑ̃nivɾe], *enneigé* [ɑ̃n(e)ʒe], *ennui* [ɑ̃nɥi]	[ɑ̃]	[ɛ̃]	*i, y, ai, ei* + *n, m* + consonant or final: *thym* [tɛ̃] (except *Poulenc* (except when *i, y, ai, ei* + *n, m* is followed by *n, m, h*, or vowel Final *-en(s)*: *bien* [bjɛ̃], verb ending *-ient* [jɛ̃], final *-oin* [wɛ̃]
on, om + consonant or final: *ombre* [õbɾə] (except when *on, om* is followed by *n, m, h*, or a vowel)	[õ]	[œ̃]	*un, um* + consonant or final: *parfum* [paɾfœ̃] (except when *un, um* is followed by *n, m, h*, or a vowel)

SCHWA [ə]

Final *-e* and *-es* (except for final *-es* of monosyllables *les, ses, mes, es*...) / in the sequence: consonant + e + consonant + vowel: *devenir* verb ending *-ent* / prefix *re-* / *fais* + vowel / schwa words: *monsieur* [məsjø] *secret* [səkɾɛ] *dessous* [dəsu] *dessus* [dəsy]

CONSONANTS

Final consonants are silent except for the consonant sounds in the word *careful.*
Common exceptions: *amen, angélus, automne, banc, blanc, bœufs, but, Carmen, cerf, clef, clerc, fils, flanc, Franc, gars, gentil, hélas, jadis, jonc, luth, lys, maïs, œufs, os, ouest, sens* (noun), *sept, sourcils, sud, tous* (stressed), *tronc*

g + *a, o, u*, or consonant: *garde* [gaɾdə] / *gu* + vowel is [g]	[g]	[k]	*c* + *a, o, u*, or consonant: *cœur* [kœɾ] / *qu* is [k] / *ch* [k] (rare
g + *e, i* or *y*: *ange* [ɑ̃ʒə] / Spelling *j*: *jour* [ʒuɾ]	[ʒ]	[s]	*c, sc* + *e, i* or *y*: *ciel* [sjɛl] / *s, ss* and *ç* / *-tion, -tiel, -tieux*
Intervocalic *s*: *brise* [bɾizə] / Spelling *z*: *azur* [azyɾ]	[z]	[ʃ]	Spelling *ch*: *chemin* [ʃəmɛ̃]
Spelling *gn*: *montagne* [mõtaɲə]	[ɲ]	[t]	Spelling: *t, th*: *rythme* [ɾitmə]

Note: Consonants are not doubled in transcription (except initial *ill-, imm-, inn-, irr-*)
b becomes [p] when followed by + *c, s, t* / *ph* is [f] / Spelling *x* + vowel or *h* is [gz], *x* + consonant is [ks] (except *luxe* and *fixe*)

LIAISON AND ELISION

In order to maintain a regular consonant/vowel flow, initial vowel words are often preceded by an enunciated consonant within the phrase

Elision: a final schwa is dropped when followed by an initial vowel word (observe the composer's setting of schwa)
Liaison: a final consonant is enunciated when followed by an initial vowel word (phonetic changes occur: *d, f, g, s, x* become *t, v, k, z*)

FORBIDDEN AND COMPULSORY LIAISON

Liaison should not be made in the following cases: after a noun in the singular, after words ending in *-rs* (except plural forms), *-rt, -rd* (link the normally sounded *r*), after *et* (and), between contrasting ideas (*et* may not always link two thoughts as it does in English), following a proper name, no liaison over a breath or rest except when phrases are linked grammatically, before or after interjections, before an aspirate *h* or before numerical words (except composite numbers). Special words in liaison: *donc* (prevocalic and dramatic), *puis* (except *puis on*), *Soit* (interjection), *toujours* (enunciate *s* only when a following initial vowel word is directly related in meaning).

Liaison is compulsory in the following cases: after a plural noun and words which indicate the plural noun, after an article, adjective, personal pronoun, verb, adverb, preposition, or conjunction. When *n* is linked, *bon, moyen* and *villain* lose their nasalization.

REVIEW OF LATIN TRANSCRIPTION RULES

A summary of the rules for frequently occurring words

Review of Latin Transcription Rules

VOWELS

CLOSED FRONT [i]	[j] GLIDE
Spelling *i*: *mitis* ['mitis] *pietate* [pi-ɛ-'tɑ-tɛ] Spelling *y*: *Kyrie* ['ki-ɾi-ɛ]	Spelling *j*: *jubilate* [jubi'lɑtɛ] Intervocalic *i*: *cuius* ['ku-jus] Initial *i* + vowel: *iudico* ['judikɔ]

CLOSED BACK [u]	[w] GLIDE
Spelling *u*: *numerus* ['numɛɾus] *tuum* ['tu-um]	Spelling *qu*: *qui* [kwi] Spelling *ngu* + vowel: *languor* ['lɑŋgwɔɾ]

OPEN FRONT [ɛ]	OPEN BACK [ɔ]
Spelling *e*: *miserere* [mizɛ'ɾɛɾɛ] *leonis* [lɛ-'ɔ-nis] Spelling *ae* and *œ*: *saecula* ['sɛkulɑ] *cœli* ['tʃɛli]	Spelling *o*: *oculos* ['ɔkulɔs] *introire* [in-tɾɔ-'i-ɾɛ]

DARK [ɑ]	DIPHTHONG [ɑu]
Spelling *a*: *amara* [ɑ'mɑɾɑ]	Spelling *au*: *laudate* [lɑu-'dɑ-tɛ]

Diphthongs that are rarely occurring:
Spellings *ay, ei, eu*: *Raymundi, Hei, euge*

CONSONANTS

ROLLED [r]	FLIPPED [ɾ]
Initial *r*: *rubet* ['rubɛt]	All other *r*: *propter* ['pɾɔptɛɾ] *terris* ['tɛɾɾis]

VOICED DENTAL FRICATIVE [z]	VOICELESS DENTAL FRICATIVE [s]
Intervocalic *s*: *visita* ['vizitɑ] Voiced consonant + final *s*: *potens* ['pɔtɛnz]	All other *s*: *solus* ['sɔlus] *passionis* [pɑs-si-'ɔ-nis]

PREPALATAL NASAL [ɲ]	PALATAL NASAL [ŋ]
Spelling *gn*: *regnum* ['rɛɲum]	Spelling *ngu* + vowel: *distinguo* [dis'tiŋgwɔ] Spelling *nct*: *punctum* ['puŋktum]

VOICELESS AFFRICATE [ts]
t + *i* + vowel: *rationis* [rɑ-tsi-'ɔ-nis] (Except when preceded by *s*: *ostium* ['ɔs-ti-um])

VOICELESS VELAR PLOSIVE [k]	VOICELESS AFFRICATE [tʃ]
c + back vowel, consonant, or final: *canticum* ['kɑntikum] (back vowel spellings: *u, o,* and central *a*)	*c* + front vowel: *cymbalis* ['tʃimbɑlis] (front vowel spellings: *i, y, e, ae, oe*)

VOICED VELAR PLOSIVE [g]	VOICED AFFRICATE [dʒ]
g + back vowel, consonant, or final: *congrego* ['kɔngɾɛgɔ] (back vowel spellings: *u, o,* and central *a*)	*g* + front vowel: *agens* ['ɑdʒɛnz] (front vowel spellings: *i, y, e, ae, oe*)

VOICELESS PREPALATAL FRICATIVE [ʃ]
sc + front vowel: *ascendat* [ɑ'ʃɛndɑt] *conscius* ['kɔn-ʃi-us] Initial *ex* + *c* + front vowel is [kʃ]: *excelsis* [ɛk'ʃɛlsis] (front vowel spellings: *i, y, e, ae, oe*)

Transcription of *x*

VOICED AFFRICATE [gz]	VOICELESS AFFRICATE [ks]
Initial *ex* + vowel: *exemplar* [ɛgz'ɛmplɑɾ] Initial *ex* + s + vowel: *exsultate* [ɛgzul'tɑtɛ] Initial *ex* + *h*: *exhilaro* [ɛgz'ilɑɾɔ]	Initial *ex* + consonant: *excolo* ['ɛkskɔlɔ] Initial *ex* + *c* + front vowel is [kʃ]: *excelsis* [ɛk'ʃɛlsis] *All other x*: dilexit [di'lɛksit] calix ['kɑliks]

TRANSCRIPTION OF *h*	VOICELESS AFFRICATE [ps]
Spelling *ihi* is [iki]: *mihi* ['miki] Spelling *ph* is [f], *th* is [t], *ch* is [k] *h* is silent for all other spellings	Spelling *ps*: *psalmi* ['psɑlmi] **VOICED AFFRICATE [dz]** Spelling z: *Lazarus* ['lɑdzɑɾus]

REVIEW OF ENGLISH TRANSCRIPTION RULES

A summary of the rules for frequently occurring words

Review of English Transcription Rules

VOWEL SPELLINGS OF MONOPHTHONGS											
[i]	[ɪ]	[ɛ]	[æ]	[ɑ]	British [ɑ]	[ɔ]	[u]	[ju]	[ʊ]	[ʌ]	[ɜ]
eat	give	bed	glad	fond	**after**	**all**	soon	due	book	up	her
breeze	build	guest	plaid	charm	class	fawns	through	new	could	blood	search
we	myth	head		**wander**	**Blanch**	born	lose	tune	full	love	bird
field	been	friend	*a* + [ɾ]	**what**	**danced**	**August**	flew	lute	woman	young	word
ski		said	arrow	**balm**	**rather**	**fought**	blue	illumine			hurt
receive		many	carol	tomorrow	plant	**war**	two	suit			further
people		bury	carry	father	command	broad		enthuse			
			marry	Ah!	sample	water		Spelling: *d, n, t, l, s, th* + *u* or *ew*			
					(see exceptions in III)			Except consonant blends with *l*: *blue*			

VOWEL SPELLINGS OF DIPHTHONGS AND TRIPHTHONGS											
[ɑɪ]	[ɑɪə]	[ɛɪ]	[ɔɪ]	[ɑʊ]	[ɑʊə]	[oʊ]	[ɪə]	[ɛə]	[ɔə]	[ʊə]	[jʊə]
chime	fire	day	choice	cloud	flour	hope	cheer	air	adore	poor	pure
sky	lyre	plain	joy	town	power	coast	dear	share	soar	tour	sure
neither		great					fierce	where	your, pour		

VOWEL SPELLINGS OF UNSTRESSED SYLLABLES								
[ɪ]	[ʌ]	[ɜ]	[ɔ]	[ʊ]	Unstr. *o*	Unstr. *u*	[ɪ]	[oʊ]
believe	**a**gree	p**er**ceive	f**or**give	f**u**lfill	**o**bey	cher**u**bim	merc**y**	shad**ow**
endure	c**o**mplete	s**ur**prise	h**o**rizon		mel**o**dy	spec**u**late	sing**ing**	[ɛɪ]
divine	c**o**ncern		t**or**mented		Exceptions	Exceptions	piti**ed**	alw**ay**s
	uncertain				mem**o**ry ɔ	cent**u**ry ʊ	prair**ie**	[ɑɪ]
	uplifting				purp**o**se ə	feat**u**re ə	marr**ie**s	parad**i**se

CONSONANT SPELLINGS											
[ɾ]	[ɹ]	[θ]	[ð]	[ʃ]	[ʒ]	[tʃ]	[dʒ]	[ŋ]	[ŋg]	[j]	[ʍ]
merry	dream	three	this	share	vision	chair	gesture	young	youngest	yellow	when
star above	ring	thing	father	precious	azure	ancient	age	sing	finger	music	wheat
thread	every	breath	breathe	devotion	occasion	search	gentle	singer		beyond	whether
Dramatic	[ˈʔɛvɹɪ]		with		treasure	choose	judge	ink			
cruel											
grim											

[ru]	Silent *r*	[ʔ]
fruit	heart	age
prove	sword	eyes
[ɾɾu]	were kind	own
ruby	dear	

Pronounced *r* is flipped for opera and oratorio (except for *dr* and *tr* combinations)

Changes in voicing occur with final consonants					
[t]	[d]	[s]	[z]	[θ]	[ð]
missed	pleased	notes	leaves	path	paths
looked	loved	works	birds	youth	youths
Voicing matches previous consonant				Plural form is voiced	

WHEN TO SING [ɑ]

Specified spellings that have an [æ] sound in American English are pronounced with a dark [ɑ] for British English

I. Spelling: *a* + [f], [s], [ntʃ], [ns], *th*

a + [f]		*a* + [s]				*a* + [ntʃ]		*a* + [ns]		*a* + *th*	
after	[ˈʔɑftə]	ask	[ʔɑsk]	master	[ˈmɑstə]	blanch	[blɑntʃ]	advance	[ʔædˈvɑns]	bath	[bɑθ]
laugh	[lɑf]	fast	[fɑst]	pass	[pɑs]	branches	[ˈbɹɑntʃ]	chance	[tʃɑns]	path	[pɑθ]
staff	[stɑf]	glass	[glɑs]	past	[pɑst]	ranch	[ɹɑntʃ]	dance	[dɑns]	rather	[ˈɹɑðə]
wafted	[ˈwɑftəd]	last	[lɑst]	vast	[vɑst]	scranch	[skɹɑntʃ]	*trance	[tɹɑns]	wrath	[ɹɑθ]

*Prefix *trans-* is transcribed with [æ]

II. Spellings *-and, -ant* and *-ample* are [ɑ] in the following words only:

-and: *command, demand, reprimand* *-ant*: *can't, shan't, aunt, advantage, chant, enchant, grant, plant, slant*

-ample: *sample, example*

III. Exceptions to section I: words with an [æ] pronunciation

a + *f*	*a* + *s*		*a* + *ns*	*a* + *th*	may be either [æ] or [ɑ]	
baffle	aspect	fantastic	cancel	fathom	alas	contrast
daffodil	aspiration	hast	circumstance	gather	ant	enhance
graphic	cascade	passage	expanse	hath	asp	lass
scaffold	chastise	passenger	fancy	math	aspen	mass
riffraff	classic	passive	romance		ass	pasture
traffic	classify	sarcastic	stance		blaspheme	ranch

BIBLIOGRAPHY

ITALIAN BIBLIOGRAPHY

Colorni, Evelina. *Singer's Italian.* New York: G. Schirmer, 1970. *Dizionario d'Ortografia e di Pronuncia.* B. Migliorini, C. Tagliavini, and P. Fiorelli. Torino: ERI/Edizioni RAI, 1981.

Garzanti italiano / [progettazione e coordinamento generale: Pasquale Stoppelli]. CD-ROM. Milano: Garzanti Linguistica, 2003.

Il Nuovo Zingarelli: Vocabolario della Lingua Italiana di Nicola Zingarelli. 11th Edition; general revision by Miro Dogliotti and Luigi Rosiello. Milano: Zanichelli, 1983.

GERMAN BIBLIOGRAPHY

Adams, David. *A Handbook of Diction for Singers.* New York: Oxford University Press, 1999.

Adler, Kurt. *Phonetics and Diction in Singing.* Minneapolis: University of Minnesota Press, 1967.

Langenscheidt's Wörterbuch. Deutsch-English English-Deutsch, New York: Simon & Schuster Inc., 1993.

Moriarty, John. *Diction.* Boston: Schirmer Music Co., 1975.

Odom, William and Benno Schollum. *German for Singers.* Belmont, CA: Thomas Learning, 1997.

Siebs, Theodor. *Deutsche Hochsprache.* Berlin: Walter De Gruyter & Co., 1969.

FRENCH BIBLIOGRAPHY

Bernac, Pierre. *The Interpretation of French Song* Praeger Publishers, New York 1970.

Davis, Eileen. *Sing French* Éclairé Press, Columbus, Ohio, 2003

Du Mont, Francis M. *French Grammar* Barnes and Noble, Inc., New York 1960.

Girard, Denis. *Cassell's French Dictionary* Macmillan Publishing Co., New York 1981.

Grubb, Thomas. *Singing in French* Schirmer Books, New York 1979.

Janes, Michael, Dora Latiri-Carpenter, and Edwin Carpenter, eds. *Oxford French Dictionary & Grammar* Oxford University Press, Oxford 2001.

Nitze, William, and Ernest Wilkins. *A Handbook of French Phonetics* Holt, Rinehart and Winston, Inc., New York 1961.

Robert, Paul. *Le petit Robert [electronic resource]: de la langue française Nouvelle édition,* Vivendi Universal Interactive Publishing, France 2001.

LATIN BIBLIOGRAPHY

Hines, Robert S. *Singer's Manual of Latin Diction and Phonetics.* New York: Schirmer Books, 1975.

Jeffers, Ron. *Translations and Annotations of Choral Repertoire: The Latin Vulgate Bible, The Holy Bible in Latin Language with Douay-Rheims English Translation,* Vulgate.org. Accessed 5/12/2016.

ENGLISH BIBLIOGRAPHY

Marshall, Madeleine. *The Singer's Manual of English Diction* G. Schirmer, Inc., New York 1953.

Ross, WM. T. *Voice Culture and Elocution* The Baker & Taylor Co., New York 1890.

Cambridge Dictionary, Dictionary.cambridge.org. Accessed 7/23/2016.